The UK Stock Market
Almanac
2013

Edited by Stephen Eckett

HARRIMAN HOUSE LTD

3A Penns Road

Petersfield

Hampshire

GU32 2EW

GREAT BRITAIN

Tel: +44 (0)1730 233870

Fax: +44 (0)1730 233880

Email: enquiries@harriman-house.com

Website: www.harriman-house.com

First edition published in Great Britain in 2004

This 5th edition published in 2012

Copyright © Harriman House Ltd

978-0-857192-523

British Library Cataloguing in Publication Data

A CIP catalogue record for this book can be obtained from the British Library.

Printed and bound by CPI Group (UK) Ltd, Croydon, CR0 4YY

Set in Gill Sans

CONTENTS

INTRODUCTION

Welcome to the 2013 edition of the UK Stock Market Almanac – where we celebrate the Efficient Market Theory. Or rather, the failure of said theory. This book could alternatively be titled, The Inefficient Almanac, as it revels in the trends and anomalies of the market that the Efficient Market Theory says shouldn't exist.

Almanac studies and strategies

This edition of the Almanac updates some of the seasonality trends and anomaly studies that have featured in previous editions. Including-

- **Market performance by month** – December is still the strongest month in the year and June the weakest; the greatest change from five years ago has been the fall of January from fourth to eighth in the month rankings. [p. 106]
- **Day of the week performance** – Wednesday is the new weakest day of the week (Monday used to be), and the strongest days are Tuesday and Friday. [p. 117]
- **Share performance** – The behaviour of certain shares that have performed consistently well (or badly) in specific times of the year (i.e. January, summer, December) is highlighted. [pp. 4, 50 and 98]
- **Bounceback stocks** – The Bounceback Strategy (buying last year's dog stocks) continues to perform well, out-performing the market every year since 2002. [p. 100]
- **Quarterly sector performance** – The strongest/weakest sectors for each quarter are identified; and the **Quarterly Sector Strategy** continues to beat the market. [pp. 6, 30, 56 and 82 (quarter performance) and pp. 40 and 42 (strategies)]
- **First/last trading day of the month** – The first trading day of July (December) is found to be unusually strong (weak); while the last trading of October (February) is found to be unusually strong (weak). [pp. 18 and 46]
- **FTSE 100 Index quarterly reviews** – As before, it is found that share prices tend to rise immediately before a company joins the index and are then flat or fall back; and that share prices tend to fall in the period before a company leaves the index and then rise afterwards. [pp. 48 and 74]
- **FTSE 100 and FTSE 250 indices** – The FTSE 100 Index greatly under-performs the mid-cap index in January and February and out-performs it in September and October. [p. 60]
- **Triple Witching** – The three days around triple witching have higher volatility than other days, and the FTSE 100 Index return on triple witching days is abnormally strong. [p. 22]
- **Market momentum** – A reference grid is presented giving the historic tendency of the market to rise (fall) following a series of consecutive daily/weekly/monthly/yearly rises (falls). [pp. 120 and 121]
- **UK and US markets** – The correlation between the UK and US markets has been increasing since the 1950s, and in the years since 2010 has been stronger than ever. [p. 154]
- **Trading around Christmas and New Year** – The nine trading days around Christmas and New Year are some of the strongest in the whole year. [pp. 102 and 104]

Six-month effect

The extraordinary **six-month effect** (also called the Sell in May effect in the UK and the Halloween effect in the US) remains strong. Over the last 10 years the market in the winter months has out-performed the market in the summer months by an average 5% annually. The **six-month strategy** is therefore still performing well – beating the market (inc. dividends) by 44% since 1994.

In this edition of the Almanac a method is presented to improve further the returns on the six-month strategy by finessing the date of entry into the market in spring using the MACD indicator.

New research

New studies appearing in the Almanac for the first time include-

- **Comparative performance of the FTSE 100 and S&P 500 indices** – The strong/weak months for the FTSE 100 Index relative to the S&P 500 Index are identified; and a strategy of switching between the two markets is found that produces twice the returns than either market individually. [p. 32]

- **Low vs high share prices** – A portfolio of the 20 lowest priced shares in the market has out-performed a portfolio of the 20 highest priced shares by an average 57 percentage points each year since 2002. [p. 64]

- **Monthly share momentum** – A rolling portfolio of the 10 top performing stocks the previous month beats the market each month by an average of 1.1 percentage points. [p. 78]

- **Holidays and the market** – In the last ten years the market has been significantly strong on the days immediately before and after holidays and weak fours days before and three days after holidays. [p. 26]

- **Small Cap Stocks in January** – On average small cap stocks significantly out-perform large cap stocks in January, and under-perform in October. [p. 8]

- **Tuesday reverses Monday** – Since the year 2000 market returns on Tuesdays have been the reverse of those on Mondays. A strategy using this effect has significantly out-performed the FTSE 100 Index over this period. [p. 24]

- **Turn of the month** – The market tends to be weak a few days either side of the turn of the month, but abnormally strong on the first trading day of the new month (except December). [p. 52]

- **Defensive stocks** – 10 stocks are identified that have performed best during the 10 worst monthly falls in the market since 2002. [p. 72]

- **Ultimate death cross** – An imminent *ultimate death cross* could be very bearish (or bullish) for the market! [p. 155]

- **Gold and UK stock market** – What would the stock market look like if it was priced in gold? [p. 159]

- **Sun and the stock market** – Does the number of sun hours in a day affect market returns? [p. 168]

Failed studies

On the basis that negative results can still be useful, a few studies we researched that didn't make it into the Almanac this year are-

- **Overnight moves** – Academics in the US have found a strong negative correlation for stocks between overnight moves (close to open) and the intraday return (open to close). We couldn't find any similar strong effect with UK stocks; it was a little more apparent with smaller cap stocks but still not very strong.

- **Friday-Monday strategy** – Previous Almanacs have highlighted a strategy exploiting strong Fridays and weak Mondays, but this no longer seems to be working as markets have been stronger on Mondays in recent years.

- **Friday 13th** – Does the market behave oddly on, or around, Friday 13ths? No.

And a study just not included...

First five days of January – In the US this is held – along with the Halloween effect – to be one of the best, and most persistent, of market predictors. The effect largely works the same for the UK market as well: the direction of the market in the first five days of the year forecasts the direction of the market for the whole year. A variant refers to the direction of the market in the whole of January rather than just the first five days.

Outlook for 2013

After the excitement of 2012, with the Olympics and the US election, what have we to look forward to in 2013? Apart from it being the International Year of Quinoa(!), we'll be celebrating the 200th anniversary of the publication of Jane Austen's *Pride and Prejudice*, the 100th anniversary of Ford introducing the first moving assembly line and the 50th anniversaries of Coca-Cola introducing its first diet drink, TaB cola, and The Beatles recording their debut album *Please Please Me* in a single session. Apart from that, there are no major (planned) events coming up this year that will obviously affect the stock market.

The consequences of the US election will be the most interesting influence to study. As pointed out in this Almanac, the UK market is strongly correlated with that in the US, so US elections have a large effect on UK shares as well. A well-known effect of the US election cycle is that stock returns in the last two years of political terms have been higher than in the first two years. This is not surprising as incumbent politicians pursue policies that stimulate the economy leading up to an election. Another significant result (that will affect us in 2013) is that stocks have lower mean returns in the 13 months after an election. An interesting finding is that small cap stocks have significantly higher returns during Democratic administrations. A simple (and historically profitable) strategy proposed in an academic paper[1] of 2011 was to invest in small caps with a Democrat president and large caps with a Republican one.

Elsewhere, there will be three lunar eclipses in the coming year (the significance of which can be read about later in these pages).

The big question for investors is when the bear market will end and the anticipated surge upwards commence? In 2013, 2014, 2015, or later?

Historically, the third year in the decade has seen stock returns of, on average, 5% since 1801. The market returns in years 1983, 1993, 2003, were 23.1%, 23.3% and 16.6% respectively. Which is all very bullish. However, various market cycle theories point to 2013 being the sell-off low point of the current bear market. In addition, the Chinese New Year, starting 10 February, will be the Year of the Snake, and this does not bode well for the market (see later). And, for fans of numerology, 2013 does have an eerie connection with a previously traumatic year for the market (it is the first year to have all digits different from each other since 1987).

While waiting for the great turning point, investors will have to be careful not to be tempted by mini-rallies in the market. As Caroline Bingley says in *Pride and Prejudice*-

> I can't help thinking that at some point someone is going to produce a piglet and we'll all have to chase it.

Stephen Eckett

---

[1] Ziemba, William T. and Dzahabarov, Constantine N., 'Seasonal Anomalies' (12 February 2011).

PREFACE

Definition

almanac (noun): an annual calendar containing dates and statistical information

What the book covers

Topics in the Almanac cover a wide spectrum. The diary includes essential information on upcoming company announcements and financial events such as exchange holidays and economic releases. There are also the results of a unique seasonality analysis of historic market performance for every day and week of the year – our Sinclair numbers. Besides this, there is information of a lighter nature, such as important social and sporting events and notable events in history.

Accompanying the diary is a series of articles about the stock market. Many of these articles focus on seasonality effects, such as the likely performance of the market in each month, momentum effects, and the difference in market performance between summer and winter.

In short, the Almanac is a unique work providing everything from essential reference information to informative and entertaining articles on the UK stock market.

How the book is structured

The Almanac has two major parts:

1. **Diary**

   This is in week-per-page format. There are 52 pages, one for each week in the year. (See the next page for a detailed explanation of the layout of each diary page.) Opposite each diary page is a short article about the stock market. These articles are strategy-oriented – they aim to reveal trading patterns and anomlies in the stock market that investors and traders can exploit to make money.

2. **Reference**

   This section contains further seasonality and anomaly studies as well background information on the profile characteristcs of the market - the indices, the sectors and companies.

Supporting website

The website supporting this book can be found at **stockmarketalmanac.co.uk.**

UNDERSTANDING THE DIARY PAGES

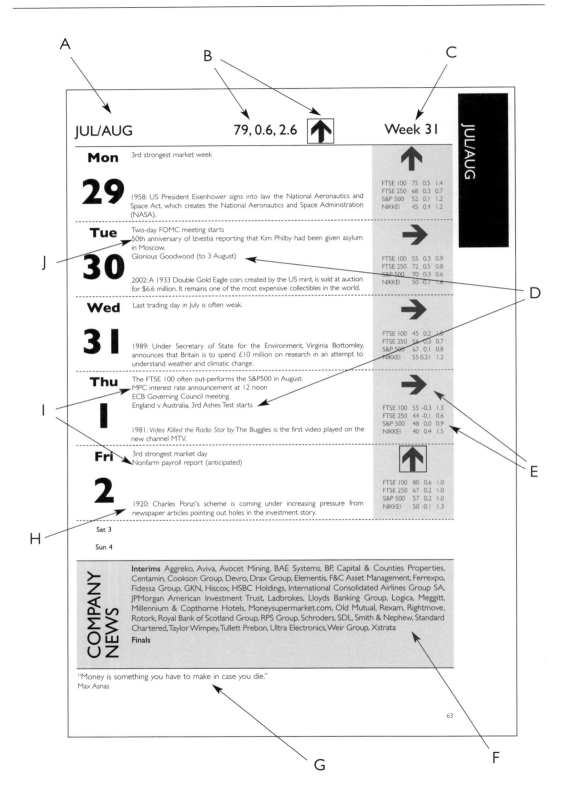

A — JUL/AUG

B — 79, 0.6, 2.6 ⬆

C — Week 31

JUL/AUG

Mon 29
3rd strongest market week

1958: US President Eisenhower signs into law the National Aeronautics and Space Act, which creates the National Aeronautics and Space Administration (NASA).

⬆
FTSE 100	75	0.5	1.4
FTSE 250	68	0.3	0.7
S&P 500	52	0.1	1.2
NIKKEI	45	0.4	1.2

Tue 30
Two-day FOMC meeting starts
50th anniversary of Izvestia reporting that Kim Philby had been given asylum in Moscow.
Glorious Goodwood (to 3 August)

2002: A 1933 Double Gold Eagle coin, created by the US mint, is sold at auction for $6.6 million. It remains one of the most expensive collectibles in the world.

J →

➡
FTSE 100	55	0.3	0.9
FTSE 250	72	0.5	0.8
S&P 500	70	0.3	0.6
NIKKEI	50	-0.1	1.6

D

Wed 31
Last trading day in July is often weak.

1989: Under Secretary of State for the Environment, Virginia Bottomley, announces that Britain is to spend £10 million on research in an attempt to understand weather and climatic change.

➡
FTSE 100	45	0.2	1.0
FTSE 250	56	0.3	0.7
S&P 500	67	0.1	0.8
NIKKEI	55	0.21	1.2

Thu 1
The FTSE 100 often out-performs the S&P500 in August.
MPC interest rate announcement at 12 noon
ECB Governing Council meeting
England v Australia, 3rd Ashes Test starts

1981: *Video Killed the Radio Star* by The Buggles is the first video played on the new channel MTV.

I

➡
FTSE 100	55	-0.3	1.3
FTSE 250	44	-0.1	0.6
S&P 500	48	0.0	0.9
NIKKEI	40	0.4	1.5

E

Fri 2
3rd strongest market day
Nonfarm payroll report (anticipated)

1920: Charles Ponzi's scheme is coming under increasing pressure from newspaper articles pointing out holes in the investment story.

⬆
FTSE 100	80	0.6	1.0
FTSE 250	67	0.2	1.0
S&P 500	57	0.2	1.0
NIKKEI	50	-0.1	1.3

H

Sat 3

Sun 4

COMPANY NEWS

Interims Aggreko, Aviva, Avocet Mining, BAE Systems, BP, Capital & Counties Properties, Centamin, Cookson Group, Devro, Drax Group, Elementis, F&C Asset Management, Ferrexpo, Fidessa Group, GKN, Hiscox, HSBC Holdings, International Consolidated Airlines Group SA, JPMorgan American Investment Trust, Ladbrokes, Lloyds Banking Group, Logica, Meggitt, Millennium & Copthorne Hotels, Moneysupermarket.com, Old Mutual, Rexam, Rightmove, Rotork, Royal Bank of Scotland Group, RPS Group, Schroders, SDL, Smith & Nephew, Standard Chartered, Taylor Wimpey, Tullett Prebon, Ultra Electronics, Weir Group, Xstrata

Finals

F

"Money is something you have to make in case you die."
Max Asnas

G

63

A – Diary page title

The diary is a week-per-page format.

B – Weekly performance analysis (Sinclair numbers)

These figures and arrow show the results of the analysis on the historic performance of the FTSE 100 during this week. The ten best and worst performing weeks are marked with a square box around the Sinclair arrow here. [See the next page for further explanation and the reference section for full data tables of FTSE 100 Index daily, Sinclair numbers.]

C – Week number

The week number of the year is indicated at the top right of every diary page.

D – Social and sporting events

Notable social and sporting events, including public holidays, are included each day.

E – Daily performance analysis (Sinclair numbers)

These figures and arrow show the results of the analysis on the historic performance of four world stock indices on this calendar day. The ten best and worst performing days for the FTSE 100 are marked with a square box around the Sinclair arrow here. [See the next page for further explanation and the reference section for full data tables of FTSE 100 Index Sinclair numbers.]

F – Likely company announcements

The box at the foot of each page contains a list of companies expected to announce interim or final results during the week. The list is only provisional, using the date of announcements in the previous year as a guide.

G – Quotation

H – On this day

Events that happened on this calendar day in history.

I – Financial events

Indicates days of financial and economic significance. For example, exchange holidays and important economic releases.

J – Anniversary

Significant anniversaries that occur on this day.

Abbreviations

FOMC – Federal Open Market Committee
MPC – Monetary Policy Committee

SINCLAIR NUMBERS – MARKET PERFORMANCE ANALYSIS

Sinclair numbers

We have conducted a unique analysis of the historic performance of four stock indices – the FTSE 100, FTSE 250, S&P 500 and Nikkei 225 – for each day, week and month of the year.

This analysis produces three numbers (which we call Sinclair numbers) for each day, week and month:

1. **Up(%)**

   The percentage of historic moves in this period (day, week or month) that were up. For example, for 2 April, in our sample the FTSE 100 increased 12 times on this day out of a total of 18 market days on 2 April, so the Up(%) is 67%. If you flick to Week 14 in the diary you will see this 67% recorded in the Sinclair table in the FTSE 100 row.

2. **Avg Change(%)**

   The average percentage change of the market in this period. For example, on 2 April, the market has risen 0.7% on average on the 18 market days.

3. **StdDev**

   This is the standard deviation of all the changes in this period away from the average. For example, for 2 April, the standard deviation is 1.2. This means that 66% of all the market moves on 2 April fell between -0.5% and +1.9% (i.e. average move of 0.7% -/+ standard deviation). The standard deviation measures how closely all the moves in the period cluster around the average. A high number for standard deviation suggests that clustering was not close, and therefore confidence in future moves being close to the average is decreased. Conversely, a low standard deviation figure suggests good clustering and increases one's confidence in future moves being close to the calculated historic average.

Sample data

- **FTSE 100 Index**: from April 1984
- **FTSE 250 Index**: from December 1985
- **S&P 500 Index**: from January 1950
- **Nikkei 225 Index**: from January 1984

Sinclair arrows

The figures for Up(%) are displayed for the respective days and weeks on the Diary pages employing the following arrow symbols:

Daily arrows	Weekly arrows
↑ the Up(%) is over 74%	↑ the Up(%) is over 70%
↗ the Up(%) is 63% to 74%	↗ the Up(%) is 60% to 70%
→ the Up(%) is 41% to 63%	→ the Up(%) is 50% to 60%
↘ the Up(%) is 30% to 41%	↘ the Up(%) is 40% to 50%
↓ the Up(%) is under 30%	↓ the Up(%) is under 40%

These daily ranges were calculated on the following basis: the average Up(%) for all days in the year is 52% and the standard deviation is 11. Adding two standard deviations to the average gives 74, adding one standard deviation gives 63, subtracting one standard deviation gives 41 and subtracting two standard deviations gives 30. The weekly ranges have been modified slightly from these figures so as to present the data with more variation.

The top ten days and weeks – with the highest Up(%) and the weakest ten days and weeks – with the lowest Up(%) – are all highlighted with a square box around the arrow.

See the reference section for full data tables of FTSE 100 Index Sinclair numbers.

I
DIARY

JANUARY MARKET

FTSE 100	57	0.3	5.2
FTSE 250	59	1.7	4.8
S&P 500	61	1.1	4.9
NIKKEI	57	0.6	5.9

Market performance this month

January is the eighth strongest month for the market in the year (its ranking has fallen a fair bit since 2007, when it was the fourth strongest month). The market has risen in 57% of all years in January, with an average rise of 0.3% this month. January is the weakest month in the strong six-month period (November–April) of the year.

January is better for mid-cap and small-cap stocks. On average, the FTSE 250 Index outperforms the FTSE 100 by 1.6 percentage points in January – the best outperformance (with February) of all months. Small caps do even better, outperforming the FTSE 100 Index by on average 3.7 percentage points in the first month.

A famous market predictor in the US has it that the direction of the market in the whole year will be the same as that for the first five days of January.

In January consider buying the worst-performing stocks of 2012 to hold for three months (see *Bounceback stocks*, week 50).

Historic performance of the market in January

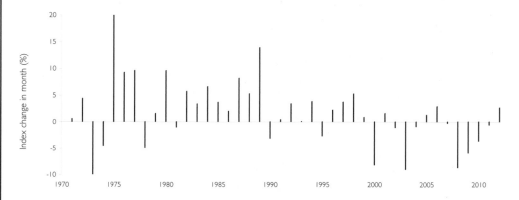

January summary

Month's performance ranking	8th
Average market change this month (standard deviation)	0.3% (5.2)
First trading day: Up / average change	60.7% / 0.4%
Last trading day: Up / average change	64.3% / 0.2%
Main features of the month	The FTSE 250 is particularly strong relative to the FTSE 100 in this month.
	Small cap stocks often outperform large cap stocks in January (January Effect).
	The FTSE 100 often underperforms the S&P 500 in January
	Week beginning 31 Dec: the 6th strongest market week.
	Week beginning 7 Jan: the weakest market week in the year.
	The last trading day in January (31 Jan) is often strong.
	Strong sectors in this first quarter are: Oil Equipment Services & Distribution, Forestry & Paper, and Industrial Engineering.
	Weak sectors in this first quarter are: Fixed Line Telecommunications, Pharmaceuticals & Biotechnology, and Food & Drug Retailers.
Significant dates	01 Jan: LSE closed
	03 Jan: MPC interest rate announcement at 12h00 (anticipated)
	04 Jan: US Nonfarm payroll report (anticipated)
	20 Jan: Inauguration of the US President
	21 Jan: Martin Luther King Day (US) – NYSE closed
	30 Jan: FOMC monetary policy statement
	Don't forget: the last date to file your 2012 tax return online is 31 January.

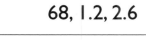
Mon
31

New Year's Eve
LSE closes early at 12h30
TSE closed
6th strongest market week

FTSE 100	56	0.1	1.1
FTSE 250	69	0.0	0.7
S&P 500	68	0.5	0.3
NIKKEI			

1781: The first bank in the US opens – Bank of North America.

Tue
1

UK Holiday: New Year's Day
LSE, NYSE, HKEX, TSE closed
Due date for payment of corporation tax for period ended 31 March 2012.
The FTSE 100 often underperforms the S&P 500 in January.

2002: Euro bank notes and coins become legal tender in twelve of the European Union's member states.

Wed
2

TSE closed
Small cap stocks often outperform large cap stocks in January.

FTSE 100	56	0.3	1.1
FTSE 250	73	0.5	1.1
S&P 500	62	0.3	1.3
NIKKEI			

1980: UK steel workers stage their first national strike for more than fifty years.

Thu
3

TSE closed
MPC interest rate announcement at 12h00

FTSE 100	69	0.3	1.2
FTSE 250	67	0.4	1.1
S&P 500	50	0.3	1.2
NIKKEI			

1997: China announces it will spend $27.7 billion to fight erosion and pollution in the Yangtze and Yellow River valleys.

Fri
4

Nonfarm payroll report (anticipated)
One market predictor holds that the direction of the market in a year is the same as that for the first five days of January.

FTSE 100	55	0.2	1.4
FTSE 250	68	0.4	1.1
S&P 500	54	0.1	1.2
NIKKEI	65	0.0	1.8

1999: The Euro begins trading at $1.1747, and hits a high of $1.1906.

Sat 5

Sun 6

COMPANY NEWS

Interims
Finals

"Inflation is when you pay fifteen dollars for a ten dollar haircut you used to get for five dollars when you had hair."
Sam Ewing

SHARE PERFORMANCE IN JANUARY

Stocks that like January

The share prices of only five companies have risen at least nine times in the last ten years in the month of January. The table below shows these five companies and the percentage price change for the stock in the month of January for that year (for example, Beazley increased 4.9% in January 2004).

Company	2003	2004	2005	2006	2007	2008	2009	2010	2011	2012	Avg
AVEVA Group	-10.2	8.9	3.3	11.5	10.3	3.1	5.4	8.4	2.4	10.3	5.3
Beazley	1.5	4.9	2.9	10.1	4.7	3.2	-5.5	4.8	3.4	4.4	3.4
Gresham Computing	-20	20.2	6	18.8	2	20.7	21.8	6.5	23.3	12.9	11.2
SIG	5.8	8.3	3.1	11.6	12.9	12.4	-32.9	2.2	13.3	18.6	5.5
Tullett Prebon	5.7	6.4	8.4	8.9	-0.8	10.2	12.3	10.3	1.4	10.3	7.3
average:	-3.4	9.7	4.7	12.2	5.8	9.9	0.2	6.4	8.8	11.3	6.6
FTSE All Share:	-9.1	-0.9	1.3	2.9	-0.3	-8.7	-5.9	-3.3	-0.6	2.6	-2.2
difference:	5.7	10.6	3.4	9.3	6.1	18.6	6.1	9.7	9.4	8.7	8.8

A portfolio of these five companies would have outperformed the FTSE All Share Index in every January for the past ten years. The average outperformance each year would have been 8.8 percentage points.

On average, the best performing companies in January have been Gresham Computing (average January increase of +11.2%) and Tullet Prebon (+7.3%).

Stocks that don't like January

The six stocks in the table below have fallen in at least nine of the past ten Januaries – these are the worst January stocks among listed companies on the LSE.

Company	2003	2004	2005	2006	2007	2008	2009	2010	2011	2012	Avg
Berkeley Group Holdings	-5.4	-3.4	2.7	-0.3	-12.4	-25.4	-9.2	-2.4	-0.6	-0.7	-5.7
Diageo	-8	-2	-2.6	-0.7	-1.2	-6.3	-1.8	-2.7	1.4	-0.3	-2.4
Fortune Oil	20	-18.2	-12.3	-9.9	-4.4	-3.7	-12	-9	-12.5	-8.3	-7.0
GlaxoSmithKline	-4	-7.8	-3.8	-2.1	1.6	-7.6	-5.1	-7.8	-9	-4.2	-5.0
Pennon Group	-1.2	-6.2	-2.5	1.1	-0.6	-2.4	-9.4	-4.3	-5.8	-2.6	-3.4
Tesco	-14.7	-7.5	-4.2	-4.1	3.3	-12.6	-0.5	-0.6	-5.2	-20.8	-6.7
average:	-2.2	-7.5	-3.8	-2.7	-2.3	-9.7	-6.3	-4.5	-5.3	-6.2	-5.0
FTSE All Share:	-9.1	-0.9	1.3	2.9	-0.3	-8.7	-5.9	-3.3	-0.6	2.6	-2.2
difference:	6.9	-6.6	-5.1	-5.6	-2.0	-1.0	-0.4	-1.2	-4.7	-8.8	-2.8

A portfolio of these six stocks would have underperformed the FTSE All Share Index in every January of the last ten years except 2003. The average underperformance was 2.8 percentage points.

Note: A similar analysis for the month of December can be found later in the Almanac, in week 49.

Mon 7

Christmas (Eastern Orthodox Churches)
Weakest market week
6th weakest day

1789: The first national Presidential election in the US occurs.

FTSE 100	30	-0.2	1.0
FTSE 250	58	0.1	0.9
S&P 500	41	-0.1	0.9
NIKKEI	45	0.6	1.0

Tue 8

1987: The Dow Jones closes above 2000 for first time (2002.25)

FTSE 100	45	-0.1	0.7
FTSE 250	47	0.0	0.7
S&P 500	43	-0.3	1.3
NIKKEI	39	-0.2	1.6

Wed 9

Time to consider putting together a bounceback portfolio.
100th anniversary of the birth of Richard M. Nixon, the 37th President of the United States.

2009: Legislation is put forward in the US House of Financial Services to reinstate the Uptick Rule, which prevents short sellers from adding to the downward momentum when the price of an asset is already experiencing sharp declines.

FTSE 100	40	-0.1	1.0
FTSE 250	47	-0.1	0.7
S&P 500	51	-0.1	1.0
NIKKEI	47	-0.8	1.2

Thu 10

MPC interest rate announcement at 12h00
ECB Governing Council meeting

2006: Apple introduces its first Intel-based machines – the iMac and the MacBook Pro.

FTSE 100	35	-0.1	0.9
FTSE 250	32	-0.2	0.7
S&P 500	51	0.1	0.8
NIKKEI	39	0.0	1.5

Fri 11

New moon

1596: The first recorded lottery in England takes place.

FTSE 100	35	-0.2	0.7
FTSE 250	63	0.0	0.7
S&P 500	61	0.0	0.8
NIKKEI	50	-0.7	1.3

Sat 12   60th anniversary of the LSE flotation of Scottish Mortgage Investment Trust

Sun 13

COMPANY NEWS

Interims
Finals

"A bank is a place that will lend you money if you can prove that you don't need it."
Bob Hope

5

SECTOR PERFORMANCE – FIRST QUARTER

The table below shows the performance of FTSE 350 sectors in the first quarter (31 December to 31 March) of each year 2003 to 2012. The table is ranked by the final column – the average performance for each sector over the ten years. For each year the top five performing sectors are highlighted in light grey, the bottom five in dark grey.

Sector	2003	2004	2005	2006	2007	2008	2009	2010	2011	2012	Avg
Industrial Metals	-66.4	37.5	6.9	49.2	14.4	21.0	80.7	39.5	0.1	5.1	18.8
Oil Equip; Srvs & Dist					4.0	-0.3	19.6	11.1	2.5	20.1	9.5
Forestry & Paper	1.7	10.9	1.1			-1.6	-27.4	38.5	16.7	29.6	8.7
Industrial Engineering	-7.4	3.4	5.1	14.1	9.6	3.2	10.2	21.0	1.6	7.8	6.9
Technology Hard & Equip	6.7	-0.3	-7.4	12.5	5.2	-28.1	27.1	19.7	22.9	8.2	6.7
Construction & Materials	1.7	9.1	8.4	15.1	5.2	-2.7	-2.3	10.8	5.8	1.5	5.3
Mining	-5.4	-0.4	9.5	16.5	9.5	-0.9	13.4	11.5	-4.2	2.7	5.2
Chemicals	-24.6	3.8	5.9	13.9	10.0	7.4	-3.0	14.0	-4.1	25.5	4.9
Industrial Transportation	-6.0	4.1	3.6	20.1	-3.2	-12.6	3.2	19.7	3.0	15.8	4.8
Automobiles & Parts	-11.6	-0.2	4.3	15.5	37.2	7.9	-29.6	17.9	-9.6	12.6	4.4
General Industrials					5.9	-4.7	-20.6	12.6	5.9	21.1	3.4
Household Goods					5.8	-4.4	3.6	5.6	-5.0	14.2	3.3
Personal Goods	-13.9	6.3	6.0	6.6	2.7	-18.6	6.7	11.7	1.8	21.2	3.1
Support Services	-13.2	3.6	5.8	12.3	5.7	-4.8	-6.9	8.7	1.5	14.7	2.7
Real Estate Inv & Srvs								-0.6	2.8	5.9	2.7
Aerospace & Defense	-10.9	14.2	6.7	5.8	8.2	-9.4	-12.2	10.1	0.1	9.9	2.3
Health Care Equip & Srvs	-12.7	7.8	-6.0	-3.7	22.6	6.9	-2.3	2.1	3.1	1.2	1.9
Financial Services	-9.4	8.4	-2.6	22.5	4.6	-15.6	-2.9	-1.2	-4.0	17.5	1.7
Media	-17.5	7.8	6.0	4.8	7.5	-13.5	-4.2	11.3	3.8	9.4	1.5
Software & Comp Srvs	-20.0	-1.0	-1.4	1.0	2.2	-11.7	10.8	15.8	0.9	14.5	1.1
General Retailers	-8.6	2.2	-2.2	7.4	3.4	-19.1	20.6	-3.8	-9.0	19.9	1.1
Equity Inv Instruments	-10.5	0.5	2.2	9.1	3.1	-5.8	-2.4	6.7	-0.1	7.7	1.1
Travel & Leisure	-0.6	8.6	-0.6	2.5	4.2	-16.5	-6.5	17.8	-8.3	8.5	0.9
Tobacco	-4.0	7.1	0.2	2.6	9.7	-7.9	-12.1	9.3	0.5	3.4	0.9
Electricity	-1.7	3.7	2.9	12.9	1.3	-7.0	-10.5	-3.3	2.1	2.5	0.3
Electronic & Elect Equip	-56.0	5.6	10.2	10.0	8.6	-2.0	-20.8	12.3	3.8	25.6	-0.3
Real Estate Inv Trusts				19.7	-5.0	1.8	-31.5	-2.1	4.8	9.6	-0.4
Nonlife Insurance	-19.0	3.7	2.4	7.9	1.5	-10.4	-8.2	7.5	2.3	7.7	-0.5
Gas; Water & Multiutilities		5.7	-1.8	4.0	5.3	-13.6	-18.6	1.0	1.5	5.1	-1.3
Oil & Gas Producers	-6.5	-2.0	8.3	6.0	-3.4	-14.4	-7.2	2.6	5.7	-2.7	-1.4
Beverages	-10.0	0.6	0.3	7.4	1.2	-9.2	-15.5	3.9	-1.2	8.6	-1.4
Food Producers	-6.4	3.7	4.6	1.6	6.7	-9.7	-15.6	2.6	-3.3	-2.0	-1.8
Life Insurance	-25.7	2.1	5.4	16.2	-2.8	-10.7	-28.5	-4.6	9.5	15.3	-2.4
Banks	-8.2	-4.2	-3.9	6.2	-3.1	-10.1	-27.4	6.7	-2.3	17.0	-2.9
Food & Drug Retailers	-9.0	-3.1	-0.1	0.4	16.3	-19.3	-7.2	2.3	-7.6	-12.5	-4.0
Mobile Telecom					-4.1	-19.6	-11.2	5.9	5.9	-3.4	-4.4
Pharm & Biotech	-5.4	-11.5	2.8	2.9	2.3	-15.3	-14.3	-0.7	-1.7	-5.5	-4.6
Fixed Line Telecoms	-3.1	-4.6	-0.3	-0.5	1.8	-19.9	-32.5	-4.6	-0.5	17.1	-4.7

Observations

1. The general clustering of light grey highlights at the top of the table, and dark grey at the bottom, suggests that certain sectors consistently perform well (or badly) in this quarter. Of the four quarters in the year, this effect is the strongest in the first quarter.

2. **Strong sectors** in this quarter are: Oil Equipment Services & Distribution, Forestry & Paper, and Industrial Engineering.

3. **Weak sectors** in this quarter are: Fixed Line Telecommunications, Pharmaceuticals & Biotechnology, and Food & Drug Retailers.

Mon

14

Coming of Age Day (Japan) – TSE closed
50th anniversary of the last scheduled run by The Flying Scotsman.

FTSE 100	60	-0.1	1.5
FTSE 250	53	0.0	1.0
S&P 500	73	0.3	0.9
NIKKEI			

1960: The Reserve Bank of Australia, the country's central bank, is established.

Tue

15

FTSE 100	60	0.2	1.3
FTSE 250	44	-0.1	1.1
S&P 500	64	0.2	0.9
NIKKEI	50	0.7	2.1

1889: The Coca-Cola Company, then known as the Pemberton Medicine Company, is originally incorporated in Atlanta, Georgia.

Wed

16

MPC meeting minutes published
Beige Book published

FTSE 100	60	0.2	0.9
FTSE 250	63	0.0	0.7
S&P 500	56	0.1	0.7
NIKKEI	50	-0.8	2.2

1913: The House of Commons accepts Home-Rule for Ireland.

Thu

17

FTSE 100	55	0.2	0.9
FTSE 250	63	0.4	0.6
S&P 500	57	0.0	1.0
NIKKEI	52	0.2	1.5

2007: The Doomsday Clock is set to five minutes to midnight in response to North Korea's nuclear testing.

Fri

18

FTSE 100	60	0.2	1.1
FTSE 250	68	0.2	0.7
S&P 500	57	0.1	0.7
NIKKEI	57	0.2	1.1

2008: The FTSE 100 suffers from its biggest ever points fall.

Sat 19

Sun 20   Inauguration of the President of the United States

COMPANY NEWS

Interims IG Group Holdings
Finals Bankers Investment Trust

"If Richard Branson had worn a pair of steel-rimmed glasses, a double breasted suit and shaved off his beard, I would have taken him seriously. As it was, I couldn't."
Lord King

SMALL CAP STOCKS IN JANUARY

In 1976 an academic paper[1] found that equally-weighted indices of all the stocks on the NYSE had significantly higher returns in January than in the other 11 months during 1904-1974. This indicated that small capitalisation stocks outperformed larger stocks in January. Over the following years, many further papers were written confirming this finding. In 2006, a paper[2] tested this effect (now called the January Effect) on data from 1802 and found the effect was consistent up to the present time.

Does the January Effect work for UK stocks?

The FTSE Small Cap Index comprises those stocks in the FTSE All Share Index that are not big enough to qualify for the FTSE 350 Index. At the time of writing the index comprised 248 stocks.

The following table shows the outperformance of the FTSE Small Cap Index sector over the FTSE 100 Index for every month since August 1999. For example, in January 2000 the Small Cap Index rose 2.0% while the FTSE 100 Index fell -9.6%, giving an outperformance of the former over the latter of 11.6 percentage points. In months where the Small Cap Index underperformed the FTSE 100 Index (i.e. the outperformance is negative) the cell is highlighted.

	Jan	Feb	Mar	Apr	May	Jun	Jul	Aug	Sep	Oct	Nov	Dec
1999								3.4	-1.4	-5.4	3.5	2.8
2000	11.6	6.1	-4.5	-2.1	-0.1	6.0	-0.2	0.5	1.7	-6.2	2.1	-1.9
2001	3.3	1.9	-4.8	-0.1	4.7	-3.1	-4.8	2.3	-11.4	4.0	8.7	-0.9
2002	-1.0	-1.4	0.3	2.9	2.0	-2.0	-2.0	-0.6	-0.8	-8.0	3.9	0.4
2003	4.5	-3.5	-2.6	2.6	7.6	4.0	4.6	6.2	-0.5	0.2	-2.3	-2.0
2004	7.8	0.7	0.0	-2.7	-3.1	2.2	-2.8	-1.5	1.0	0.6	1.5	0.4
2005	3.5	-0.2	0.3	-1.7	-2.5	0.3	0.6	2.0	-1.6	-0.8	3.2	-0.3
2006	3.1	1.7	-1.8	-0.6	-0.6	-2.8	-1.9	2.3	1.8	-0.1	1.7	4.1
2007	1.4	1.0	-1.1	-0.1	-0.7	-3.6	2.2	-1.9	-4.5	-1.2	-6.8	-1.2
2008	0.2	4.1	-2.9	-3.5	0.2	-1.7	-0.1	-0.8	-1.8	-9.4	-5.9	0.5
2009	2.5	3.6	0.4	17.8	-1.0	2.7	-2.4	6.5	2.2	-1.6	-5.5	-2.0
2010	5.1	-3.8	-2.6	4.8	-0.6	3.1	-3.5	0.8	0.7	1.0	-0.1	1.1
2011	1.5	-2.8	0.9	0.0	0.8	0.1	1.9	-0.1	-2.2	-6.2	-3.0	-1.4
2012	4.3	2.7	3.1	-0.1	0.5	-2.3	-0.2					
average:	3.7	0.8	-1.2	1.3	0.5	0.2	-0.7	1.5	-1.3	-2.6	0.1	0.0

The following chart plots the average change in the Small Cap Index for each month.

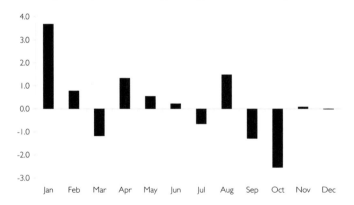

Observations

1. The UK market experiences the same January Effect (i.e. the outperformance of small cap stocks in January) as seen in the US market. The small cap outperformance in January is significantly strong. The Small Cap Index has underperformed the FTSE 100 Index in January in just one year out of the past 13.

2. The Small Cap Index significantly underperforms the FTSE 100 Index in October.

---

[1] Rozeff and Kinney, 'Capital market seasonality: The case of stock returns', *Journal of Financial Economics* 3 (1976), 379–402.
[2] Haug, M. and M. Hirschey, 'The January effect', *Financial Analysts Journal* 62:5 (2006), 78–88.

Mon

21

Martin Luther King Day (US) – NYSE closed

1976: From London's Heathrow Airport and Orly Airport outside Paris, the first Concordes with commercial passengers simultaneously take flight.

FTSE 100	40	-0.5	1.3
FTSE 250	32	-0.5	1.0
S&P 500			
NIKKEI	40	-0.5	1.4

Tue

22

1981: Rupert Murdoch bids to take over *The Times* and *The Sunday Times* newspapers.

FTSE 100	50	0.0	1.3
FTSE 250	47	0.1	1.1
S&P 500	52	-0.1	0.9
NIKKEI	40	-0.2	2.1

Wed

23

1957: American inventor Walter Frederick Morrison sells the rights to his 'flying disc' to the Wham-O toy company, who later rename it the 'Frisbee'.

FTSE 100	35	-0.4	0.9
FTSE 250	22	-0.3	0.6
S&P 500	64	0.2	0.7
NIKKEI	38	-0.3	1.8

Thu

24

ECB Governing Council Meeting
200th anniversary of the founding of The Royal Philharmonic Society in London.

1916: The US Supreme Court rules that a federal income tax is legal, despite the fact that the US Constitution explicitly forbids the direct taxation of citizens.

FTSE 100	60	0.5	1.2
FTSE 250	58	0.3	1.0
S&P 500	60	0.0	1.0
NIKKEI	62	-0.3	1.6

Fri

25

Burns Night

2011: The first wave of the Egyptian Revolution begins in Egypt as part of the Arab Spring.

FTSE 100	35	-0.2	0.7
FTSE 250	37	-0.1	0.6
S&P 500	58	0.0	0.7
NIKKEI	67	0.0	1.2

Sat 26

Sun 27   Full moon

COMPANY NEWS

Interims PZ Cussons, Renishaw

Finals Aberforth Smaller Companies Trust, Chemring Group

"Whenever I think about the budgetary problems, I think about the problems of Errol Flynn… reconciling net income with gross habits."
Sir Malcolm Rifkind

FEBRUARY MARKET

FTSE 100	57	0.9	4.1
FTSE 250	74	2.3	4.0
S&P 500	54	-0.1	3.5
NIKKEI	59	0.7	4.9

Market performance this month

The performance of the market in this month has improved in recent years. Five years ago it ranked ninth of all months, whereas today it is fourth. The market has risen in February in 57% of all years, with an average rise of 0.9%.

With January, February is the best month for mid-cap stocks relative to the large caps. On average, the FTSE 250 Index outperforms the FTSE 100 Index by 1.3 percentage points in this month.

This is one of the four months in the year that the FTSE 100 Index has historically outperformed the S&P 500 Index; in February this is by 0.6 percentage points on average.

Historically, this is the second strongest month in the year for the mining sector.

Historic performance of the market in February

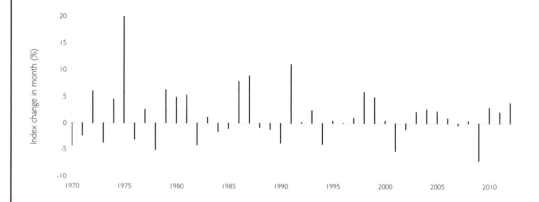

February summary

Month's performance ranking	4th
Average market change this month (standard deviation)	0.9% (4.1)
First trading day: Up / average change	57.1% / 0.6%
Last trading day: Up / average change	42.9% / -0.1%
Main features of the month	The FTSE 250 is particularly strong relative to the FTSE 100 in this month.
	The FTSE 100 often outperforms the S&P 500 in February.
	The mining sector is often strong in February.
	The last trading day in February (28 Feb) is often weak.
Significant dates	01 Feb: US Nonfarm payroll report (anticipated)
	07 Feb: MPC interest rate announcement at 12h00 (anticipated)
	10 Feb: Chinese New Year
	13 Feb: MSCI quarterly index review
	18 Feb: Washington's Birthday (US) – NYSE closed

Mon

28

200th anniversary of the publication of Jane Austen's *Pride and Prejudice*.

1958: The Lego company patents their design of Lego bricks; the original bricks are still compatible with the bricks produced today.

FTSE 100	55	0.1	1.1
FTSE 250	47	0.2	0.9
S&P 500	61	0.2	1.1
NIKKEI	55	0.2	1.6

Tue

29

Two-day FOMC meeting starts
50th anniversary of Charles de Gaulle blocking the United Kingdom's entry into the European Economic Community (EEC).

1989: Global Motors, the American company that imported the Yugo (the car you could "punch holes in the body with a wooden pencil"), files for bankruptcy.

FTSE 100	40	-0.2	1.0
FTSE 250	58	0.0	1.1
S&P 500	55	0.1	1.0
NIKKEI	55	0.3	1.4

Wed

30

World Economic Forum Annual Meeting (Davos)

2005: Reuters shares plunge as allegations emerge that it has been stealing data from Bloomberg.

FTSE 100	60	0.3	1.1
FTSE 250	63	0.1	0.7
S&P 500	56	0.0	0.9
NIKKEI	52	0.2	1.4

Thu

31

World Economic Forum Annual Meeting (Davos)
The last trading day in January is often strong.
Last day to file the 2012 Tax Return online without incurring penalties.

2010: *Avatar* becomes the first film to gross over $2 billion worldwide.

FTSE 100	65	0.3	0.8
FTSE 250	63	0.2	0.6
S&P 500	64	0.4	0.8
NIKKEI	71	-0.1	1.9

Fri

1

Nonfarm payroll report (anticipated)
World Economic Forum Annual Meeting (Davos)
The FTSE 100 often outperforms the S&P 500 in February.
100th anniversary of the reopening of New York City's Grand Central Terminal.

1884: The first volume (A to ant) of the Oxford English Dictionary is published.

FTSE 100	65	0.6	1.0
FTSE 250	84	0.7	0.9
S&P 500	59	0.1	0.8
NIKKEI	52	0.7	0.7

Sat 2   Groundhog Day, World Economic Forum Annual Meeting (Davos)

Sun 3   Super Bowl XLVII – New Orleans

COMPANY NEWS

Interims British Sky Broadcasting
Finals ARM Holdings, AstraZeneca, Centamin, Ocado, Royal Dutch Shell

"Budget: a mathematical confirmation of your suspicions."
A. A. Latimer

CHINESE CALENDAR AND THE STOCK MARKET

When we look at the annual performance of the stock market we naturally take our start and end points as 1 January and 31 December. For example, a long-term chart of an index will normally plot the index values on 31 December for each year.

But using different start and end points may be interesting. While the overall performance of the market will obviously not change, the path to the final point may show up differently, and thus possibly reveal a pattern of behaviour not previously noticed.

This week sees the start of the Chinese New Year on 10 February. The start of the Chinese Year moves around (on the Western calendar) from year to year, but always falls between 21 January and 21 February. The calculation of the actual date of the Chinese New Year is sinologically complex. For example:

> Rule 5: In a leap suì, the first month that does not contain a zhongqì is the leap month, rùnyuè. The leap month takes the same number as the previous month.

That quote comes from a 52-page academic paper on *The Mathematics of the Chinese Calendar*[1]. However, we shall skip lightly over such details and focus on a key aspect of the Chinese calendar which is the sexagenary cycle. This is a combination of ten heavenly stems and the 12 earthly branches. The branches are often associated with the sequence of 12 animals. (At last – the animals!) Cutting to the chase, the Chinese calendar encompasses a 12-year cycle, where each year is associated with an animal.

Can we detect any significant behavioural patterns in the stock market correlated with the sexagenary cycle? In other words, are there monkey years in the market?

The following chart plots the average performance of the stock market[2] for each animal year since 1950. For example, Ox years started in 1961, 1973, 1985, 1997, 2009; and the average performance of the market in those (Chinese) years was +14.0%.

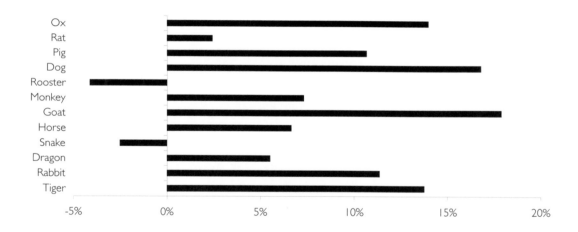

As can be seen, the best performing market animals have been the goat and dog. And, coincidentally (or is it?), the worst performing animals have been the rooster (perhaps a mistranslation for turkey?) and snake.

The Chinese New Year starting this week is… the Year of the Snake! The Chinese calendar is therefore forecasting the market will fall 2.5% from 10 February 2013 to 30 January 2014.

As the famous Chinese proverb says,

> *If the wind comes from an empty cave, it's not without a reason.*

---

[1] Helmer Aslaksen, 'The Mathematics of the Chinese Calendar', www.math.nus.edu.sg/aslaksen (2010).

[2] The S&P 500 Index was used for this study; as the correlation between the US and UK markets is so high, this index is a sufficient proxy for the UK market for the purposes here.

Mon

4

The mining sector is often strong in February.

1998: Noel Godin throws a pie into Bill Gates' face as the co-founder of Microsoft makes his way to a meeting with EU officials, in Brussels, Belgium.

→

FTSE 100	45	-0.2	1.0
FTSE 250	53	0.2	1.0
S&P 500	43	-0.2	1.1
NIKKEI	45	0.0	1.2

Tue

5

40th anniversary of the LSE flotation of CRH

1963: The European Court of Justice's ruling in Van Gend en Loos vs Nederlandse Administratie der Belastingen establishes the principle of direct effect; one of the most important decisions in the development of European Union law.

→

FTSE 100	45	-0.2	1.3
FTSE 250	58	-0.2	1.0
S&P 500	43	-0.1	0.9
NIKKEI	30	0.1	1.2

Wed

6

1959: Jack Kilby of Texas Instruments files the first patent for an integrated circuit.

→

FTSE 100	60	0.0	0.9
FTSE 250	53	0.2	0.8
S&P 500	55	0.1	0.8
NIKKEI	62	-0.5	1.2

Thu

7

MPC interest rate announcement at 12h00
ECB Governing Council meeting

1990: The Central Committee of the Soviet Communist Party agrees to give up its monopoly on power, heralding the collapse of the Soviet Union.

→

FTSE 100	55	0.1	1.2
FTSE 250	58	0.1	0.8
S&P 500	49	0.0	0.6
NIKKEI	57	-0.1	0.8

Fri

8

2012: Following the implementation of America's Foreign Account Tax Compliance Act (FACTA), the US Treasury and the IRS issue proposed regulations regarding information reporting by foreign financial institutions.

→

FTSE 100	55	0.2	1.0
FTSE 250	63	0.0	0.9
S&P 500	46	-0.1	0.8
NIKKEI	62	0.1	1.0

Sat 9

Sun 10   Chinese New Year (Year of the Snake), New moon

COMPANY NEWS

Interims Aquarius Platinum Ltd, BHP Billiton, Dunelm Group, Rank Group, City of London Investment Trust, Hargreaves Lansdown

Finals Barclays, Beazley, BP, Catlin, GlaxoSmithKline, Randgold Resources, Reckitt Benckiser, Shire, Smith & Nephew, SVG Capital, Unilever, Xstrata

"Never call an accountant a credit to his profession; a good accountant is a debit to his profession."
Charles J. C. Lyall

SUPER BOWL INDICATOR

Sunday 3 February 2013 was the date for Super Bowl XLVII in New Orleans.

One of the most famous market predictors in the US is the Super Bowl Indicator. This holds that if the Super Bowl is won by a team from the old National Football League the stock market will end the year higher than it began, and if a team from the old American Football League wins then the market will end lower.

Unlikely? Well, it certainly sounds far-fetched that a game of mutant rugby could affect the economy and stock market. However, in 1990 two academics published a paper[1] finding that the indicator was accurate 91% of the time.

And then in 2010 George Kester, a finance professor at Washington and Lee University, published a paper[2] with new research that found that the Super Bowl Indicator still worked (although its accuracy had fallen to 79%). Kester also calculated that a portfolio that switched between stocks and treasury bills governed by the Super Bowl Indicator would be worth twice that of a simple portfolio invested continuously in the S&P 500.

And the connection between American football and the UK stock market is…?

Seeing how closely correlated the US and UK stock markets are, it might be interesting to see how the Super Bowl Indicator applies to the UK market. The chart to the right shows the annual percentage change of the FTSE All Share index since 1967 (when the Super Bowl started). For clarity, the Y-axis has been capped at +50% and -40%, which truncates the bars for the years 1974 (-55%) and 1975 (+136%). The years for which the Super Bowl Indicator failed to accurately predict the direction of the market are shown with white bars in the chart.

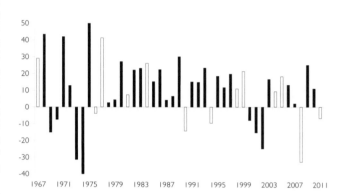

Overall, the indicator was accurate in 73% of years (only slightly less than its accuracy rate in the US).

The chart to the right shows the market behaviour around the time of the Super Bowl; the bars represent the average daily change in the FTSE All Share Index since 1967 for the three days before, and three days following, the Super Bowl (which always takes place on a Sunday).

The average change in the index for all days since 1967 was 0.03%; we can see therefore that the market is abnormally weak two days before a Super Bowl and abnormally strong one day before it.

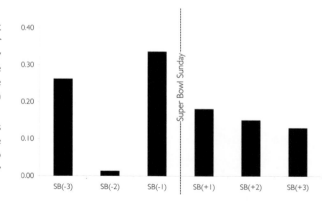

Finally, if you need any reassuring about the spookily close relationship between American football and numbers:

"Men, I want you just thinking of one word all season. One word and one word only: Super Bowl."
Bill Peterson, football coach

---

[1] Krueger, T. and Kennedy, W., 'An Examination of the Super Bowl Stock Market Predictor', *The Journal of Finance* 45:2 (1990), 691-697.
[2] Kester, George W., 'What Happened to the Super Bowl Stock Market Predictor?', *The Journal of Investing* 19:1 (2010), 82-87.

Mon 11

National Foundation Day (Japan) – TSE closed
HKEX closed
50th anniversary of The Beatles recording their debut album *Please Please Me* in a single session.

2010: The EU promises to act over Greek debts and advises Greece to make spending cuts. The austerity plans spark strikes and riots in the streets.

FTSE 100	60	0.4	1.0
FTSE 250	84	0.4	0.7
S&P 500	55	0.0	0.9
NIKKEI			

Tue 12

Shrove Tuesday (Pancake Day)
HKEX closed

2001: NEAR Shoemaker spacecraft becomes the first spacecraft to land on an asteroid.

FTSE 100	35	-0.1	1.2
FTSE 250	53	0.1	0.9
S&P 500	53	0.1	0.8
NIKKEI	75	0.7	1.4

Wed 13

Ash Wednesday
HKEX closed
MSCI quarterly index review (announcement date)

2011: For the first time in over 100 years, the Umatilla, an American Indian tribe, are able to hunt and harvest a bison just outside of Yellowstone National Park, restoring an ancient tradition guaranteed by a treaty signed in 1855.

FTSE 100	65	0.2	0.6
FTSE 250	68	0.1	0.5
S&P 500	55	0.2	0.7
NIKKEI	48	0.4	1.0

Thu 14

St Valentine's Day
100th anniversary of the birth of Jimmy Hoffa, American labour leader.

1946: The unveiling at the University of Philadelphia of ENIAC, the world's first computer, which has 18,000 vacuum tubes and fills a room measuring 30ft by 60ft.

FTSE 100	45	0.1	0.7
FTSE 250	63	0.2	0.5
S&P 500	42	0.0	0.8
NIKKEI	71	-0.2	1.5

Fri 15

2003: Protests against the Iraq War take place in over 600 cities worldwide. An estimated 8 million to 30 million people participate, making it the largest peace demonstration in history.

FTSE 100	60	0.1	0.7
FTSE 250	58	0.0	0.6
S&P 500	53	0.1	0.6
NIKKEI	57	0.3	1.1

Sat 16

Sun 17

COMPANY NEWS

Interims Diageo, Essar Energy, Murray Income Trust
Finals African Barrick Gold, Anglo American, BAE Systems, BG Group, Domino's Pizza, Fidessa Group, Herald Investment Trust, InterContinental Hotels Group, Ladbrokes, Morgan Crucible, Reed Elsevier, Rio Tinto, Rolls-Royce, Spectris, Telecity Group

"An economist is someone who sees something working in practice and asks whether it would work in principle."
Stephen M. Goldfeld

MARKET BEHAVIOUR – BY DAY

The two tables below list the historic ten best and worst days for the market.

For example, historically the very best day of the whole year has been 27 December; the market has risen on this day in 83% of all years. And on this day the market has risen by an average of 0.5%. The second strongest day of the year is 26 January.

Conversely, the very worst day of the year is 30 May; the market has only risen on this day in 18% of previous years and has fallen by an average of 0.5% on this day.

The performance figures below are ranked by the Up(%) – the percentage of years that the market has historically risen on the day.

10 strongest days in the year

Day	Up(%)	Avg Chng(%)	StdDev
27 Dec	83	0.5	1.2
26 Jan	80	0.7	1.1
02 Aug	80	0.6	1.0
31 Oct	80	0.5	1.0
23 Dec	80	0.4	0.6
24 Dec	80	0.2	0.6
27 Sep	75	0.7	1.1
02 May	75	0.6	0.9
16 Dec	75	0.6	0.8
01 Apr	75	0.5	1.2

10 weakest days in the year

Day	Up(%)	Avg Chng(%)	StdDev
30 May	18	-0.5	1.3
08 Apr	22	-0.3	0.7
08 Jul	25	-0.2	0.9
14 Apr	28	-0.3	0.9
07 Jan	30	-0.2	1.0
20 Jan	30	-0.5	0.8
04 Aug	30	-0.4	1.0
10 Aug	30	-0.6	1.4
09 Sep	30	-0.3	0.8
19 Nov	30	-0.6	1.5

Note: The above best and worst days for the market are marked on the diary pages with a square around the arrow icon.

Analysis of Up-Days

Average Up(%)	52
Standard deviation	11

On average, in previous years the market has risen 52% of all days.

The standard deviation is 11, which means that:

- days that have an Up(%) over 63 (the average plus one standard deviation) can be considered **strong** days, and

- days that have an Up(%) under 41 (the average minus one standard deviation) can be considered **weak** days.

50, 0, 2.4   Week 8

Mon

18

Washington's Birthday (US) – NYSE closed

FTSE 100	42	0.0	0.7
FTSE 250	68	0.4	0.7
S&P 500			
NIKKEI	47	0.5	1.2

1981: Margaret Thatcher's Conservative government withdraws plans to close 23 coal mining pits in its first major U-turn since coming to power.

Tue

19

FTSE 100	45	-0.1	1.1
FTSE 250	53	0.0	0.6
S&P 500	47	-0.1	0.9
NIKKEI	55	0.0	1.0

1674: England and the Netherlands sign the Peace of Westminster, ending the Third Anglo-Dutch War. A provision of the agreement transfers the Dutch colony of New Amsterdam to England, and it is renamed New York.

Wed

20

MPC meeting minutes published
40th anniversary of the LSE flotation of Premier Oil.

FTSE 100	40	-0.3	1.1
FTSE 250	42	-0.2	0.9
S&P 500	54	0	0.9
NIKKEI	38	-0.1	1.2

2002: Palindrome day. At 20:02 hours the time and date reads 20:02, 20, 02, 2002. Or 2002 2002 2002.

Thu

21

ECB Governing Council Meeting

FTSE 100	45	0.0	0.8
FTSE 250	37	-0.2	0.5
S&P 500	33	-0.1	0.7
NIKKEI	43	-0.2	1.8

1965: Black nationalist leader, Malcolm X, is assassinated.

Fri

22

FTSE 100	40	-0.1	0.6
FTSE 250	58	-0.1	0.6
S&P 500	42	0.0	1.0
NIKKEI	48	0.3	1.0

1997: Scientists in Scotland reveal the birth of Dolly the sheep – the world's first successfully cloned mammal.

Sat 23

Sun 24

COMPANY NEWS

Interims Genesis Emerging Markets Fund Ltd, Dechra Pharmaceuticals, Genus, Barratt Developments, Galliford Try, Hays, Ashmore Group, Kier Group, Redrow

Finals AMEC, Berendsen, BlackRock World Mining Trust, Bodycote, Capita Group, Centrica, COLT Group SA, Croda International, CSR, Devro, Drax Group, Filtrona, Hammerson, Lancashire Holdings, Lloyds Banking Group, Logica, Millennium & Copthorne Hotels, New World Resources, Rathbone Brothers, Rexam, Rightmove, Royal Bank of Scotland Group, Segro, St James's Place, Talvivaara Mining, Temple Bar Investment Trust, Travis Perkins, William Hill

"Wealth – any income that is at least one hundred dollars more a year than the income of one's wife's sister's husband."
H. L. Mencken

LAST TRADING DAYS OF THE MONTH

In week 23 we look at how the market behaves on the first trading day of each month. This page looks at the last trading days of each month.

FTSE 100 Index daily data was analysed from 1984 to discover if the UK equity market had a tendency to significantly increase or decrease on the last trading day of each month. The results are shown in the table below.

	Number of days	Positive	Positive (%)	Average (%)
All days	7135	3723	52.2	0.03
Last trading day of each month	339	187	55.2	0.13
Last trading day of each month (from 2000)	150	71	47.3	0.10

Analysis

Overall, since 1984, the market has had a tendency to increase by an above average amount on the last trading day of each month. On average, the market has risen 0.13% on months' last trading days against 0.03% for all days in the month. However, in recent years (since 2000), the effect has somewhat reversed, with the majority of last trading days seeing falls in the market.

This behaviour is very different from that of the first trading days in the month, which strongly outperform the average for all days, and where the effect has strengthened in recent years.

The table below shows the analysis of last trading days by month from 1984.

	Jan	Feb	Mar	Apr	May	Jun	Jul	Aug	Sep	Oct	Nov	Dec
Positive(%)	64.3	42.9	50.0	55.2	51.7	69.0	46.4	64.3	46.4	75.0	46.4	50.0
Average(%)	0.2	-0.1	0.1	0.2	0.1	0.2	0.2	0.2	0.0	0.6	-0.1	0.1

The difference in performance between the months is quite significant. The last trading days in January, June and October are all abnormally strong – in the case of October the market rises 75% of all years. By contrast, the last trading days of February, July, September and November are very weak.

A summary of the last trading day effect (by month) is shown in the chart below.

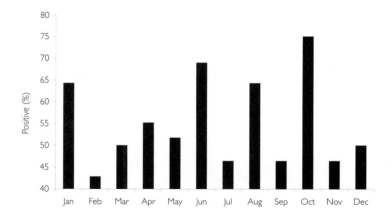

Note: See also *First trading days of the month*, week 23.

Mon

Full moon (market often strong this day)
100th anniversary of the birth of Gert Fröbe, the German actor.

25

1986: Corazon Aquino becomes the Philippines' first female president after the dictator Ferdinand Marcos flees the country, ending his 20-year rule.

FTSE 100	70	0.4	1.1
FTSE 250	68	0.5	1.0
S&P 500	52	0.1	0.8
NIKKEI	85	-0.4	1.2

Tue

26

1995: Barings PLC, the country's oldest merchant bank, declares bankruptcy after discovering that Nicholas Leeson, the firm's chief trader in Singapore, has lost approximately £625 million to £1 billion of the bank's assets on unauthorised futures and options transactions.

FTSE 100	60	0.3	0.8
FTSE 250	63	0.3	0.6
S&P 500	59	0.1	0.8
NIKKEI	50	0.7	1.3

Wed

27

FTSE 100	45	-0.2	0.9
FTSE 250	68	-0.1	1.1
S&P 500	47	-0.2	0.9
NIKKEI	57	0.0	1.6

1900: The British Labour Party is founded.

Thu

The last trading day in February is often weak.

28

FTSE 100	45	-0.2	1.1
FTSE 250	58	0.0	0.7
S&P 500	58	0.0	0.6
NIKKEI	62	0.3	1.2

1885: The American Telephone and Telegraph Company is incorporated as the subsidiary of American Bell Telephone.

Fri

St David's Day
MSCI quarterly index review (effective date)

1

FTSE 100	65	0.3	1.1
FTSE 250	74	0.4	0.8
S&P 500	64	0.3	0.7
NIKKEI	48	0.0	1.3

1946: The Bank of England is nationalised.

Sat 2

Sun 3

COMPANY NEWS

Interims Go-Ahead Group, JPMorgan Emerging Markets Inv Trust, Petra Diamonds Ltd

Finals Avocet Mining, AZ Electronic Materials SA, BBA Aviation, Bovis Homes, British American Tobacco, Bunzl, Capital & Counties Properties, Capital Shopping Centres, Carillion, Cookson Group, CRH, Derwent London, Dialight, Elementis, GKN, Henderson Group, Hiscox, Howden Joinery, HSBC Holdings, IMI, Informa, International Consolidated Airlines Group SA, International Personal Finance, Interserve, ITV, Jardine Lloyd Thompson, Man Group, Mondi, Moneysupermarket.com, Murray International Trust, National Express, NMC Health, Pearson, Perform Group, Persimmon, Provident Financial, Rentokil Initial, Restaurant Group, Rotork, RSA Insurance, SDL, Senior, Serco Group, Spirent Communications, Standard Chartered, Taylor Wimpey, UBM, Ultra Electronics, Weir Group, WPP Group

"Inflation is taxation without legislation."
Milton Friedman

MARCH MARKET

FTSE 100	57	0.6	3.5
FTSE 250	59	1.4	4.1
S&P 500	65	1.2	3.4
NIKKEI	59	1.5	6.8

Market performance this month

March is a middling month for the market, ranking sixth of all months in performance. On average, the market rises 0.6% this month. The probability of a positive return in the month is 57%.

Historically, mid-cap stocks have performed marginally better than large cap stocks in March.

Historic performance of the market in March

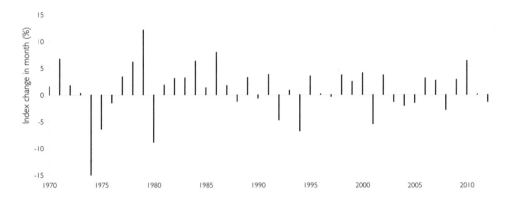

March summary

Month's performance ranking	6th
Average market change this month (standard deviation)	0.6% (3.5)
First trading day: Up / average change	57.1% / 0.0%
Last trading day: Up / average change	50.0% / 0.1%
Main features of the month	25 Mar: Start of the 9th weakest market week of the year
Significant dates	01 Mar: US Nonfarm payroll report (anticipated)
	06 Mar: FTSE 100 Index review announced
	07 Mar: MPC interest rate announcement at 12h00 (anticipated)
	15 Mar: Triple Witching
	20 Mar: FOMC monetary policy statement
	20 Mar: Chancellor's Budget 2013 (anticipated)
	29 Mar: Good Friday – LSE closed

Mon 4

100th anniversary of Woodrow Wilson becoming US President.

1980: Nationalist leader, Robert Mugabe, wins a sweeping election victory to become Zimbabwe's first black prime minister.

FTSE 100	60	0.4	1.2
FTSE 250	84	0.5	1.0
S&P 500	52	0.2	0.9
NIKKEI	75	-0.3	1.4

Tue 5

2009: The Bank of England, led by Sir Mervyn King, announces it will begin a policy of quantitative easing – effectively printing £75 billion of money – by buying bonds. Four days later the FTSE 100 hits a six-year low of 3460.

FTSE 100	50	0.0	1.3
FTSE 250	58	-0.1	1.1
S&P 500	58	0.1	1.0
NIKKEI	48	0.5	1.7

Wed 6

Beige Book published
FTSE 100 quarterly review

2000: Celltech shares peak at 1843.5p, having risen over four times in value in the previous four months.

FTSE 100	55	0.2	1.0
FTSE 250	63	0.0	1.1
S&P 500	47	0.0	1.0
NIKKEI	57	0.2	1.4

Thu 7

MPC interest rate announcement at 12h00
ECB Governing Council meeting

2009: The Kepler space observatory, designed to discover Earth-like planets orbiting other stars, is launched.

FTSE 100	45	-0.2	0.8
FTSE 250	58	-0.1	1.0
S&P 500	44	-0.2	0.7
NIKKEI	43	0.2	1.3

Fri 8

Nonfarm payroll report (anticipated)

1985: The impact of President Reagan's high-level tax cuts is made clear when the IRS announce that over 400,000 Americans have reached the millionaire rank.

FTSE 100	65	0.1	0.8
FTSE 250	53	0.1	0.8
S&P 500	60	0.1	0.9
NIKKEI	48	-0.4	1.6

Sat 9

Sun 10   Mothering Sunday

COMPANY NEWS

Interims J D Wetherspoon

Finals Admiral Group, Aggreko, Alliance Trust, Amlin, Aviva, Balfour Beatty, Cape, Cobham, Dignity, Fidelity European Values, Foreign & Colonial Investment Trust, Fresnillo, Glencore International, Hunting, Inmarsat, Intertek, IP Group, John Wood Group, Jupiter Fund Management, Laird, Meggitt, Melrose, Menzies (John), Michael Page International, Old Mutual, Petrofac, RPS Group, Schroders, Spirax-Sarco Engineering, Tullett Prebon

"They say there are two sides to everything. But there is only one side in the stock market; and it is not the bull side or the bear side, but the right side."
Edwin Lefèvre

TRIPLE WITCHING

Derivatives contract expiry

Exchange-traded options and futures are financial contracts that expire on a certain day. On this expiry day the underlying assets (in the case we're interested in here, stocks and stock indices) can experience an increased level of volatility. This can be for a couple of reasons:

1. Traders that have positions in the derivative instruments (e.g. options) may try to influence the closing price of the underlying stocks to which the settlement prices of the derivatives are related. For example, if a trader is long call (or short put) options, they might try to ramp the underlying stock in the closing period of trading. Conversely, traders of long puts (or short calls) might try to sell the stock down in the closing period.

2. If traders with arbitrage positions (i.e. matched holdings in derivatives and underlying stocks) unwind their positions at contract expiry this can create buying or selling pressure on the stocks.

Triple witching

The derivatives contracts that are relevant here are: stock index futures, stock index options and stock options. The expiries of these contracts happen in a programmed calendar throughout the year. However, on four days a year these three different types of derivative all expire on the same day – the third Friday of the months of March, June, September and December. The final hour of these days has come to be known in the US as *triple witching hour*. And with the recent introduction of single stock futures, triple witching has become *quadruple witching*.

Triple witching days 2013
15 March
21 June
20 September
20 December

Due to the correlation of the US and UK markets, the UK would be affected by US triple witching anyway; however, the UK also has it own version of triple witching, as the expiries of stock options and futures on LIFFE also coincide on the same four days as those in the US.

The first chart shows the recent average trading range (defined as the percentage range between the high and low prices on the day) for the FTSE 100 Index on the triple witching day (day 2) and that for the day immediately prior to it and following it (days 1 and 3 respectively). The dotted line shows the average trading range for all days since the year 2000.

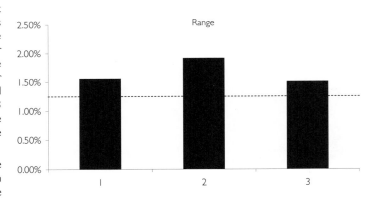

As can be seen, the trading range for the three days is higher than that for normal days, with the greatest volatility seen on the triple witching day itself.

The second chart shows the average change in the FTSE 100 Index on the three days around triple witching (which occurs on day 2). The dotted line shows the average change for all days since the year 2000.

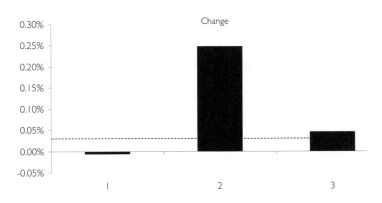

It can be seen that the average change on triple witching day is significantly above normal.

Mon

11

New moon
60th anniversary of the LSE flotation of TR Property Investment Trust.

➡

FTSE 100	45	-0.2	1.0
FTSE 250	58	0.0	1.1
S&P 500	59	0.2	0.9
NIKKEI	60	-0.2	1.5

2003: Sainsbury's shares trade at 217p – a low price not seen since 1989.

Tue

12

Cheltenham National Hunt Festival (until 15th)

↘

FTSE 100	40	-0.3	1.4
FTSE 250	63	0.1	0.9
S&P 500	53	0.0	1.1
NIKKEI	52	-0.1	1.4

2003: Pearson shares hit a ten year low of 429.5p, having fallen over 80% in the preceding three years.

Wed

13

➡

FTSE 100	45	0.1	1.6
FTSE 250	58	0.1	1.1
S&P 500	62	0.0	0.9
NIKKEI	43	-0.2	2.0

2008: Gold prices on the New York Mercantile Exchange hit $1,000 per ounce for the first time.

Thu

14

➡

FTSE 100	60	0.3	1.3
FTSE 250	58	0.0	1.1
S&P 500	47	-0.1	0.9
NIKKEI	52	-0.3	1.8

1794: Eli Whitney, a pioneer in the mass production of cotton, is granted a patent for the cotton gin.

Fri

15

Triple Witching (market often strong on this day)

➡

FTSE 100	50	0.1	1.0
FTSE 250	53	0.0	1.0
S&P 500	69	0.3	0.8
NIKKEI	81	-0.2	2.6

1990: Mikhail Gorbachev announces that he will be introducing free market principles into the former USSR. For many people around the world, this represents the failure of Communism as an economic system.

Sat 16

Sun 17   St Patrick's Day

COMPANY NEWS

Interims Close Brothers, Smiths Group
Finals Aegis Group, Antofagasta, Computacenter, F&C Asset Management, Ferrexpo, G4S, Greggs, Hikma Pharmaceuticals, Inchcape, John Laing Infrastructure Fund, Law Debenture, Legal & General, Morrison (Wm) Supermarkets, Premier Farnell, Prudential, Raven Russia, Savills, SIG, SOCO International, Standard Life, Tullow Oil, Witan Investment Trust, Yule Catto & Co

"My idea of a group decision is to look in the mirror."
Warren Buffett

TUESDAY REVERSES MONDAY

Some traders believe that Tuesday's market reverses Monday's. In other words, if the market rises on Monday it will fall the following day, and vice versa.

Is this true?

The first chart shows the change in the FTSE 100 Index on:

1. Tuesdays when the market has **risen** the previous day (*Monday up*), and

2. Tuesdays when market has **fallen** the previous day (*Monday down*).

The data analysed covers two periods: 1984-2012 and 2000-2012.

For example, in the period 1984-2012, the market rose on average 0.02% on Tuesdays following a Monday increase.

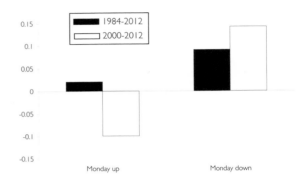

As can be seen, for the longer period of 1984-2012 the theory that Tuesday reverses Monday does not seem to hold. For this period, when the market falls on Monday the return is positive the next day (which is fine), but when the market rises on Monday, average Tuesday returns are positive as well (i.e. no reversal).

However, since 2000 the theory appears to be working rather well. Tuesday returns have on average been the reverse of Monday. In fact, when the market is down on Monday, the average returns the following day have been five times greater than the average returns on all days since 2000.

How can this be exploited?

The line graph to the right shows the value of three portfolios since 2000 (all starting with a value of 100):

1. Portfolio 1: tracks the FTSE 100 Index

2. Portfolio 2: if the market is down on Monday this portfolio goes long the market at the end of Monday and closes the position at the end of Tuesday (for four days out of five the portfolio is in cash)

3. Portfolio 3: similar to the above, with the addition that it also goes short the market on Tuesday if Monday was up

By 2012 the market portfolio (portfolio 1) value would be 82, portfolio 2 would be worth 148 and portfolio 3 would be worth 196.

It's interesting to observe that both portfolios 2 and 3 performed well during the steep market fall in 2007-2008. Although, of late, the profitability of portfolio 3 has been falling.

The bar chart to the right looks at the effectiveness of the theory on a year-by-year basis for the period 2008-2011.

It can be seen that while the theory worked well in the years 2008 and 2010, it did not in 2009 and 2011. The difference in profitability of portfolios 2 and 3 in 2011 is attributable to the market rising (relatively) strongly on Tuesdays following a positive Monday.

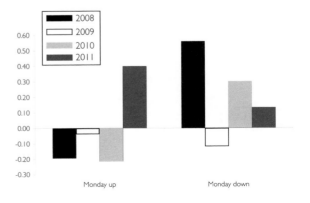

Mon

18

1985: Capital Cities Communications buys American Broadcasting Co. (ABC). Capital Cities tenders $3.5 billion in cash and warrants, making it the largest corporate merger in history up to that point.

FTSE 100	50	0.1	1.2
FTSE 250	53	0.3	0.9
S&P 500	57	0.3	0.9
NIKKEI	65	0.3	1.0

Tue

19

Two-day FOMC meeting starts
200th anniversary of the birth of David Livingstone, the Scottish missionary and explorer.

1999: The DJIA breaks the 10,000 mark for the first time.

FTSE 100	65	0.1	0.8
FTSE 250	58	0.2	0.8
S&P 500	44	-0.1	0.8
NIKKEI	57	0.3	1.7

Wed

20

Spring Equinox, also known as Ostara
Vernal Equinox (Japan) – TSE closed
Chancellor's Budget 2013 (anticipated)
MPC meeting minutes published

1602: The Dutch East India Company is established with a royal charter – the world's first IPO. The spice merchants issue shares that pay dividends between 12-63%, based on the fate of the company's trading ships.

FTSE 100	50	0.1	1.0
FTSE 250	58	-0.1	0.8
S&P 500	47	0.0	0.8
NIKKEI			

Thu

21

600th anniversary of Henry V becoming King of England.
50th anniversary of the closing of Alcatraz Island Federal Penitentiary in San Francisco Bay.

1991: Environment Secretary Michael Heseltine scraps the controversial poll tax and replaces it with a property tax.

FTSE 100	47	0.1	1.0
FTSE 250	61	0.1	0.8
S&P 500	39	-0.1	0.9
NIKKEI	75	0.0	2.6

Fri

22

1960: Arthur Leonard Schawlow and Charles Hard Townes receive the first patent for a laser.

FTSE 100	40	-0.4	1.2
FTSE 250	37	-0.4	0.8
S&P 500	47	0.0	0.6
NIKKEI	42	1.5	1.6

Sat 23

Sun 24   Palm Sunday

COMPANY NEWS

Interims
Finals Bank of Georgia, Bank of Georgia Holdings plc, BH Global Ltd, BH Macro Ltd, Cairn Energy, Eurasian Natural Resources Corporation, Gem Diamonds, Hochschild Mining, Kingfisher, Next, Ophir Energy, Phoenix Group, Premier Oil, Regus, Ted Baker, UK Commercial Property Trust

"For the merchant, even honesty is a financial speculation."
Charles Baudelaire

HOLIDAYS AND THE MARKET

In 1990 an academic paper[1] was published with the finding that the trading day prior to holidays in the US market had an average return 14 times greater than the average for the other days in the year. Furthermore, the paper found that over one-third of the total annual return in the market was attributable to the eight trading days that fell before holidays. This, and other papers, found that the day immediately before holidays had the highest returns (in the period around holidays), with the third day before the holidays having the next highest return and the day following the holiday having negative returns.

In 2010, research on this was updated in a paper[2] that found that the holiday effect had diminished in the 1990s and 2000s and that the outperformance was occurring largely in just the third day before holidays.

Does a holiday effect exist in the UK market?

The chart below shows the results of research on the daily returns of the FTSE 100 Index from 1984 to 2012. The four trading days immediately prior to holidays, H(-4) to H(-1), and the three trading days after holidays, H(+1) to H(+3), were analysed. A holiday was defined as a three day (or longer) period with no trading. The bars in the chart show the average return on the seven days around holidays.

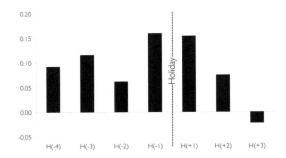

As with the US studies, H(-3) and H(-1) were found to be strong over the period analysed. Although, unlike the US studies, the day after a holiday, H(+1), was also found to be strong.

The period 2000-2012 was also analysed (the results can be seen in the following chart).

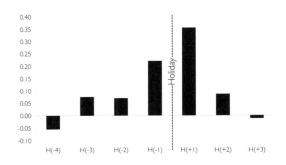

As can be seen, the UK holiday effect has changed in recent years. In the last ten years or so, the market has been significantly strong on the days immediately before and after holidays and weak four days before and three days after holidays. Some more statistics for the 2000-2012 analysis are given in the following table.

	All days	H(-4)	H(-3)	H(-2)	H(-1)	H(+1)	H(+2)	H(+3)
Days tested	3198	69	69	69	69	69	69	69
Average return(%)	0.00	-0.05	0.08	0.07	0.22	0.36	0.09	-0.01
Standard Deviation	1.31	1.27	1.06	1.01	0.92	1.31	1.12	0.87
Positive(%)	51	57	46	54	58	62	52	49

---

[1] Ariel, R. A., 'High stock returns before holidays: existence and evidence on possible causes', *Journal of Finance* (1990).

[2] Ziemba, William T. and Dzahabarov, Constantine N., 'Seasonal Anomalies' (12 February 2011).

Mon

25

Passover (until 2 April)
9th weakest market week

1995: WikiWikiWeb, the world's first wiki and part of the Portland Pattern Repository, is made public by Ward Cunningham.

FTSE 100	47	0.2	1.2
FTSE 250	39	0.1	1.1
S&P 500	42	0.1	0.8
NIKKEI	65	-0.1	1.3

Tue

26

1996: The International Monetary Fund approves a $10.2 billion loan for Russia.

FTSE 100	55	0.2	1.0
FTSE 250	42	0.1	0.5
S&P 500	56	0.1	0.8
NIKKEI	70	0.5	1.7

Wed

27

Full moon (market often strong on this day)
300th anniversary of the signing of First Treaty of Utrecht between Britain and Spain.
50th anniversary of the publication of the Beeching Report.
50th anniversary of the birth of Quentin Tarantino.

2011: Nintendo launches the 3DS in North America.

FTSE 100	53	0.0	1.0
FTSE 250	61	0.2	0.7
S&P 500	40	-0.1	0.9
NIKKEI	57	0.8	1.4

Thu

28

1994: BBC Radio 5 closes and is replaced with a new news and sport station called BBC Radio 5 Live.

FTSE 100	35	-0.3	0.7
FTSE 250	50	-0.1	0.6
S&P 500	48	-0.1	0.8
NIKKEI	60	0.4	1.2

Fri

29

UK Holiday: Good Friday
LSE, NYSE, HKEX closed
100th anniversary of the birth of R. S. Thomas, the Welsh poet.

2008: J. P. Morgan Chase's plans to acquire Bear Stearns for $1.2 billion are approved.

FTSE 100			
FTSE 250			
S&P 500			
NIKKEI	43	0.4	1.6

Sat 30

Sun 31   Easter (Western Christianity), End corporation tax financial year, Start of BST (clocks go forward)

COMPANY NEWS

Interims Bellway, Wolseley

Finals Afren, Barr (A G), Bumi, Bwin.Party Digital Entertainment, EnQuest, Evraz, F&C Commercial Property Trust, Hansteen Holdings, JPMorgan American Investment Trust, Kazakhmys, Kenmare Resources, Kentz Corporation Ltd, Mercantile Investment Trust, Merchants Trust, Petropavlovsk, Resolution, RusPetro, Salamander Energy

"Compound interest."
Albert Einstein, when asked what he thought was man's greatest invention

APRIL MARKET

FTSE 100	68	1.8	3.7
FTSE 250	67	2.3	5.3
S&P 500	68	1.5	3.8
NIKKEI	59	1.3	5.7

Market performance this month

Five years ago, April was the strongest month for the market in the year, but it is now ranked third. On average, the market rises 1.8% in this month. The probability of a positive return in the month is 68%. From 1971 the market rose in April every year for 15 years – a recent record for any month. Although the number of years with negative returns in the month has been increasing lately.

In any one year the relative performance of large and mid-cap stocks can diverge significantly in this month, but overall mid-caps marginally outperform large caps in April.

Six month effect

This is the last month in the six-month cycle, when the November-April market greatly outperforms the May-October market. For investors impressed with this phenomenon, the end of April is the time to sell out, or reduce exposure to the equity market.

Historic performance of the market in April

April summary

Month's performance ranking	3rd
Average market change this month (standard deviation)	1.8% (3.7)
First trading day: Up / average change	67.9% / 0.4%
Last trading day: Up / average change	55.2% / 0.2%
Main features of the month	Strong sectors in this second quarter are: Electronic & Electrical Equipment, Personal Goods, and Electricity.
	Weak sectors in this second quarter are: Construction & Materials, Health Care Equipment & Services, and General Industrials.
	April is the only month that the mining sector has historically underperformed the FTSE 100 Index.
	02 Apr: First trading day (FTD) in April – the second strongest FTD-of-the-month in the year
	08 Apr: 2nd weakest market day of the year
	15 Apr: Start of the 10th strongest market week of the year
Significant dates	01 Apr: Easter Monday – LSE closed
	04 Apr: MPC interest rate announcement at 12h00 (anticipated)
	05 Apr: US Nonfarm payroll report (anticipated)

		FTSE 100		

Mon

1

UK Holiday: Easter Monday
LSE, HKEX closed
3rd strongest market month
April is the only month that the mining sector has historically underperformed in the FTSE 100 Index.

2004: Google introduces its Gmail product to the public. The launch is met with scepticism on account of the launch date.

FTSE 100			
FTSE 250			
S&P 500	71	0.4	0.9
NIKKEI	60	-0.6	1.7

Tue

2

First trading day (FTD) in April – the second strongest FTD-of-the-month in the year.

1993: Phillip Morris, the maker of Marlboro cigarettes, sees its stock tumble by 26%, reducing the company's market cap by $10 billion, after slashing the prices of its products.

FTSE 100	67	0.7	1.2
FTSE 250	88	0.6	1.0
S&P 500	51	0.1	1.0
NIKKEI	62	0.3	2.4

Wed

3

2000: Microsoft is ruled to have violated United States antitrust laws by keeping "an oppressive thumb" on its competitors.

FTSE 100	43	-0.3	1.1
FTSE 250	53	0.0	1.0
S&P 500	52	0.0	1.0
NIKKEI	67	0.2	1.7

Thu

4

Ching Ming Festival (HK) – HKSE closed
MPC interest rate announcement at 12h00
ECB Governing Council meeting

1964: The Beatles occupy the top five positions on the Billboard Hot 100 pop chart.

FTSE 100	53	0.1	0.9
FTSE 250	59	-0.1	0.8
S&P 500	52	-0.1	0.6
NIKKEI	43	0.3	1.0

Fri

5

Nonfarm payroll report (anticipated)

1993: President Roosevelt introduces Presidential Executive Order 6102 as part of the New Deal controls. Gold, or gold certificates, over $100 in value that are owned by private individuals are to be turned in to the Federal Reserve, in return for paper currency.

FTSE 100	71	0.3	0.7
FTSE 250	63	0.1	0.5
S&P 500	60	0.3	1.0
NIKKEI	52	-0.1	0.9

Sat 6   Grand National

Sun 7

COMPANY NEWS

Interims
Finals

"Bankruptcy is a legal proceeding in which you put your money in your pants' pocket and give your coat to your creditors."
Joey Adams

SECTOR PERFORMANCE – SECOND QUARTER

The table below shows the performance of FTSE 350 sectors in the second quarter (31 March to 30 June) of each year from 2003 to 2012. The table is ranked by the final column – the average performance for each sector over the ten years. For each year the top five performing sectors are highlighted in light grey, the bottom five in dark grey.

Sector	2003	2004	2005	2006	2007	2008	2009	2010	2011	2012	Avg
Electronic & Elect Equip	51.2	-1.1	-14.5	-7.3	13.2	9.1	23.6	12.1	13.7	-4.6	9.5
Automobiles & Parts	33.6	10.0	1.9	-17.9	4.4	-26.7	81.7	-15.7	15.4	-12.4	7.4
Personal Goods	7.3	15.4	-2.0	-6.9	5.0	-1.1	35.2	7.0	17.1	-11.5	6.6
Software & Comp Srvs	47.4	-6.7	5.4	-14.4	-3.5	7.1	20.8	-8.2	5.1	-0.5	5.3
Electricity	1.7	2.1	19.2	1.7	-0.8	6.8	2.8	-0.7	12.3	4.4	5.0
Industrial Engineering	23.1	5.2	-2.3	-0.7	6.2	14.7	4.8	-1.2	8.7	-11.4	4.7
Technology Hard & Equip	36.1	-0.9	-13.2	-6.4	14.5	-4.8	31.5	4.4	0.4	-15.2	4.6
Pharm & Biotech	11.2	1.8	10.8	4.2	-3.9	6.0	2.3	-2.8	10.4	2.2	4.2
Fixed Line Telecoms	10.6	-3.8	1.0	6.4	10.0	-6.5	16.9	2.8	5.4	-2.9	4.0
Beverages	2.1	6.3	10.5	-4.2	5.1	-5.2	13.9	-3.1	5.2	5.7	3.6
Chemicals	13.5	3.2	-0.5	0.8	15.2	-6.5	7.6	-4.6	9.4	-3.4	3.5
Oil Equip; Srvs & Dist				-7.8	8.4	21.0	21.8	-3.8	-1.3	-17.8	2.9
Tobacco	9.7	2.6	12.0	-1.9	5.0	-7.8	2.8	-6.1	8.7	1.1	2.6
Aerospace & Defense	24.1	10.4	10.6	-10.3	-1.5	-9.6	8.2	-9.5	1.7	0.4	2.5
Nonlife Insurance	32.7	-4.2	6.5	-6.6	-6.5	-7.8	-3.3	0.4	5.8	3.8	2.1
Oil & Gas Producers	5.2	8.8	8.9	-1.4	15.1	16.4	1.4	-25.9	-3.2	-5.0	2.0
Equity Inv Instruments	20.9	-0.9	5.3	-7.1	2.5	-2.7	10.7	-6.3	1.7	-4.7	1.9
Travel & Leisure	22.4	6.0	4.2	-0.9	-3.9	-7.6	6.3	-11.7	3.1	1.3	1.9
Financial Services	26.9	-8.9	2.9	-4.4	1.3	-3.6	21.7	-8.1	-1.5	-8.7	1.8
Gas; Water & Multiutilities	8.0	1.1	8.4	0.6	-3.8	-2.1	2.4	-5.4	2.7	5.4	1.7
General Retailers	26.1	9.7	-3.6	-0.5	-8.8	-15.9	14.5	-10.3	9.8	-5.8	1.5
Mining	1.4	-6.5	2.1	0.5	18.5	16.9	17.2	-21.6	-2.0	-13.2	1.3
Industrial Transportation	16.8	0.9	3.0	10.0	-4.0	-19.0	14.6	-7.0	3.8	-6.8	1.2
Life Insurance	21.4	4.9	-1.7	-9.2	-0.7	-18.5	31.8	-13.1	0.9	-6.5	0.9
Food & Drug Retailers	17.0	4.3	-0.7	2.1	-1.2	-3.4	2.9	-10.7	4.5	-6.3	0.9
Mobile Telecom				-4.5	23.4	-0.7	-4.0	-8.3	-6.4	4.2	0.5
Banks	17.9	-1.0	3.4	-4.2	-1.0	-21.2	34.9	-11.9	-4.7	-7.6	0.5
Support Services	16.3	-2.1	0.3	-8.2	2.3	-9.4	11.0	-5.0	3.1	-4.8	0.4
Media	24.1	-1.0	-4.8	-3.9	3.2	-14.5	1.0	-5.8	3.1	-3.2	-0.2
Food Producers	-6.0	4.6	2.1	-6.5	3.9	-13.1	7.2	-6.2	5.0	2.7	-0.6
Industrial Metals		-3.6	-22.2	3.7		-2.9	79.2	-25.0	-8.1	-29.4	-1.0
Forestry & Paper	11.1	-3.6	-7.3			-29.1	39.9	-17.2	3.5	-7.5	-1.3
Real Estate Inv & Srvs								-14.5	8.6	1.2	-1.6
General Industrials				-8.9	-1.7	-1.8	13.1	-6.6	0.9	-6.2	-1.6
Health Care Equip & Srvs	4.9	7.4	10.7	-17.7	-0.5	-22.0	6.8	-2.6	-4.3	0.9	-1.6
Construction & Materials	21.2	-2.8	4.5	-8.2	14.4	-16.5	0.0	-17.8	-9.8	-1.7	-1.7
Real Estate Inv Trusts				-5.0	-15.3	-21.7	15.9	-13.9	9.0	3.1	-4.0
Household Goods				-4.8	-6.3	-24.9	5.3	-15.3	7.1	-3.8	-6.1

Observations

1. The general clustering of light grey highlights at the top of the table, and dark grey at the bottom, suggests that certain sectors consistently perform well (or badly) in this quarter. This effect is the strongest in the first quarter.

2. **Strong sectors** in this quarter are: Electronic & Electrical Equipment, Personal Goods, and Electricity.

3. **Weak sectors** in this quarter are: Construction & Materials, Health Care Equipment & Services, and General Industrials.

Mon	2nd weekest market day	
8		FTSE 100 22 -0.3 0.7
		FTSE 250 39 -0.2 0.5
	1904: Longacre Square in Midtown Manhattan is renamed Times Square after *The New York Times* Newspaper.	S&P 500 59 0.2 0.8
		NIKKEI 55 0.3 1.5

Tue		
9		FTSE 100 65 0.3 0.8
		FTSE 250 53 0.4 1.1
		S&P 500 53 0.2 1.0
	1967: The first Boeing 737 (a 100 series) makes its maiden flight.	NIKKEI 43 -0.1 2.0

Wed	New moon	
10		FTSE 100 53 0.3 1.7
		FTSE 250 47 0.2 2.0
	1790: George Washington gives the United States its first patent laws. The original patent law covers inventions and processes and only lasts 14 years.	S&P 500 63 0.2 0.8
		NIKKEI 43 -0.3 2.1

Thu		
11		FTSE 100 38 -0.2 0.9
		FTSE 250 53 -0.1 0.7
		S&P 500 48 -0.1 0.8
	1855: Britain's first pillar-boxes are put up in London; there are just six of them, and they are painted green.	NIKKEI 48 0.3 1.4

Fri		
12		FTSE 100 58 0.1 0.7
		FTSE 250 53 0.0 0.6
		S&P 500 67 0.3 0.7
	2009: Zimbabwe abandons the Zimbabwe Dollar as its official currency.	NIKKEI 57 0.3 1.0

Sat 13

Sun 14

COMPANY NEWS

Interims
Finals HICL, JD Sports Fashion

"The market, like the Lord, helps those who help themselves. But, unlike the Lord, the market does not forgive those who know not what they do."
Warren Buffett

MONTHLY COMPARATIVE PERFORMANCE – FTSE 100 & S&P 500

The table below shows the monthly outperformance of the FTSE 100 Index over the S&P 500 Index since 1984. For example, in January 1984, the FTSE 100 increased 6.3%, while the S&P 500 fell -0.9%; the outperformance of the former over the latter was therefore 7.2 percentage points.

The cells are highlighted if the number is negative (i.e. the S&P 500 outperformed the FTSE 100).

	Jan	Feb	Mar	Apr	May	Jun	Jul	Aug	Sep	Oct	Nov	Dec
1984	7.2	1.8	5.6	1.8	-4.4	0.3	-1.4	-1.3	3.6	0.9	4.1	2.1
1985	-3.5	-2.5	1.7	1.6	-3.7	-7.2	2.7	7.5	-0.3	2.5	-2.0	-6.3
1986	1.3	0.4	2.8	0.9	-8.5	1.5	0.3	-0.5	2.2	-0.6	-1.9	5.4
1987	-5.5	5.8	-1.7	3.8	6.8	-1.1	-1.5	-8.2	7.6	-4.3	-1.2	1.1
1988	0.5	-5.4	1.8	2.5	-1.3	-0.2	0.3	-1.5	0.2	-1.2	-1.3	-1.4
1989	7.3	0.5	1.5	-2.9	-3.7	2.5	-2.0	2.4	-3.1	-4.3	4.6	4.3
1990	3.4	-4.4	-2.8	-3.7	2.3	2.1	-1.5	2.4	-2.9	3.7	-1.2	-2.8
1991	-2.9	3.0	1.0	1.2	-3.3	1.4	2.7	0.2	1.0	-3.3	-1.3	-8.1
1992	5.1	-1.3	-2.6	6.0	1.9	-5.1	-8.8	-1.2	9.5	3.9	1.5	1.4
1993	-2.1	1.1	-1.5	0.3	-1.3	2.0	1.4	2.5	-1.0	2.5	1.2	6.9
1994	-1.1	-1.7	-2.7	0.1	-6.2	1.0	2.4	1.7	-4.2	0.3	3.4	-1.7
1995	-4.8	-3.0	1.5	-0.3	-0.4	-2.3	1.3	0.5	-3.1	1.1	-0.3	-1.1
1996	-1.4	-1.5	-1.5	1.9	-4.1	-1.2	4.4	2.6	-3.2	-2.0	-5.4	3.6
1997	-2.3	0.2	4.4	-3.0	-1.7	-4.7	-1.2	3.9	3.5	-4.2	-4.7	4.7
1998	5.3	-1.4	-2.1	-1.0	0.9	-4.6	1.2	4.5	-9.8	-0.6	-0.3	-3.2
1999	-3.9	8.0	-1.9	0.3	-2.5	-4.0	1.8	0.9	-0.6	-2.5	3.6	-0.7
2000	-4.5	1.4	-4.7	-0.2	2.7	-3.1	2.5	-1.2	-0.3	2.8	3.4	0.9
2001	-2.3	3.2	1.6	-1.8	-3.4	-0.1	-0.9	3.1	-0.1	1.0	-4.3	-0.5
2002	0.5	0.8	-0.3	4.1	-0.7	-1.2	-0.9	-0.9	-1.0	-0.1	-2.5	0.5
2003	-6.7	4.2	-2.0	0.5	-2.0	-1.5	1.5	-1.7	-0.5	-0.7	0.6	-2.0
2004	-3.7	1.1	-0.7	4.1	-2.5	-1.0	2.3	0.8	1.6	-0.2	-2.2	-0.9
2005	3.3	0.5	0.4	0.1	0.4	3.0	-0.3	1.5	2.6	-1.2	-1.5	3.7
2006	0.0	0.5	1.9	-0.2	-1.9	1.9	1.1	-2.5	-1.5	-0.3	-3.0	1.6
2007	-1.7	1.7	1.2	-2.1	-0.6	1.6	-0.6	-2.2	-1.0	2.5	0.1	1.2
2008	-2.8	3.6	-2.5	2.0	-1.6	1.5	-2.8	2.9	-3.9	6.2	5.4	2.6
2009	2.1	3.3	-6.0	-1.3	-1.2	-3.8	1.0	3.2	1.0	0.2	-2.8	2.5
2010	-0.4	0.3	0.2	-3.7	1.6	0.2	0.1	4.1	-2.6	-1.4	-2.4	0.2
2011	-2.9	-1.0	-1.3	-0.1	0.0	1.1	0.0	-1.6	2.2	-2.7	-0.2	0.4
2012	-2.4	-0.7	-4.9	0.2	-1.0	0.7	2.9					
average:	-0.6	0.6	-0.5	0.4	-1.4	-0.7	0.3	0.8	-0.1	-0.1	-0.4	0.5

The average monthly outperformance of the FTSE 100 over the S&P 500 is shown in the following chart:

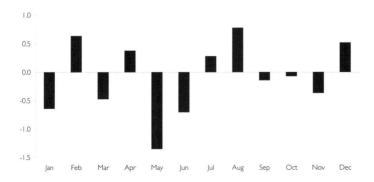

1. Although since 1984 the S&P 500 has overall greatly outperformed the FTSE 100 (+711% against +463%), there are months in the year when the FTSE 100 fairly consistently outperforms the S&P 500.

2. The five months that are relatively strong for the FTSE 100 are: February, April, July, August and December.

3. The greatest monthly difference in performance is seen in May, when the S&P 500 on average beats the FTSE 100 by 1.4 percentage points each year.

Mon

10th strongest market week
50th anniversary of the Aldermaston March.
10th anniversary of the LSE flotation of InterContinental Hotels Group.
10th anniversary of the LSE flotation of Mitchells & Butlers.

1955: Ray Kroc opens the first franchised McDonald's in Des Plaines, Illinois.

FTSE 100	65	0.4	0.9
FTSE 250	74	0.3	0.8
S&P 500	72	0.3	0.6
NIKKEI	55	-0.2	1.2

Tue
16

1956: The Council of Europe Development Bank is founded. Its headquarters are located in Paris, France.

FTSE 100	58	0.1	1.2
FTSE 250	65	0.4	0.8
S&P 500	57	0.2	0.9
NIKKEI	62	0.2	1.4

Wed
17

MPC meeting minutes published
Beige Book published

1837: John Pierpont Morgan, better known as J.P. Morgan, is born. Morgan grows up to be one of the most influential people on Wall Street, playing a part in the formation of the railroads, US Steel, and General Electric (GE).

FTSE 100	59	0.0	1.1
FTSE 250	53	-0.1	1.3
S&P 500	64	0.4	0.9
NIKKEI	48	-0.2	1.9

Thu
18

ECB Governing Council Meeting

1956: The British Chancellor, Harold Macmillan, unveils the premium bond scheme.

FTSE 100	50	0.0	1.0
FTSE 250	50	0.1	0.9
S&P 500	57	0.2	1.2
NIKKEI	62	-0.3	1.7

Fri
19

2011: Fidel Castro resigns as First Secretary of the Communist Party of Cuba's Central Committee, after 45 years of holding the title.

FTSE 100	52	0.2	0.7
FTSE 250	63	0.2	0.6
S&P 500	48	-0.1	0.6
NIKKEI	43	0.4	1.2

Sat 20

Sun 21

COMPANY NEWS

Interims Debenhams, WHSmith
Finals Heritage Oil Ltd, International Public Partnership Ltd, Tesco

"I have noticed that everyone who ever told me that the markets are efficient is poor."
Larry Hite

SIX-MONTH EFFECT

This is the strongest – and strangest – seasonality effect in the market.

As mentioned earlier (regarding the Chinese New Year), new patterns of market behaviour can be revealed when price histories are analysed using different timeframes. In this case, we are going to split the year into two six-month periods:

1. **Winter period:** 1 November to 30 April

2. **Summer period:** 1 May to 31 October

(We will call them "winter" and "summer" for the sake of giving them names.)

The following chart compares the performance since 1971 of the FTSE All Share Index for the two periods; each bar represents the outperformance of the winter period over the following summer period. For example, from 1 November 2010 to 30 April 2011 the index rose 7.5%, while during the subsequent period 1 May 2011 to 31 October 2011 the index fell 9.3%. The difference in performance was therefore 16.8 percentage points (7.5 - -9.3) and that is the figure plotted on the chart for 2011.

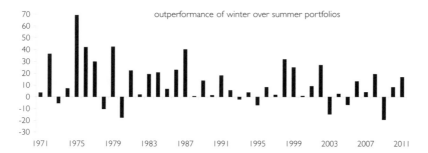

The chart shows a quite remarkable thing; namely that the market seems to perform much better in the six-month winter period than the summer period. To quantify this outperformance:

• in the 41 years since 1971, the winter period has outperformed the summer period 33 times, and

• the average annual outperformance since 1970 has been 12%!

The behaviour is extraordinary and should not exist in a modern, efficient(ish) market. But exist it does. Indeed, a similar effect also exists in other markets, such as the US.

How long has this effect been operating?

The following chart is identical to that above except the data starts from 1921.

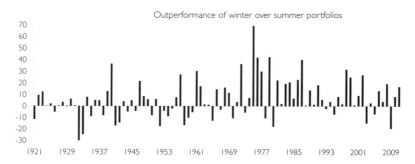

We can see from this chart that during the first half of the 20th century the market performance during the two periods was pretty equally balanced. But the behaviour changed significantly around the beginning of the 1970s.

But it may be that the above study is woefully short-termist in its approach. An academic paper[1] of 2012 found evidence of the six-month effect (also called the Sell in May effect in the UK and the Halloween effect in the US) starting from 1694 in the UK. The paper also found the effect was present in 36 of 37 developed and emerging markets.

---

[1] Jacobsen, B., Zhang, Cherry Yi, 'Are Monthly Seasonals Real? A Three Century Perspective' (15 February 2012).

Mon

22

1912: *Pravda*, the voice of the Communist Party of the Soviet Union, begins publication in Saint Petersburg.

➡️

FTSE 100	47	0.1	0.8
FTSE 250	72	0.2	0.7
S&P 500	40	0.0	1.1
NIKKEI	50	-0.1	1.0

Tue

St George's Day

23

1985: Coca-Cola announces that it has changed its traditional formula. Consumers rebel and Coke's stock and market share take multiple hits.

➡️

FTSE 100	38	-0.2	0.9
FTSE 250	63	0.1	0.9
S&P 500	44	-0.1	0.7
NIKKEI	57	-0.1	0.9

Wed

24

1844: Samuel Morse sends the message "What hath God wrought," (a biblical quotation, 23:23) from the Old Supreme Court Chamber in Washington D.C. to his assistant, Alfred Vail, in Baltimore, Maryland, to inaugurate the first telegraph line.

➡️

FTSE 100	50	0.1	1.1
FTSE 250	44	0.0	0.9
S&P 500	44	-0.1	0.8
NIKKEI	33	0.4	1.0

Thu

Full moon
Partial lunar eclipse (often sees market turning point)

25

1953: Scientists identify DNA.

➡️

FTSE 100	60	0.1	0.6
FTSE 250	50	0.0	0.5
S&P 500	56	0.1	0.9
NIKKEI	57	-0.2	1.1

Fri

26

1928: Madame Tussaud's waxworks exhibition opens in London.

↗️

FTSE 100	71	0.3	0.6
FTSE 250	74	0.2	0.5
S&P 500	56	0.1	0.6
NIKKEI	57	0.1	0.8

Sat 27 — 20th anniversary of the LSE flotation of Stagecoach Group

Sun 28

COMPANY NEWS

Interims Edinburgh Investment Trust, Associated British Foods, Fenner, Edinburgh Dragon Trust
Finals Dexion Absolute Ltd, NB Global Floating Rate Income Fund, Polymetal International, Whitbread

"Speculation is the struggle of well-equipped intelligence against the rough power of chance."
Henry Emery

MAY MARKET

FTSE 100	45	-0.3	4.5
FTSE 250	56	0.3	4.4
S&P 500	56	0.1	3.8
NIKKEI	52	-0.1	6.2

Market performance this month

We are heading into the weakest two-month period in the year. Generally, market performance in May justifies the saying, "sell in May and go away". May is the second weakest month of the year and marks the start of the underperforming half of the year. There are only three months where, since 1970, the market has an average return of below zero – this is one of them (the others are June and September). On average, the market falls -0.3% in May. The probability of a positive return in the month is below 50%, at 45%.

May is the weakest month of the year for the FTSE 100 Index relative to the S&P 500 Index; on average, the former underperforms the latter by 1.4 percentage points.

However, May is usually a good month for the mining sector, which has historically outperformed the wider market in this month.

Historic performance of the market in May

May summary

Month's performance ranking	11th
Average market change this month (standard deviation)	-0.3% (4.5)
First trading day: Up / average change	51.7% / 0.1%
Last trading day: Up / average change	51.7% / 0.1%
Main features of the month	The FTSE 100 often underperforms the S&P 500 in May.
	The mining sector is often strong in May.
	02 May: 8th strongest market day of the year
	20 May: Start of the 10th weakest market week of the year
	28 May: Start of the 6th weakest market week of the year
	30 May: Weakest market day of the year
Significant dates	03 May: US Nonfarm payroll report (anticipated)
	06 May: Early May bank holiday – LSE closed
	09 May: MPC interest rate announcement at 12h00 (anticipated)
	15 May: MSCI quarterly index review (anticipated)
	27 May: Spring bank holiday – LSE closed

Mon	Showa Day (Japan) – TSE closed		
29			FTSE 100 47 0.3 0.9 FTSE 250 61 0.3 0.9 S&P 500 50 0.2 0.9 NIKKEI
	1974: President Richard Nixon announces the release of edited transcripts of White House tape recordings related to the Watergate Scandal.		

Tue	Two-day FOMC meeting starts		
30			FTSE 100 57 0.2 0.7 FTSE 250 63 0.3 0.8 S&P 500 49 0.0 0.8 NIKKEI 50 -0.3 1.7
	1993: The World Wide Web is born at CERN in Switzerland.		

Wed	Labour Day (HK) – HKSE closed End of the strong half year (six-month effect) 2nd weakest market month 50th anniversary of Coca-Cola Company introducing its first diet drink, TaB Cola.		
1			FTSE 100 50 0.1 0.8 FTSE 250 50 0.1 0.5 S&P 500 58 0.3 0.7 NIKKEI 67 0.7 1.2
	1707: The Act of Union joins the Kingdom of England and Kingdom of Scotland to form the Kingdom of Great Britain.		

Thu	8th strongest market day ECB Governing Council meeting The FTSE 100 often underperforms the S&P 500 in May.		
2			FTSE 100 75 0.6 0.9 FTSE 250 71 0.6 0.7 S&P 500 67 0.2 0.7 NIKKEI 65 0.4 0.8
	1997: The Labour Party's Tony Blair comes to power, ending 18 years of Conservative rule.		

Fri	Constitution Memorial Day (Japan) – TSE closed Nonfarm payroll report (anticipated)		
3			FTSE 100 59 -0.2 1.1 FTSE 250 60 0.0 0.4 S&P 500 58 0.1 0.8 NIKKEI
	1867: The Hudson's Bay Company gives up all claims to Vancouver Island.		

Sat 4   **Greenery Day (Japan)**

Sun 5   **Easter Sunday (Eastern Christianity), Children's Day (Japan)**

COMPANY NEWS

Interims Aberdeen Asset Management, F&C Commercial Property Trust, Imperial Tobacco

Finals Bluecrest Allblue Fund, Brown (N) Group, Home Retail Group, Scottish Mortgage Investment Trust

"Investors are slow to learn that security analysts do not always mean what they say."
Hersh Shefrin

QUARTERLY SECTOR STRATEGY

The performance of the sectors in each quarter is analysed elsewhere in the *Almanac*. From the analysis it can be seen that four of the strongest sectors in the respective quarters are: Forestry & Paper, Electronic & Electrical Equipment, Technology Hardware & Equipment, and Mining.

The performance of these sectors, in their respective strong quarters, is shown in the table below.

Quarter	Sector	2002	2003	2004	2005	2006	2007	2008	2009	2010	2011	2012
1	Forestry & Paper		1.7	10.9	1.1	0	0	-1.6	-27.4	38.5	16.7	29.6
2	Electronic & Elect Equip		51.2	-1.1	-14.5	-7.3	13.2	9.1	23.6	12.1	13.7	-4.6
3	Technology Hard & Equip	-30.4	47.4	-19.8	15.2	-7.4	-6	6.5	23.2	29.8	-6.9	
4	Mining	15.5	18.3	-0.4	11.2	10.6	2.7	-31.5	24.1	22.8	8.5	

This behaviour suggests a strategy which cycles a portfolio through these four sectors throughout the year. In other words, the portfolio is 100% invested in the Forestry & Paper sector from 31 December to 31 March, then switches into Electronic & Electrical Equipment to 31 June, then switches into Technology Hardware & Equipment to 30 September, then switches into Mining to 31 December, and then switches back into Forestry & Paper and starts the cycle again.

The chart below illustrates the performance of such a strategy for the period 3rd Qtr 2002 to 2nd Qtr 2012, with a comparison to the FTSE All Share Index.

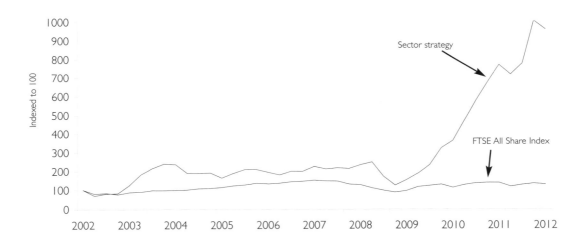

Over the ten years the strategy would have grown £1000 into £9560; while a £1000 investment in the FTSE All Share Index would have become just £1278.

Mon
6
May Day Bank Holiday (UK)
LSE, TSE closed

1997: The Bank of England is given independence from political control; the most significant change in the bank's 300-year history.

FTSE 100			
FTSE 250			
S&P 500	39	-0.1	0.8
NIKKEI			

Tue
7
The mining sector is often strong in May.

2000: Vladimir Putin is inaugurated as the President of Russia.

FTSE 100	38	-0.5	0.9
FTSE 250	33	-0.3	1.3
S&P 500	38	-0.2	0.7
NIKKEI	52	0.5	1.9

Wed
8
50th anniversary of the US premiere of *Dr. No*, the first James Bond film.

1945: Rejoicing sweeps Europe at end of the war, after Winston Churchill officially announces that a ceasefire had been signed in Rheims the day before.

FTSE 100	50	0.0	1.1
FTSE 250	56	0.0	1.1
S&P 500	56	0.2	0.8
NIKKEI	62	0.1	0.9

Thu
9
Feast of the Ascension (Western Christianity)
MPC interest rate announcement at 12h00

1873: The Vienna stock market crash heralds the Long Depression.

FTSE 100	38	-0.1	0.7
FTSE 250	47	-0.2	0.4
S&P 500	47	-0.1	0.7
NIKKEI	29	0.1	0.9

Fri
10
New moon
Solar eclipse (annular)

2010: The European Financial Stability Fund, authorised to borrow up to €440 billion, becomes operational.

FTSE 100	43	0.3	1.5
FTSE 250	47	0.2	1.5
S&P 500	47	-0.1	1.1
NIKKEI	43	-0.5	1.3

Sat 11   FA Cup Final

Sun 12

COMPANY NEWS

Interims TUI Travel, easyJet, Sage Group, British Assets Trust
Finals 3i Infrastructure, BT, Experian, Sainsbury (J)

"Money, not morality, is the principle commerce of civilised nations."
Thomas Jefferson

QUARTERLY SECTOR (HEDGE) STRATEGY

On the previous page we saw the performance of a strategy cycling investment in historically strong sectors through the calendar quarters. On this page we look at zipping up that strategy by, in each quarter, going long of the strong sector and hedging that by also going short of the quarter's weak sector.

The weakest sectors in the respective quarters are: Pharmaceuticals & Biotechnology, Construction & Materials, Support Services, and Banks.

The performance of these sectors, in their respective weak quarters, is shown in the table below.

Quarter	Weak Sector	2002	2003	2004	2005	2006	2007	2008	2009	2010	2011	2012
1	Pharm & Biotech		-5.4	-11.5	2.8	2.9	2.3	-15.3	-14.3	-0.7	-1.7	-5.5
2	Construction & Materials		21.2	-2.8	4.5	-8.2	14.4	-16.5	0	-17.8	-9.8	-1.7
3	Support Services	-29.5	7.9	-8.6	2.5	5.9	-10.9	-10.5	19.4	8.8	-13.7	
4	Banks	7.8	8.5	6.6	6.5	3.2	-10.3	-38.2	-9.2	-4	-0.3	

So, in the first quarter the strategy would be long the Forestry & Paper sector and short Pharmaceuticals & Biotechnology. On 31 March the strategy would close those positions and open new ones: long the Electronic & Electrical Equipment sector and short Construction & Materials, etc.

The hedge strategy is summarised in the following table.

Quarter	Long these sectors	Short these sectors
1	Forestry & Paper	Pharm & Biotech
2	Electronic & Elect Equip	Construction & Materials
3	Technology Hard & Equip	Support Services
4	Mining	Banks

The chart below illustrates the performance of such a strategy for the period 3rd Qtr 2002 to 2nd Qtr 2012, with a comparison to the FTSE All Share Index (the previous long-only sector strategy is also shown on the chart).

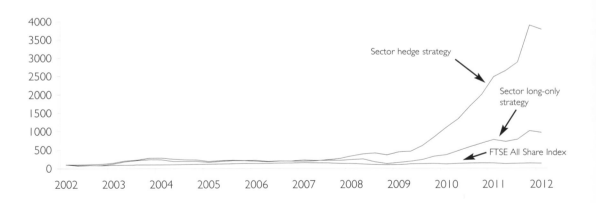

Over the ten years the hedge strategy would have grown £1000 into £37,600, while the £1000 investment in the FTSE All Share Index would have become £1278.

Mon

13

FTSE 100　55　0.2　0.9
FTSE 250　63　0.0　1.0
S&P 500　48　-0.1　0.8
NIKKEI　40　0.1　1.2

1995: A British mother of two becomes the first woman to conquer Everest without oxygen or the help of sherpas.

Tue

100th anniversary of the founding of the Rockefeller Foundation.

14

FTSE 100　33　-0.6　1.4
FTSE 250　37　-0.3　0.8
S&P 500　42　-0.2　0.9
NIKKEI　52　-0.2　1.1

1957: Petrol rationing, which was in force in Britain for five months following the Suez crisis, is abolished.

Wed

MSCI quarterly index review (announcement date)

15

FTSE 100　52　0.2　0.9
FTSE 250　53　0.0　0.8
S&P 500　53　0.0　0.9
NIKKEI　38　-0.1　1.6

1878: The Tokyo Stock Exchange (TSE) is formed.

Thu

ECB Governing Council Meeting

16

FTSE 100　43　0.1　0.6
FTSE 250　42　0.1　0.7
S&P 500　47　0.0　0.8
NIKKEI　43　0.0　1.1

1866: The US Congress eliminates the half dime coin and replaces it with the five cent piece, or the nickel.

Fri

Birthday of the Buddha (HK) – HKSE closed

17

FTSE 100　48　-0.2　1.3
FTSE 250　58　-0.2　1.0
S&P 500　56　-0.1　0.8
NIKKEI　57　-0.3　1.3

1930: The Bank of International Settlements, seen as the bank of central banks, is founded.

Sat 18　Rugby – Heineken Cup Final

Sun 19　Pentecost (Western Christianity)

COMPANY NEWS

Interims Diploma, Lonmin, Compass Group, Euromoney Institutional Investor, Grainger, Marston's, Mitchells & Butlers

Finals 3i Group, Babcock International, ICAP, Invensys, Investec, Land Securities, National Grid, Shanks, SSE, Stobart Group, TalkTalk Telecom, Vedanta Resources

"Failure is only the opportunity to begin again more intelligently."
Henry Ford

LUNAR CALENDAR AND THE STOCK MARKET

Do the phases of the moon affect the stock market?

One half of the moon is always illuminated by the sun; but its visibility from the earth varies from zero (new moon) to 100% (full moon). The time between new moons is approximately 29.5 days.

Lunar calendars are based on the phases of the moon. Most lunar calendars that are used today (e.g. the Chinese calendar, Hebrew calendar and Hindu calendar) are in fact *lunisolar*, so called as they try to reconcile a lunar calendar with the solar year. The only widely used calendar that is purely lunar is the Islamic calendar.

In folklore (and sometimes scientific studies) full moons have been said to affect human behaviour. Of course it is ridiculous to ask, but can full moons affect the behaviour of investors, and thereby influence the stock market?

The table below shows the result of some analysis into this (on FTSE 100 daily data since January 2000). "All days" refers to all market days since January 2000. FM(0) refers to the day of the full moon itself and the other columns to the one and two days before and after the full moon.

	All days	FM(-2)	FM(-1)	FM(0)	FM(+1)	FM(+2)
Number of days	3155	154	154	154	154	154
Number of days up(%)	51.0	45.5	51.3	53.9	55.2	49.4
Average daily change(%)	0.004	-0.200	0.018	0.090	0.015	-0.024
Standard deviation	0.013	1.491	1.423	1.107	1.322	1.208

It was found that on days with a full moon the FTSE 100 Index rose on average 0.09% (25 times the average increase of 0.004% for all days). The market had a tendency to rise the day after a full moon as well. By contrast, two days before and after a full moon the market tended to be weak.

Lunar eclipses

Lunar eclipses occur when the earth passes between the sun and the moon – they can only happen at full moons. The chart below shows the FTSE 100 Index since 2004 and the incidence of lunar eclipses (the vertical bars).

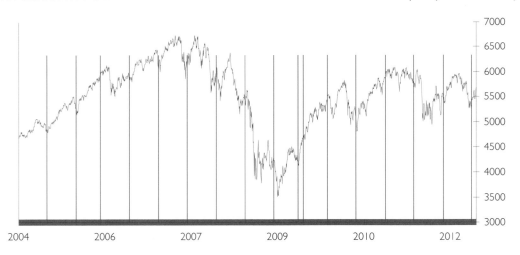

A quick look at the above chart shows that there is no close correlation between lunar eclipses and the behaviour of the stock market. However… if one was so minded, one can see some correlation on occasions. Occasionally the eclipses do accompany strong moves in the market, including significant turning points. An interesting time can be when two eclipses unusually occur in consecutive months (this happened in July 2009 when the market rose 12% in 22 days between the two eclipses). No doubt a coincidence.

There will be three lunar eclipses in 2013: 25 April, 25 May, 18 October (Note: the first two eclipses are in consecutive months!) The second of the two, on 25 May, occurs on Saturday this week.

45, -0.3, 2.1

Mon

20

10th weakest market week

FTSE 100	50	-0.2	1.0
FTSE 250	68	-0.2	1.0
S&P 500	45	-0.1	0.9
NIKKEI	45	0.3	0.9

1310: Shoes are made for right and left feet for the first time.

Tue

21

Chelsea Flower Show (until 25th)

FTSE 100	57	0.0	0.8
FTSE 250	63	-0.1	0.8
S&P 500	47	-0.1	0.8
NIKKEI	62	-0.2	1.3

1894: The Manchester Ship Canal is officially opened by Queen Victoria.

Wed

22

MPC meeting minutes published

FTSE 100	52	0.0	1.0
FTSE 250	58	-0.1	1.2
S&P 500	53	0.1	0.7
NIKKEI	52	0.1	1.2

1980: Namco releases the highly influential video game, Pacman.

Thu

23

FTSE 100	43	-0.3	1.2
FTSE 250	47	0.0	1.3
S&P 500	42	-0.2	0.8
NIKKEI	52	-0.2	1.1

1995: The first version of the Java programming language is released.

Fri

24

FTSE 100	43	-0.1	0.8
FTSE 250	47	-0.1	0.7
S&P 500	51	-0.1	0.9
NIKKEI	60	0.0	0.9

2000: BMW sells Land Rover to US car giant Ford for €3 billion, marking the end of the process of breaking up the UK car maker, Rover.

Sat 25 — Full moon, Penumbral lunar eclipse, Football – Champions League Final

Sun 26 — Roland Garros (to 9 June), Monaco Grand Prix

COMPANY NEWS

Interims ITE Group, Victrex, Paragon Group of Companies, Shaftesbury, British Empire Securities & General Trust, Britvic

Finals Big Yellow Group, Booker, British Land Co, BTG, Burberry Group, Cable & Wireless, Cable & Wireless Worldwide, Caledonia Investments, Cranswick, Dairy Crest, Electrocomponents, FirstGroup, Great Portland Estates, Homeserve, Intermediate Capital, KCOM, London Stock Exchange, Marks & Spencer Group, MITIE Group, PayPoint, QinetiQ, SABMiller, Telecom plus, TR Property Investment Trust, United Utilities, Vodafone

"If you would know the value of money, go and try to borrow some."
Benjamin Franklin

JUNE MARKET

FTSE 100	41	-0.7	3.5
FTSE 250	44	-0.6	4.8
S&P 500	51	0.0	3.5
NIKKEI	59	-0.1	5.5

Market performance this month

The weak month of May is followed by the weakest month in the year – June. On average, the market has fallen 0.7% in June (with a standard deviation of a relatively low 3.5). The probability of a positive return in the month is a lowly 41%.

After May, this is the weakest month of the year for the FTSE 100 Index relative to the S&P 500 Index.

However, June is the strongest month for the Pharmaceuticals & Biotechnology sector, relative to the wider market.

Summary: A quick glance at the chart below clearly demonstrates that since 1990 this has not been a good month for investors.

Historic performance of the market in June

June summary

Month's performance ranking	12th
Average market change this month (standard deviation)	-0.7% (3.5)
First trading day: Up / average change	55.2% / 0.2%
Last trading day: Up / average change	69.0% / 0.2%
Main features of the month	The FTSE 100 often underperforms the S&P 500 in June.
	The Pharma & Biotech sector is often strong in June.
	17 Jun: Start of the 2nd weakest market week of the year
	28 Jun: Last trading day in June is often strong
Significant dates	06 Jun: MPC interest rate announcement at 12h00 (anticipated)
	07 Jun: US Nonfarm payroll report (anticipated)
	12 Jun: FTSE 100 Index quarterly review announcement
	19 Jun: FOMC monetary policy statement
	21 Jun: Triple witching

Mon 27

Spring Bank Holiday (UK) – LSE closed
Memorial Day (US) – NYSE closed
6th weakest market week
50th anniversary of the release of *The Freewheelin' Bob Dylan*.

2000: Scottish farmers who accidentally planted genetically modified seeds say they will fight for compensation after the UK Government advises them to dig up the crop.

FTSE 100			
FTSE 250			
S&P 500			
NIKKEI	40	0.2	1.0

Tue 28

20th anniversary of the LSE flotation of RPC Group

2012: The discovery of Flame, a complex malware program targeting computers in Middle Eastern countries, is announced.

FTSE 100	53	0.1	0.7
FTSE 250	50	0.1	0.6
S&P 500	55	0.0	1.4
NIKKEI	62	0.0	0.9

Wed 29

100th anniversary of the first performance of the ballet *The Rite of Spring*, in Paris.

2010: Apple's stock market value overtakes Microsoft's.

FTSE 100	69	0.3	0.7
FTSE 250	73	0.3	0.5
S&P 500	54	0.3	1.2
NIKKEI	67	0.4	1.1

Thu 30

Weakest market day

1539: In Florida, Hernando de Sotod 600 soldiers land at Tampa Bay with the goal of finding gold.

FTSE 100	18	-0.5	1.3
FTSE 250	27	-0.4	1.0
S&P 500	58	0.1	1.1
NIKKEI	43	0.5	0.8

Fri 31

Horse Racing – The Oaks

1927: The last Ford Model T rolls off the assembly line, after a production run of 15,007,003 vehicles.

FTSE 100	59	0.1	0.6
FTSE 250	80	0.3	0.4
S&P 500	61	0.3	1.0
NIKKEI	60	0.0	1.3

Sat 1 Horse Racing – The Derby, 20th anniversary of the LSE flotation of AstraZeneca.

Sun 2

COMPANY NEWS

Interims JPMorgan Indian Investment Trust, Scottish Investment Trust, Brewin Dolphin Holdings, Electra Private Equity, JPMorgan Asian Investment Trust

Finals AVEVA Group, De La Rue, Halfords, London & Stamford Property Ltd, Pennon, Severn Trent, Tate & Lyle

"Money is lacking? Well then, create it!"
Goethe

FIRST TRADING DAYS OF THE MONTH

Does the market display any abnormal effect on the first trading day of each month?

FTSE 100 Index daily data was analysed from 1984 to discover if the UK equity market had a tendency to significantly increase or decrease on the first trading day of each month. The results are shown in the table below.

	Number of days	Positive	Positive(%)	Average(%)
All days	7135	3723	52.2	0.03
First trading day of each month	339	202	59.6	0.21
First trading day of each month (from 2000)	151	95	62.9	0.28

Analysis

Of the 339 months since 1984, the market has risen 202 times (59.6%) on the first trading day of each month, with an average rise of 0.21%. This is significantly greater than the average for all days, where the market has risen 52.2% of the time, with an average rise of 0.03%.

The effect seems to be, if anything, stronger in recent years. Since 2000, the market has increased 62.9% on months' first trading days, with an average rise of 0.28%.

The table below breaks down the performance of the market on the first trading days by month since 1984.

	Jan	Feb	Mar	Apr	May	Jun	Jul	Aug	Sep	Oct	Nov	Dec
Positive(%)	60.7	57.1	57.1	67.9	51.7	55.2	69.0	60.7	64.3	60.7	64.3	46.4
Average(%)	0.4	0.6	0.0	0.4	0.1	0.2	0.4	0.0	0.2	0.2	0.1	0.0

The strongest month is seen to be July, when the market increases on the first trading day in 69% of all years, with an average increase of 0.4% on that day. The weakest month is December – the only month when the market has fallen more often then risen on the first trading day. This is an unexpected result as December is one of the stronger months for the market.

A summary of the first trading day effect (by month) is shown in the chart below.

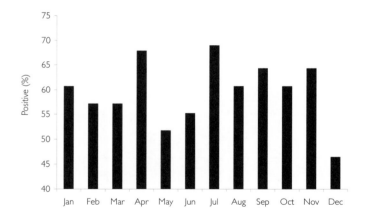

Note: See also *Last trading days of the month*, week 13.

Mon

3

Weakest market month
MSCI quarterly index review (effective date)
100th anniversary of suffragette Emily Davison running out in front of the King's horse at the Epsom Derby.

1996: The US Supreme Court rules on the case of Smiley vs. Citibank. The court finds that fees are included under the definition of interest, meaning that Citibank is free to charge its credit card customers any amount it sees fit.

FTSE 100	63	0.2	0.8
FTSE 250	56	0.1	0.6
S&P 500	48	0.0	0.8
NIKKEI	50	0.3	1.4

Tue

4

The Pharma & Biotech sector is often strong in June.
The FTSE 100 often underperforms the S&P 500 in June.

1912: Massachusetts becomes the first state in the US to set a minimum wage.

FTSE 100	53	0.0	1.0
FTSE 250	59	-0.1	0.6
S&P 500	56	-0.1	1.1
NIKKEI	62	-0.1	1.1

Wed

5

Beige Book published

1975: The UK holds its first countrywide referendum, on remaining in the European Economic Community (EEC).

FTSE 100	55	0.1	0.8
FTSE 250	56	0.1	0.6
S&P 500	62	0.1	0.9
NIKKEI	52	0.1	0.9

Thu

6

MPC interest rate announcement at 12h00
ECB Governing Council meeting

2001: Members of Friends Provident, the mutual life insurer, vote 97% in favour of floating the company on the stock market. After flotation, the shares fall steadily for two years.

FTSE 100	57	0.0	1.0
FTSE 250	74	0.0	1.3
S&P 500	53	0.2	1.1
NIKKEI	33	0.1	0.9

Fri

7

Nonfarm payroll report (anticipated)

2000: Judge Jackson orders Microsoft to be broken up into two companies and to change its conduct towards it competitors. (The Appeals Court later overturns the ruling that Microsoft be split in two.)

FTSE 100	48	0.0	0.8
FTSE 250	63	0.1	0.7
S&P 500	44	0.0	0.8
NIKKEI	62	-0.2	1.3

Sat 8 New moon

Sun 9

COMPANY NEWS

Interims

Finals Edinburgh Investment Trust, Johnson Matthey, Perpetual Income & Growth Investment Trust, RIT Capital Partners, Synergy Health

"There are people who have money, and people who are rich."
Coco Chanel

FTSE 100 REVIEWS – COMPANIES JOINING THE INDEX

The charts below show the share prices of 12 companies that have joined the FTSE 100 Index in the years 2011 and 2012. The time period for each chart is six months, starting from three months before the company joined the index. So it is possible to see the share price behaviour in the three months leading up to joining, and the three months after.

It can be seen that, in most cases, the share price rises immediately before the company joins the FTSE 100 Index, while immediately afterwards the price is usually flat or falls back again.

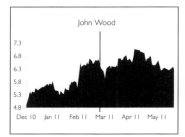

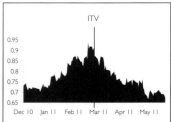

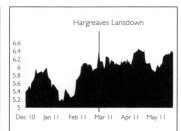

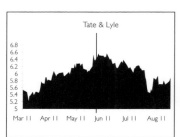

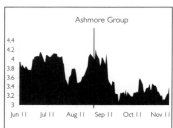

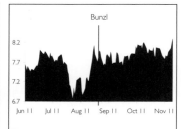

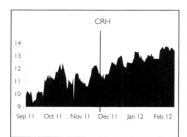

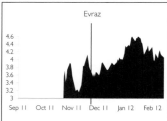

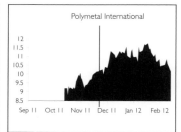

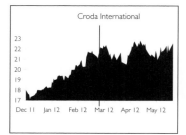

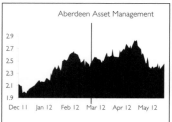

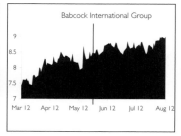

Mon

10

1997: British Airways unveil their new funky-painted tailfins. The re-painting cost £60 million. Over the following 15 months, BA shares halve in value.

FTSE 100	50	-0.1	0.7
FTSE 250	53	0.0	0.6
S&P 500	52	0.1	0.8
NIKKEI	40	-0.2	1.2

Tue

11

1962: John and Clarence Anglin and Frank Lee Morris attempt to escape from Alcatraz federal prison. Whilst they did escape from "The Rock", it is thought that they drowned in the surrounding water.

FTSE 100	52	0.0	1.0
FTSE 250	53	-0.1	0.7
S&P 500	68	0.1	0.9
NIKKEI	67	0.2	1.0

Wed

Tuen Ng Festival (HK) – HKSE closed
FTSE 100 quarterly review

12

1964: Nelson Mandela, leader of the anti-apartheid struggle in South Africa, is given a life sentence for sabotage

FTSE 100	43	-0.2	0.9
FTSE 250	37	-0.2	0.8
S&P 500	55	0.0	0.8
NIKKEI	43	0.2	1.2

Thu

US Golf Open (to 16th)

13

1990: The official demolition of the Berlin Wall begins, although the removal of 'Checkpoint Charlie' is postponed.

FTSE 100	52	-0.2	0.8
FTSE 250	37	-0.2	0.9
S&P 500	62	0.1	0.8
NIKKEI	43	-0.4	1.1

Fri

14

1996: Sumitomo Corp, announces that it has lost $1.8 billion over ten years of unauthorised trading by head copper trader, Yasuo Hamanaka. The actual losses are later reported to be over $2 billion and Hamanaka is renounced as a rogue trader.

FTSE 100	43	-0.1	1.1
FTSE 250	53	0.0	1.0
S&P 500	53	0.0	0.8
NIKKEI	57	-0.2	0.9

Sat 15

Sun 16   Father's Day

COMPANY NEWS

Interims

Finals Atkins (W S), Fidelity China Special Situation, Halma, Monks Investment Trust, Oxford Instruments, RPC Group, Utilico Emerging Markets

"If at first you don't succeed try, try again. Then quit. There's no use being a damn fool about it."
W. C. Fields

SHARE PERFORMANCE IN THE SUMMER

Here comes the summer! Usually trading volumes are low over the summer and so one must be wary of drawing too much statistical significance from price changes in this period. But, with that proviso, this page highlights those stocks that have performed unusually well (or badly) over the two summer months of July and August.

Stocks that like the summer

The share prices of only six companies have risen at least nine times in the last ten years in the two-month summer period of July and August. The table below shows these six companies and the percentage price change for the stock in the summer months for that year (for example, Shire increased 19.5% in July-August 2003).

Company	2003	2004	2005	2006	2007	2008	2009	2010	2011	2012	Avg
Games Workshop Group	25.9	6.3	8.4	33.7	12.1	63.8	7.3	13.5	4.1	13.6	18.9
Greene King	8.6	2.4	3.8	2.6	3.0	19.9	23.6	5.3	-8.7	2.7	6.3
Keller Group	11.1	10.9	26.0	17.6	2.6	26.3	17.7	8.4	-20.5	37.4	13.8
Pace	15.3	4.8	25.4	55.6	15.0	5.0	10.0	27.0	-0.9	55.8	21.3
Rotork	13.8	-1.4	14.9	6.3	10.3	0.2	16.3	22.6	2.3	11.7	9.7
Shire	19.5	0.1	13.2	13.1	4.2	17.5	22.4	2.3	2.2	5.0	10.0
average:	15.7	3.9	15.3	21.5	7.9	22.1	16.2	13.2	-3.6	21.0	13.3
FTSE All Share:	4.7	-0.6	3.9	1.3	-4.2	0.5	16.0	6.0	-9.6	3.9	2.2
difference:	11.0	4.5	11.4	20.2	12.1	21.6	0.2	7.2	6.0	17.1	11.1

On average, over the last ten years the market has risen 2.2% over the July to August period, but each of these six stocks rose by more than 6% on average. An equally-weighted portfolio of these six companies would have outperformed the FTSE All Share Index in every summer for the past ten years. The average outperformance each year would have been 11.1% percentage points.

Two of these companies (Games Workshop and Shire) managed to rise for all ten years.

Of course, in some cases (e.g. brewer Greene King) it is fairly obvious why the company's share price might rise in the summer.

Stocks that don't like the summer

The 11 stocks in the table below have all fallen in at least seven of the past ten summers and have a negative average price change.

Company	2003	2004	2005	2006	2007	2008	2009	2010	2011	2012	Avg
De La Rue	13.7	-9.8	-10.8	-1.7	-4.5	-1.3	-4.3	-26.1	5.5	5.9	-3.3
Helphire Group	-13.5	0.5	12.4	0.2	-1.4	-46.1	-1.4	-15.1	-26.7	-5.0	-9.6
Highway Capital	-13.8	-21.6	4.2	-2.9	-20.4	-24.0	48.1	-7.7	-21.6	21.4	-3.8
Man Group	2.7	-7.4	13.7	-0.6	-19.0	-8.8	-3.1	-6.8	-5.5	3.8	-3.1
Oxford BioMedica	76.3	-5.4	11.1	8.9	-1.2	-52.2	-8.2	-13.2	-8.7	-12.8	-0.5
Pennon Group	-15.1	3.2	-2.7	5.1	-2.4	-3.9	-4.5	3.6	-7.3	-3.0	-2.7
Psion	19.9	-14.5	-1.5	-23.7	-4.5	-22.5	50.6	24.3	-31.9	-1.7	-0.5
Speedy Hire	14.5	-4.1	-0.1	-0.2	-0.8	-18.1	33.6	-15.5	-17.5	3.1	-0.5
STV Group	28.1	-19.0	-0.5	-6.1	-12.6	-32.1	-2.8	27.8	-12.6	-3.5	-3.3
Titon Holdings	17.3	5.0	-5.3	-2.1	-30.7	-9.7	15.3	-4.7	-26.4	-8.2	-5.0
Walker Crips Group	8.7	-9.2	-7.4	-7.9	-9.2	-12.4	3.4	2.2	-3.9	-3.9	-4.0
average:	12.6	-7.5	1.2	-2.8	-9.7	-21.0	11.5	-2.8	-14.2	-0.4	-3.3
FTSE All Share:	4.7	-0.6	3.9	1.3	-4.2	0.5	16.0	6.0	-9.6	3.9	2.2
difference:	7.9	-6.9	-2.7	-4.1	-5.5	-21.5	-4.5	-8.8	-4.6	-4.3	-5.5

A portfolio of these 11 stocks would have underperformed the FTSE All Share Index in nine of the past ten summers by an average of 5.5 percentage points each year.

Mon
17

2nd weakest market week

FTSE 100	65	0.3	1.0
FTSE 250	58	0.1	0.8
S&P 500	50	0.1	0.8
NIKKEI	45	0.1	1.2

1991: The first trading day of the newly privatised Scottish & Southern Energy.

Tue
18

Two-day FOMC meeting starts
Royal Ascot (to 22nd)

FTSE 100	38	-0.3	0.7
FTSE 250	32	-0.3	0.7
S&P 500	40	-0.2	0.6
NIKKEI	43	0.0	1.5

1999: An anti-capitalism protest in London turns violent as some of the protesters vent their anger on the Liffe Building, which forms part of the London Stock Exchange.

Wed
19

MPC meeting minutes published
ECB Governing Council Meeting

FTSE 100	48	-0.1	1.0
FTSE 250	47	0.0	1.2
S&P 500	55	0.0	0.8
NIKKEI	48	0.1	1.4

2012: Comedian Jimmy Carr is in the spotlight after it is revealed that he participated in a legal tax avoidance scheme, which sheltered approximately £3 million a year.

Thu
20

FTSE 100	38	-0.3	0.8
FTSE 250	32	-0.2	0.7
S&P 500	47	-0.1	0.7
NIKKEI	62	-0.3	0.9

1983: Raiders escape with uncut diamonds and jewellery worth up to £6 million from a vault in Mayfair, central London, in what is believed to be Britain's biggest gemstone robbery up to this point in history.

Fri
21

Summer Solstice, also known as Midsummer or Litha
Triple Witching (market often strong on this day)
200th anniversary of the Battle of Vitoria, Peninsula War.

FTSE 100	57	0.1	0.8
FTSE 250	53	0.0	0.6
S&P 500	51	0.0	0.9
NIKKEI	62	0.1	1.5

1788: The US Constitution is ratified.

Sat 22

Sun 23   Full moon, 20th anniversary of the LSE flotation of Carpetright.

COMPANY NEWS

Interims Chemring Group, Bankers Investment Trust
Finals Ashtead Group, Dixons Retail, Imagination Technologies, Micro Focus International, Personal Assets Trust, Templeton Emerging Markets

"A bank is a place where they lend you an umbrella in fair weather, and ask for it back when it begins to rain."
Robert Frost

TURN OF THE MONTH

In week 23 we looked at the behaviour of the market on the first trading day of each month. This page analyses the behaviour of the market for the 11 days around each turn of the month (ToM). The reference day is taken to be the first trading day of the new month, ToM(0), and the days studied are from five trading days before the reference day, ToM(-5), to five trading after the reference day, ToM(+5). For the ToM coming up this week, ToM(-5) is Monday 24 June, ToM(0) is Monday 1 July, and ToM(+5) is Friday 5 July. The index analysed is the FTSE All Share.

From 1970

The charts below analyse the 512 ToMs since 1970. The left chart shows the percentage number of up days, and the right chart is the average change on the day. For example, on ToM(-5) the market has on average risen 49% of the time with an average change of -0.03%.

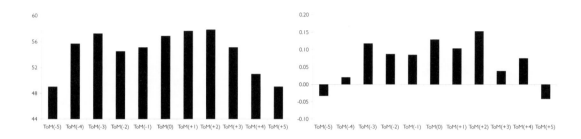

We can see that there is a definite trend for the market to be weak at the beginning of the 11-day period, to then become strong around the turn of the month, and afterwards to become weak again. The bell shape of the charts is quite evident.

Does this behaviour persist in more recent years?

From 2000

The charts below are the same configuration as above, except they look at a shorter time period: the 152 ToMs since the year 2000 to today.

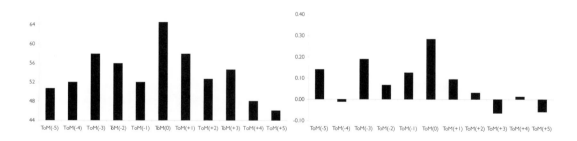

Broadly, the behaviour has been the same for the last few years as that from 1970. The main observation is that the strength of the first trading day of the month, ToM(0), has become even more pronounced. On average, the market rises on 65% of all ToM(0) with an average change of 0.28% (which is nine times the average change on all trading days).

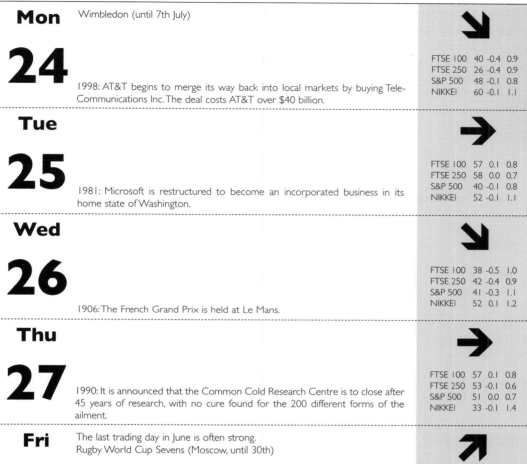
Mon

Wimbledon (until 7th July)

24

1998: AT&T begins to merge its way back into local markets by buying Tele-Communications Inc. The deal costs AT&T over $40 billion.

FTSE 100	40	-0.4	0.9
FTSE 250	26	-0.4	0.9
S&P 500	48	-0.1	0.8
NIKKEI	60	-0.1	1.1

Tue

25

1981: Microsoft is restructured to become an incorporated business in its home state of Washington.

FTSE 100	57	0.1	0.8
FTSE 250	58	0.0	0.7
S&P 500	40	-0.1	0.8
NIKKEI	52	-0.1	1.1

Wed

26

1906: The French Grand Prix is held at Le Mans.

FTSE 100	38	-0.5	1.0
FTSE 250	42	-0.4	0.9
S&P 500	41	-0.3	1.1
NIKKEI	52	0.1	1.2

Thu

27

1990: It is announced that the Common Cold Research Centre is to close after 45 years of research, with no cure found for the 200 different forms of the ailment.

FTSE 100	57	0.1	0.8
FTSE 250	53	-0.1	0.6
S&P 500	51	0.0	0.7
NIKKEI	33	-0.1	1.4

Fri

The last trading day in June is often strong.
Rugby World Cup Sevens (Moscow, until 30th)

28

2011: Christine Lagarde is confirmed as Dominique Strauss-Kahn's replacement as Managing Director of the IMF.

FTSE 100	67	0.2	0.9
FTSE 250	68	0.2	0.5
S&P 500	56	0.2	0.9
NIKKEI	62	-0.3	1.2

Sat 29   Tour de France (until 23rd July)

Sun 30   20th anniversary of the LSE flotation of Devro.

COMPANY NEWS

Interims Carnival, Domino Printing Sciences, Ocado
Finals Berkeley Group Holdings, Betfair, Carpetright, Essar Energy, Greene King, Smith (DS), Stagecoach

"Money is better than poverty, if only for financial reasons."
Woody Allen

JULY MARKET

FTSE 100	55	0.8	4.3
FTSE 250	52	0.6	5.2
S&P 500	52	0.9	4.1
NIKKEI	45	-0.5	5.2

Market performance this month

After May and June, shares tend to perform a bit better in July, but not by much. July ranks ninth of all months for performance.

On average, the market increases 0.8% in July, with a probability of a positive return of 55%.

However, the start of the month tends to be strong. The first trading day is the strongest first trading day of the month in the year and the first week of the month is among the top ten strongest in the year.

Summary: Not a month to get excited by, a glance at the chart below shows the very unpredictable market in July.

Historic performance of the market in July

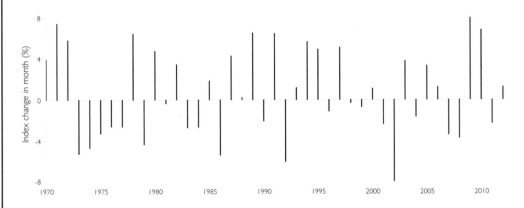

July summary

Month's performance ranking	9th
Average market change this month (standard deviation)	0.8% (4.3)
First trading day: Up / average change	69.0% / 0.4%
Last trading day: Up / average change	46.4% / 0.2%
Main features of the month	Strong sectors in this third quarter are: Technology Hardware & Equipment, Household Goods, and Gas; Water & Multiutilities.
	Weak sectors in this third quarter are: Industrial Metals, and Support Services.
	01 Jul: First trading day in July – the strongest first-trading-day-of-the-month in the year
	08 Jul: 3rd weakest market day of the year
	08 Jul: Start of the 3rd weakest market week of the year
	22 Jul: Start of the 5th weakest market week of the year
	29 Jul: Start of the 3rd strongest market week of the year
	31 Jul: Last trading day in July is often weak
Significant dates	04 Jul: MPC interest rate announcement at 12h00 (anticipated)
	04 Jul: Independence Day (US) – NYSE closed
	05 Jul: US Nonfarm payroll report (anticipated)
	31 Jul: FOMC monetary policy statement

Mon

1

Hong Kong Special Administrative Region Establishment Day (HK) – HKSE closed
8th strongest market week
First trading day in July – the strongest first-trading-day-of-the-month in the year. The market increases on this day 69% of all years.

1997: Thailand is forced to let its currency, the baht, float. It has devalued 20%. This event marks the beginning of the Asian economic crises.

FTSE 100	65	0.3	1.5
FTSE 250	74	0.0	1.0
S&P 500	68	0.2	0.8
NIKKEI	55	0.3	1.6

Tue

2

2005: The world's biggest music stars unite at Live8 concerts around the globe in order to press political leaders to tackle poverty in Africa at the G8 summit.

FTSE 100	57	0.0	1.1
FTSE 250	58	-0.1	1.1
S&P 500	53	0.0	1.0
NIKKEI	57	0.5	1.3

Wed

3

NYSE closes early at 13h00
Henley Royal Regatta (to 7th)

2012: Bob Diamond resigns as chief executive of Barclays, following controversy over the alleged fixing of Libor interest rates by traders employed by the bank.

FTSE 100	67	0.3	1.2
FTSE 250	63	0.2	0.8
S&P 500	70	0.3	0.6
NIKKEI	62	0.1	0.9

Thu

4

Independence Day (US) – NYSE closed
MPC interest rate announcement at 12h00
ECB Governing Council meeting

2012: The discovery of particles consistent with the Higgs boson, also known as the God Particle, at the Large Hadron Collider is announced at CERN.

FTSE 100	55	0.3	0.8
FTSE 250	53	0.0	0.6
S&P 500			
NIKKEI	45	0.1	0.8

Fri

5

Nonfarm payroll report (anticipated)
50th anniversary of the Roman Catholic Church accepting cremation as a funeral practice.

2012: The Shard, the tallest building in the European Union standing at 309.6m, opens.

FTSE 100	40	0.1	1.0
FTSE 250	47	0.0	0.6
S&P 500	60	0.1	1.1
NIKKEI	57	-0.2	0.8

Sat 6

Sun 7 British Grand Prix, 100th anniversary of birth of Pinetop Perkins, blues musician.

COMPANY NEWS

Interims

Finals Anite, Polar Capital Technology Trust

"Capital is money, capital is commodities. By virtue of it being value, it has acquired the occult ability to add value to itself. It brings forth living offspring, or, at the least, lays golden eggs."
Karl Marx

The table below shows the performance of FTSE 350 sectors in the third quarter (30 June to 30 September) of each year from 2002 to 2011. The table is ranked by the final column – the average performance for each sector over the ten years. For each year the top five performing sectors are highlighted in light grey, the bottom five in dark grey.

Sector	2002	2003	2004	2005	2006	2007	2008	2009	2010	2011	Avg
Technology Hard & Equip	-30.4	47.4	-19.8	15.2	-7.4	-6.0	6.5	23.2	29.8	-6.9	5.2
Personal Goods	2.1	9.6	-12.6	4.7	18.9	-3.4	-7.9	20.3	35.8	-16.4	5.1
Household Goods					10.4	-6.9	6.7	14.3	11.1	-6.4	4.9
Gas; Water & Multiutilities		-4.2	10.1	0.8	13.9	1.6	3.8	6.7	9.1	-0.3	4.6
Mobile Telecom					6.3	5.3	-17.4	18.9	12.0	0.2	4.2
Automobiles & Parts	-16.9	14.1	-14.3	12.9	5.2	-11.1	-12.2	35.9	45.7	-24.1	3.5
Real Estate Inv Trusts					6.0	-9.4	4.4	27.8	13.2	-21.9	3.4
Electricity	-7.3	-2.6	9.8	10.6	8.1	1.4	-1.0	7.7	8.3	-6.7	2.8
Tobacco	-5.8	-7.0	-3.3	9.1	5.8	0.9	1.5	16.4	8.0	1.3	2.7
Food & Drug Retailers	-14.7	9.5	-0.2	-2.7	9.3	1.9	4.0	12.3	12.7	-7.2	2.5
Mining	-19.7	17.6	17.2	31.1	-5.1	12.8	-44.1	26.5	19.1	-30.9	2.5
Industrial Engineering	-27.5	13.2	-4.5	12.0	-0.4	-1.7	-20.5	47.6	25.1	-20.4	2.3
Food Producers	-6.7	3.5	-11.2	6.1	9.4	-11.3	-0.1	30.2	2.4	0.0	2.2
Oil Equip; Srvs & Dist					4.6	7.1	-26.9	24.5	26.1	-22.3	2.2
General Industrials					-1.4	-3.8	-6.1	24.8	20.0	-21.2	2.1
Beverages	-8.5	3.6	-5.1	6.3	4.4	4.1	-1.0	15.2	5.4	-5.3	1.9
Life Insurance	-33.8	10.5	-1.2	2.9	5.4	-2.2	-3.5	35.8	26.2	-21.4	1.9
Pharm & Biotech	-19.0	3.2	1.1	9.0	-2.4	-3.4	10.4	11.9	6.2	-2.7	1.4
Chemicals	-21.5	9.1	-3.7	14.8	6.7	2.1	-21.4	23.0	25.4	-20.3	1.4
Aerospace & Defense	-34.2	9.8	1.1	17.3	5.9	8.2	-5.8	15.6	6.7	-12.4	1.2
Banks	-24.2	0.4	5.7	1.4	4.8	-8.5	-1.4	39.2	10.7	-24.1	0.4
Construction & Materials	-20.4	11.1	6.8	4.9	16.8	-0.6	-24.2	10.9	13.1	-15.7	0.3
Health Care Equip & Srvs	-8.1	11.8	-12.5	-11.8	15.3	-5.8	5.6	24.6	-7.3	-12.0	0.0
Software & Comp Srvs	-44.4	18.6	-7.6	1.7	2.3	3.6	-5.4	23.8	14.0	-7.1	0.0
Travel & Leisure	-13.1	6.0	0.5	2.6	7.8	-9.2	-11.2	22.1	8.5	-16.8	-0.3
Fixed Line Telecoms	-16.3	-0.5	4.7	6.9	11.4	-7.0	-14.1	21.5	2.9	-14.6	-0.5
Equity Inv Instruments	-26.4	3.8	0.9	12.1	4.0	2.5	-14.4	16.5	8.5	-13.6	-0.6
Electronic & Elect Equip	-31.2	24.2	-18.7	22.6	4.0	-8.8	-18.1	24.4	22.0	-26.9	-0.7
Nonlife Insurance	-46.3	-17.8	-7.5	13.3	13.9	3.8	18.3	16.5	8.5	-16.1	-1.3
General Retailers	-13.6	3.0	0.5	-4.0	6.5	-10.7	-12.1	16.2	10.8	-10.8	-1.4
Financial Services	-21.5	7.2	-9.0	13.9	6.5	-4.0	-21.9	21.6	12.4	-21.8	-1.7
Oil & Gas Producers	-22.3	-3.4	6.5	12.7	-6.0	-2.5	-21.9	13.0	19.2	-12.2	-1.7
Industrial Transportation	-20.4	5.7	-2.7	7.6	3.0	-9.9	-19.1	26.9	7.1	-19.3	-2.1
Media	-24.1	1.9	-9.4	1.5	1.6	-5.2	-8.2	24.7	9.2	-16.1	-2.4
Forestry & Paper	-20.4	0.6	-8.0	3.6		-45.0	-13.0	49.2	33.9	-23.7	-2.5
Support Services	-29.5	7.9	-8.6	2.5	5.9	-10.9	-10.5	19.4	8.8	-13.7	-2.9
Real Estate Inv & Srvs									7.9	-18.8	-5.5
Industrial Metals	-59.2	35.0	28.3	22.6	-15.0	-65.5	-60.8	10.9	30.6	-44.7	-11.8

Observations

1. **Strong sectors** in this quarter are: Technology Hardware & Equipment, Household Goods, and Gas; Water & Multiutilities.

2. **Weak sectors** in this quarter are: Industrial Metals, and Support Services.

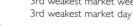

Mon

8

New moon
3rd weakest market week
3rd weakest market day

1889: The first issue of *The Wall Street Journal* is published in New York. The paper grew out of a two-page newsletter run by Edward Jones and Charles Dow.

FTSE 100	25	-0.2	0.9
FTSE 250	47	-0.1	1.0
S&P 500	52	0.1	0.9
NIKKEI	50	0.3	1.4

Tue

9

Ramadan (until 7 August)

1984: York Minster is struck by a lightning bolt and the resulting fire rampages through most of the building. However, the cathedral's valuables are rescued by clergymen and the Rose Window is not affected.

FTSE 100	60	0.1	0.8
FTSE 250	58	0.1	0.6
S&P 500	64	0.2	0.8
NIKKEI	52	-0.2	1.0

Wed

10

Cricket – England v Australia, 1st Ashes Test starts

1979: Chuck Berry is sentenced to four months imprisonment for tax evasion.

FTSE 100	35	-0.5	0.9
FTSE 250	47	-0.1	0.7
S&P 500	50	-0.2	0.9
NIKKEI	48	0.2	1.0

Thu

11

1995: A colony of great-crested newts halts work on a £200 million rail depot near Rugby. They have to be moved to ponds as they are protected under European and British law.

FTSE 100	50	-0.3	1.5
FTSE 250	47	-0.3	1.1
S&P 500	56	0.1	0.8
NIKKEI	38	0.0	1.3

Fri

12

1982: *E.T.: The Extra-Terrestrial* breaks all box office records in the history of motion pictures, by surpassing the $100 million mark of ticket sales in the first 31 days.

FTSE 100	35	-0.1	0.7
FTSE 250	53	0.1	0.5
S&P 500	47	0.1	1.0
NIKKEI	48	-0.4	1.2

Sat 13   20th anniversary of the LSE flotation of Cranswick.

Sun 14   100th anniversary of the birth of Gerald Ford, 38th US President.

COMPANY NEWS

Interims
Finals Daejan Holdings

"Anyone who lives within their means suffers from a lack of imagination."
Oscar Wilde

SECTOR MONTHLY PERFORMANCE – PHARMA & BIOTECH

Elsewhere in the *Almanac* we look at the quarterly performance of sectors; on this page we look in greater detail at the monthly performance of the Pharmaceuticals & Biotechnology sector.

The FTSE 350 Pharmaceuticals & Biotechnology sector is comprised of the stocks shown in the table on the right.

The following table shows the outperformance of the FTSE 350 Pharmaceuticals & Biotechnology sector over the FTSE 100 Index for every month since August 1999. For example, in January 2000 the Pharmaceuticals & Biotechnology sector index fell -8.0%, while the FTSE 100 Index fell -9.5%, giving an outperformance of the former over the latter of 1.5 percentage points. In months where the sector underperforms the FTSE 100 Index (i.e. the outperformance is negative) the cell is highlighted.

Company	TIDM
Dechra Pharmaceuticals	DPH
GlaxoSmithKline	GSK
Hikma Pharmaceuticals	HIK
Shire	SHP
AstraZeneca	AZN
BTG	BTG

	Jan	Feb	Mar	Apr	May	Jun	Jul	Aug	Sep	Oct	Nov	Dec
1999								5.0	-1.0	7.5	-0.9	-12.0
2000	1.5	-3.6	12.4	10.1	-2.0	5.6	-3.0	0.8	11.4	-6.9	9.8	-8.1
2001	-7.8	11.9	3.7	-6.5	5.8	5.6	3.7	-4.9	8.9	-5.1	-6.4	-1.9
2002	0.9	4.9	-6.8	-0.9	-9.7	4.9	-4.8	-7.2	13.4	-1.7	-3.4	1.5
2003	3.8	-4.1	3.0	4.1	-4.8	0.7	-3.5	-0.1	5.3	-0.6	-0.8	-3.7
2004	-3.7	-5.6	-0.6	4.3	-1.2	-2.9	0.9	1.1	-3.2	-3.9	-6.8	2.1
2005	-1.5	2.0	0.6	9.8	-0.1	-3.6	-0.3	-0.6	2.7	2.6	-2.0	0.4
2006	-4.5	-1.3	2.8	2.6	-0.5	4.5	-2.5	2.3	-4.3	-6.2	-2.3	-5.5
2007	2.5	3.8	-5.2	0.7	-9.3	0.2	-0.2	1.8	-2.9	-7.7	5.8	-2.8
2008	1.8	-6.7	0.7	0.2	0.9	5.9	12.1	5.9	5.6	11.8	-3.9	11.1
2009	1.8	-6.1	1.7	-11.0	-1.6	6.6	-2.0	-2.6	-3.5	1.9	-2.4	1.3
2010	-0.2	-2.8	-2.7	-0.8	4.2	7.9	-7.1	5.3	-4.5	-4.6	0.6	-6.1
2011	-2.6	0.1	0.6	4.4	4.5	0.6	2.6	3.7	5.4	-4.0	1.2	2.4
2012	-4.0	-6.0	0.9	1.0	6.1	-1.7	1.2					
average:	-0.9	-1.0	0.9	1.4	-0.6	2.6	-0.2	0.8	2.6	-1.3	-0.9	-1.6

The following chart plots the average change in the sector index for each month.

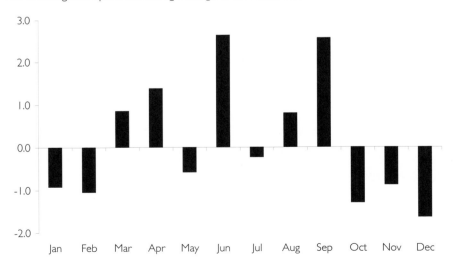

Observations

1. The sector is significantly strong in the months of June and September.

2. The sector is weak for the period October to February.

3. This pattern of behaviour is the reverse of that seen for the general market (i.e. the six-month effect).

Mon	Marine Day (Japan) – TSE closed	➡			

15

2003: AOL Time Warner disbands Netscape Communications Corporation. The Mozilla Foundation is established on the same day.

FTSE 100	45	-0.1	1.7
FTSE 250	53	-0.1	1.1
S&P 500	55	0.0	0.8
NIKKEI			

Tue ➡

16

1661: The Swedish bank, Stockholms Banco, issues the first banknotes in Europe.

FTSE 100	50	0.1	0.8
FTSE 250	47	0.0	0.9
S&P 500	49	0.0	0.9
NIKKEI	53	-0.2	1.1

Wed
MPC meeting minutes published
Beige Book published ↗

17

1989: The result of ten years of work, the Stealth bomber – the world's most revolutionary warplane – makes its maiden flight after 18 months delay.

FTSE 100	65	0.3	1.3
FTSE 250	63	0.1	1.0
S&P 500	59	0.1	0.9
NIKKEI	60	-0.1	1.2

Thu
ECB Governing Council Meeting
Cricket – England v Australia, 2nd Ashes Test starts
British Golf Open (until 21st) ↘

18

1983: A gigantic new dinosaur skeleton is unveiled to the media at the Natural History Museum in London.

FTSE 100	35	-0.2	1.1
FTSE 250	42	0.0	1.0
S&P 500	33	-0.2	0.8
NIKKEI	26	-0.1	1.1

Fri ➡

19

1873: William Gosse becomes the first European to discover Ayres Rock (Uluru) in Australia and names it in honour of the South Australian Premier, Sir Henry Ayres.

FTSE 100	50	-0.1	1.3
FTSE 250	63	0.3	0.9
S&P 500	49	0.0	0.9
NIKKEI	53	-0.6	1.0

Sat 20

Sun 21

COMPANY NEWS

Interims Computacenter, Howden Joinery, Aberforth Smaller Companies Trust, Capita Group
Finals IG Group Holdings, Sports Direct International

"I've got all the money I'll ever need if I die by four o'clock this afternoon."
Henry Youngman

MONTHLY COMPARATIVE PERFORMANCE – FTSE 100 & FTSE 250

The table below shows the monthly outperformance of the FTSE 100 Index over the mid-cap FTSE 250 Index. For example, in January 1986, the FTSE 100 Index increased 1.6%, while the FTSE 250 Index increased 2.6%. The outperformance of the former over the latter was therefore -1.0. In August 1986, the FTSE 100 Index increased 6.6%, while the FTSE 250 Index increased 4.3%. The outperformance of the former over the latter was therefore 2.3. The cells are highlighted if the number is negative (i.e. the FTSE 250 outperformed the FTSE 100).

Monthly comparative performance of FTSE 100 and FTSE 250 indices

Year	Jan	Feb	Mar	Apr	May	Jun	Jul	Aug	Sep	Oct	Nov	Dec
1986	-1.0	-1.1	0.4	-4.0	-0.1	-1.5	-1.0	2.3	-0.8	-0.3	-2.3	1.5
1987	-1.8	2.6	-2.1	1.3	1.3	-4.8	-2.7	-0.1	-1.3	2.6	1.0	-4.1
1988	-2.0	-1.0	-0.3	-0.5	-1.4	-0.6	-1.3	0.9	0.5	-2.0	0.3	2.0
1989	1.3	-3.6	1.5	2.8	-1.3	2.6	0.1	3.2	-2.1	2.2	2.6	1.8
1990	-1.0	1.4	0.7	-0.3	2.8	-0.8	0.3	4.8	1.9	-1.7	2.9	-1.2
1991	2.7	-4.8	-1.4	1.6	2.2	0.0	2.0	-1.9	-1.9	0.4	0.4	4.0
1992	-1.6	-2.3	-0.2	-3.9	-0.4	1.4	4.8	1.1	1.0	-1.1	-0.1	-6.1
1993	-4.6	-0.6	-2.0	-3.1	-0.1	-0.1	-1.3	-0.3	0.2	1.6	1.1	-0.9
1994	-5.6	-1.6	-2.0	0.5	0.8	2.5	-1.0	0.6	1.5	1.7	0.0	-0.6
1995	1.3	0.2	2.8	-0.3	-0.3	1.5	-2.0	-1.9	0.0	2.0	2.2	-0.9
1996	-0.7	-3.0	-3.4	-2.0	-0.9	2.5	2.6	0.1	2.8	-0.1	1.8	0.1
1997	1.5	-0.5	1.8	4.5	4.2	1.1	5.2	-4.3	3.9	-3.8	-0.5	3.5
1998	4.7	-1.3	-3.4	-1.6	-6.2	6.1	0.5	2.6	1.5	1.5	3.7	3.4
1999	-3.3	0.3	-2.4	-2.8	-1.4	-2.4	-3.3	-0.6	2.0	4.9	-4.7	1.0
2000	-5.5	-4.9	4.6	1.1	0.0	-6.7	-1.9	0.7	-0.3	3.0	-1.4	-0.7
2001	-1.7	-4.7	3.5	0.8	-5.4	1.5	1.4	-3.9	8.1	-2.0	-5.8	-1.3
2002	0.5	-1.0	-2.5	-1.2	-0.3	0.7	4.2	-2.0	-0.2	5.5	0.0	-0.3
2003	-2.5	1.9	0.8	-2.2	-6.6	-3.5	-4.2	-4.9	0.7	-0.1	1.5	1.5
2004	-5.7	-1.8	-2.2	3.1	1.2	-3.0	2.9	0.0	-0.5	0.3	-2.3	-3.1
2005	-2.5	1.2	0.2	3.7	-2.3	-0.6	0.1	-1.6	0.8	0.1	-6.0	-2.0
2006	-1.8	-2.5	-1.3	0.7	0.9	0.6	2.3	-3.0	-3.2	-0.9	-4.2	-1.9
2007	0.4	-0.4	-3.3	0.2	1.1	4.6	-2.1	-0.6	5.0	-1.8	3.6	1.2
2008	-1.7	-1.8	-2.6	5.7	0.2	1.9	-0.6	-1.8	2.9	9.6	1.0	-1.0
2009	-4.7	-4.5	-2.9	-10.0	3.5	-1.7	0.6	-3.7	0.9	1.1	2.5	-0.1
2010	-3.4	2.0	-2.7	-4.2	0.5	-2.4	0.7	0.6	-1.0	-0.7	-0.4	-2.2
2011	0.1	0.9	-1.2	-0.9	-1.7	0.3	1.0	1.6	1.8	1.4	0.9	3.3
2012	-4.6	-3.0	-2.5	0.5	0.4	1.0	1.6					
average:	-1.6	-1.3	-0.8	-0.4	-0.3	0.0	0.3	-0.5	0.9	0.9	-0.1	-0.1

The average monthly outperformance of the FTSE 100 over the FTSE 250 is shown in the following chart.

Observations

By looking at the clustering of the highlighted cells in the table, it can be seen that:

1. The FTSE 250 tends to outperform the FTSE 100 in the first three months of the year and in August.

2. The FTSE 250 is particularly strong relative to the FTSE 100 in January and February.

3. The FTSE 100 is particularly strong relative to the FTSE 250 in September and October.

Mon

22

Full moon (market often strong this day)
5th weakest market week

FTSE 100	45	-0.5	1.5
FTSE 250	37	-0.2	0.9
S&P 500	45	-0.1	0.9
NIKKEI	25	0.0	1.4

1944: The International Monetary Fund (IMF) is created.

Tue

23

100th anniversary of the birth of Michael Foot, the Labour politician.

FTSE 100	60	0.1	1.0
FTSE 250	53	0.0	1.1
S&P 500	49	-0.1	0.9
NIKKEI	48	-0.6	1.6

1926: Fox Film buys the patents of the Movietone sound system for recording sound onto film.

Wed

24

FTSE 100	45	-0.4	1.1
FTSE 250	42	-0.4	1.1
S&P 500	43	0.0	1.2
NIKKEI	67	-0.1	1.8

2002: The SEC files charges against the Rigas family for their part in bringing down the bankrupt cable giant, Adelphia.

Thu

25

FTSE 100	45	0.2	1.2
FTSE 250	42	-0.2	0.7
S&P 500	54	0.1	0.8
NIKKEI	48	0.3	1.0

1603: James VI of Scotland is crowned as king of England (James I of England), bringing the Kingdom of England and Kingdom of Scotland into personal union.

Fri

26

FTSE 100	55	0.0	1.0
FTSE 250	56	-0.2	0.9
S&P 500	61	0.1	0.8
NIKKEI	52	-0.2	1.1

1995: Bob Monkhouse offers a reward of £10,000 for the return of two joke books stolen from the BBC television centre, which contain gags and scripts jotted down over 25 years.

Sat 27

Sun 28

COMPANY NEWS

Interims African Barrick Gold, Anglo American, ARM Holdings, AstraZeneca, Barclays, Beazley, BG, Bodycote, British American Tobacco, Capital Shopping Centres, Centrica, COLT Group SA, Croda International, CSR, Dialight, Dignity, Domino's Pizza, Fidelity European Values, Foreign & Colonial Investment Trust, GlaxoSmithKline, Hammerson, Herald Investment Trust, Inchcape, Informa, International Personal Finance, Intertek, ITV, Jardine Lloyd Thompson, Laird, Lancashire Holdings, Law Debenture, Legal & General, Morgan Crucible, National Express, Pearson, Provident Financial, Rathbone Brothers, Reckitt Benckiser, Reed Elsevier, Rentokil Initial, Rolls-Royce, Royal Dutch Shell, Senior, Shire, Spectris, St James's Place, Temple Bar Investment Trust, Travis Perkins, Tullow Oil, UBM

Finals British Sky Broadcasting, PZ Cussons, Renishaw

"I told the Inland Revenue I didn't owe them a penny because I lived near the seaside."
Ken Dodd

AUGUST MARKET

FTSE 100	57	0.6	4.8
FTSE 250	69	0.5	5.6
S&P 500	55	0.0	4.7
NIKKEI	46	-0.7	7.3

Market performance this month

Not surprisingly perhaps, during the low-volume summer doldrums the performance of shares in August is very similar to that in July. Five years ago, August was ranked fifth best month in the year, but now it has slipped to seventh position.

The average index change in the month is 0.6%, while the probability of a positive return in August is 57%. There have been some nasty surprises though, most recently with large falls in 1998 and 2011.

This is the strongest month of the year for the FTSE 100 Index relative to the S&P 500 Index, with the former outperforming the latter by an average of 0.8 percentage points.

Historic performance of the market in August

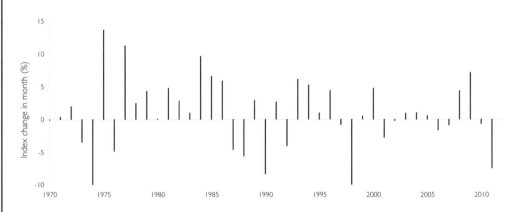

August summary

Month's performance ranking	7th
Average market change this month (standard deviation)	0.6% (4.8)
First trading day: Up / average change	60.7% / 0.0%
Last trading day: Up / average change	64.3% / 0.2%
Main features of the month	The FTSE 100 often outperforms the S&P 500 in August.
	02 Aug: 3rd strongest market day of the year
	19 Aug: Start of the 4th strongest market week of the year
Significant dates	02 Aug: US Nonfarm payroll report (anticipated)
	08 Aug: MPC interest rate announcement at 12h00 (anticipated)
	14 Aug: MSCI quarterly index review announcement
	26 Aug: Summer bank holiday – LSE closed

JUL/AUG   79, 0.6, 2.6   Week 31

Mon
29

3rd strongest market week

1958: US President Eisenhower signs into law the National Aeronautics and Space Act, which creates the National Aeronautics and Space Administration (NASA).

FTSE 100	75	0.5	1.4
FTSE 250	68	0.3	0.7
S&P 500	52	0.1	1.2
NIKKEI	45	0.4	1.2

Tue
30

Two-day FOMC meeting starts
50th anniversary of Izvestia reporting that Kim Philby had been given asylum in Moscow.
Races – Glorious Goodwood Festival (until 3 August)

2002: A 1933 Double Gold Eagle coin, created by the US mint, sells at auction for $6.6 million. It remains one of the most expensive collectibles in the world.

FTSE 100	55	0.3	0.9
FTSE 250	72	0.5	0.8
S&P 500	70	0.3	0.6
NIKKEI	50	-0.1	1.6

Wed
31

The last trading day in July is often weak.

1989: Under Secretary of State for the Environment, Virginia Bottomley, announces that Britain is to spend £10 million on research in an attempt to understand weather and climatic change.

FTSE 100	45	0.2	1.0
FTSE 250	56	0.3	0.7
S&P 500	67	0.1	0.8
NIKKEI	55	0.21	1.2

Thu
1

The FTSE 100 often outperforms the S&P 500 in August.
MPC interest rate announcement at 12h00
ECB Governing Council meeting
Cricket – England v Australia, 3rd Ashes Test starts

1981: *Video Killed the Radio Star* by The Buggles is the first video played on the new channel MTV.

FTSE 100	55	-0.3	1.3
FTSE 250	44	-0.1	0.6
S&P 500	48	0.0	0.9
NIKKEI	40	0.4	1.5

Fri
2

3rd strongest market day
Nonfarm payroll report (anticipated)

1920: Charles Ponzi's scheme is coming under increasing pressure from newspaper articles pointing out holes in the investment story.

FTSE 100	80	0.6	1.0
FTSE 250	67	0.2	1.0
S&P 500	57	0.2	1.0
NIKKEI	50	-0.1	1.3

Sat 3

Sun 4

COMPANY NEWS

Interims Aggreko, Aviva, Avocet Mining, BAE Systems, BP, Capital & Counties Properties, Centamin, Cookson Group, Devro, Drax Group, Elementis, F&C Asset Management, Ferrexpo, Fidessa Group, GKN, Hiscox, HSBC Holdings, International Consolidated Airlines Group SA, JPMorgan American Investment Trust, Ladbrokes, Lloyds Banking Group, Logica, Meggitt, Millennium & Copthorne Hotels, Moneysupermarket.com, Old Mutual, Rexam, Rightmove, Rotork, Royal Bank of Scotland Group, RPS Group, Schroders, SDL, Smith & Nephew, Standard Chartered, Taylor Wimpey, Tullett Prebon, Ultra Electronics, Weir Group, Xstrata
Finals

"Money is something you have to make in case you die."
Max Asnas

LOW VS HIGH SHARE PRICES

Do investors like low share prices? That is the reason often given for companies having share splits or bonus issues. But surely rational investors understand that price is independent of value?

Apparently not. An academic paper[1] in 2008 found that in the US equity market share returns are inversely proportional to share price (i.e. the lower the share price the higher the future return). A fairly remarkable finding. In addition, the paper found that a portfolio that was long of stocks under $5 and short of stocks over $20 and rebalanced annually generated average monthly returns of 0.53%. Lengthening the rebalancing period to two years increased the returns and reduced the costs.

Would a similar strategy work in the UK market?

The table to the right shows the annual percentage returns on two portfolios for the period 2002-2011:

	2002	2003	2004	2005	2006	2007	2008	2009	2010	2011
Low-price_20	16.4	190.9	82.8	40.9	34.7	33.1	-47.4	241.4	27.0	-1.8
High-price_20	-15.4	22.9	19.3	19.7	22.9	-11.6	-43.6	30.3	10.9	-4.6

1. **Low-price_20**: This portfolio buys equal amounts of the 20 lowest priced shares in the FTSE All Share Index at close on 31 December, holds the same portfolio for one year, and then rebalances the next 31 December.

2. **High-price_20**: As above, but this portfolio buys the 20 highest priced shares.

The chart displays the outperformance of the Low-price_20 portfolio over the High-price_20. For example, in 2002 the former outperformed the latter by 31.8 percentage points.

The outperformance of the low-priced shares is striking. On average, the low-price portfolio outperformed the high-price portfolio by 57 percentage points each year. And, no, the performance of the low-price portfolio in 2003 and 2009 is not a mistake − they really did having storming years; when markets bounce back low-price shares can fly.

Of course, a problem with low-priced shares is that their wide bid-offer spread can increase dealing costs. For example, for the low-price portfolio in the table to the right, the average spread for the 20 stocks (at 10h00 on a Monday morning) was 3.6%. However, the low-price portfolio would still easily outperform the high-price portfolio even with 5% spreads.

The table shows the shares that would have been held by the portfolios in 2012 based on share prices at close 31 December 2011.

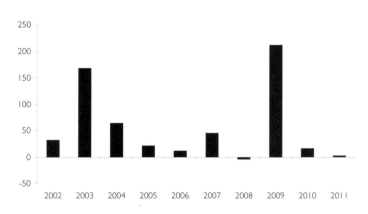

Low-price portfolio	Price (£)	High-price portfolio	Price (£)
Findel	0.04	Personal Assets Trust	334.55
Pendragon	0.08	Camellia	99.64
Lonrho	0.09	Randgold Resources Ltd	65.85
Dixons Retail	0.10	Reckitt Benckiser Group	31.80
Punch Taverns	0.10	Rio Tinto	31.25
Norcros	0.12	Capital Gearing Trust	31.18
Fortune Oil	0.12	British American Tobacco	30.56
BATM Advanced Comms Ltd	0.15	AstraZeneca	29.75
Thomas Cook Group	0.15	Daejan Holdings	27.75
International Ferro Metals Ltd	0.19	Next	27.37
Ashley (Laura) Holdings	0.20	Royal Dutch Shell	24.54
Speedy Hire	0.20	Imperial Tobacco Group	24.35
Innovation Group (The)	0.20	Anglo American	23.79
Invista European Real Estate Trust	0.24	SABMiller	22.67
Lloyds Banking Group	0.26	Shire	22.43
Renold	0.26	Unilever	21.63
Topps Tiles	0.27	Wolseley	21.32
Enterprise Inns	0.28	Carnival	21.26
BlackRock New Energy IT	0.30	Intertek Group	20.35
Management Consulting Group	0.31	Weir Group	20.32

[1] Hwang, Soosung and Lu, 'Chensheng, Is Share Price Relevant?' (25 September 2008).

Mon

5

1962: The actress Marilyn Monroe is found dead in her bed with an empty bottle of sleeping tablets by her side.

FTSE 100	50	-0.2	1.3
FTSE 250	63	-0.1	1.2
S&P 500	43	-0.1	0.9
NIKKEI	35	0.2	-0.4

Tue

New moon

6

1991: Tim Berners-Lee releases files describing his idea for the World Wide Web. WWW debuts as a publicly available service on the Internet.

FTSE 100	40	-0.2	1.4
FTSE 250	28	-0.5	1.1
S&P 500	52	0.0	1.1
NIKKEI	30	-0.3	1.4

Wed

Ramadan ends

7

2011: The European Central Bank says it will buy Italian and Spanish government bonds, as concern grows that the debt crisis may spread to the larger economies of Italy and Spain.

FTSE 100	65	0.3	0.9
FTSE 250	56	0.1	1.1
S&P 500	63	0.3	0.8
NIKKEI	40	-0.3	1.5

Thu

MPC interest rate announcement at 12h00
50th anniversary of The Great Train Robbery.

8

2002: Worldcom auditors announce another $3.3 billion in accounting errors, adding to the $3.85 billion worth of accounting fraud that sunk the company.

FTSE 100	60	0.1	1.3
FTSE 250	67	0.1	1.3
S&P 500	50	-0.1	1.4
NIKKEI	60	-0.3	1.2

Fri

Cricket – England v Australia, 4th Ashes Test starts

9

2007: French bank BNP Paribas says investors will not be able to take money out of two of its funds because it cannot value the assets in them due to a "complete evaporation of liquidity".

FTSE 100	55	0.1	1.0
FTSE 250	61	0.1	1.0
S&P 500	45	0.0	1.1
NIKKEI	50	0.2	1.4

Sat 10

Sun 11

COMPANY NEWS

Interims BBA Aviation, BlackRock World Mining Trust, Bumi, Catlin, Cobham, Greggs, Inmarsat, InterContinental Hotels Group, Mondi, Murray International Trust, Prudential, Randgold Resources, Rio Tinto, RSA Insurance, Spirent Communications, SVG Capital, Telecity Group, Unilever, William Hill
Finals Aquarius Platinum Ltd

"An economist is someone who states the obvious in terms that are incomprehensible."
Alfred A. Knopf

SIX-MONTH STRATEGY

In week 17 we looked at the six-month effect. Let's look at how to exploit that effect in practice.

Consider two portfolios:

- **Winter portfolio**: This portfolio only invests in the UK stock market in the previously defined winter period (1 November to 30 April), and for the other six months of the year the portfolio is all in cash.

- **Summer portfolio**: Does the reverse of the above portfolio – it invests in shares only in the summer period (1 May to 31 October) and is in cash for the rest of the time.

For the purposes of this simple study, we'll assume that the portfolios' investments in the stock market track the FTSE All Share Index. The chart below shows the comparative performance of the two portfolios, each starting with £1000, since 1970.

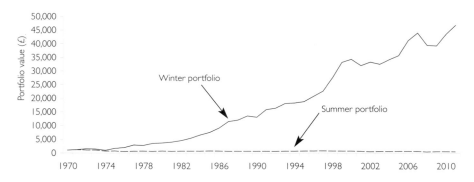

The chart needs little commentary. Starting with £1000 in 1970 the,

- **Summer portfolio** would be worth £445 by 2011; but the

- **Winter portfolio** would be worth £46,529 (over 100 times more!)

This isn't just a feature of the 1970s; the effect is still working today. If, instead of starting in 1970, the portfolios had started in 1995, then the summer portfolio would be worth £662 by 2011; but the winter portfolio would be worth £2494.

This bizarre effect suggests a strategy of investing in the stock market during the period 1 November to 30 April and then selling up and putting the cash in a deposit account or buying sterling T-bills for the other six months of the year. The chart below illustrates the result of doing this methodically since 1994, comparing the performance of this strategy to the FTSE 100 Total Return Index (i.e. compares it to a strategy of being fully invested in the market all year and receiving dividends).

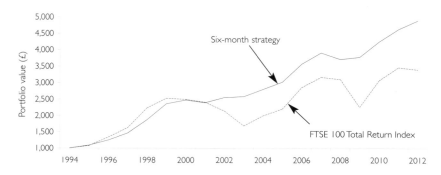

Starting in 1994 with £1000, the six-month strategy would have increased in value to £4884 by 2012; over the same period a portfolio tracking the FTSE 100 Index year-round would have increased to just £3389 (inc. dividends).

Note: There is evidence that the profitability of the strategy can be further enhanced by using an indicator like the MACD to time the exact entry and exit points for the equity investment (see week 43).

Mon

12

1982: Mexico announces it is unable to pay its enormous external debt, marking the beginning of a debt crisis that will spread to all of Latin America and the Third World.

FTSE 100	70	0.4	1.1
FTSE 250	72	0.3	0.8
S&P 500	45	0.0	0.7
NIKKEI	40	0.0	1.1

Tue

13

1991: Prosecutors announce the discovery of one of the largest bank frauds in Japan's history, involving $2.5 billion in fraudulently obtained loans.

FTSE 100	60	0.2	1.1
FTSE 250	61	0.2	1.0
S&P 500	52	0.0	0.8
NIKKEI	50	-0.1	1.4

Wed

14

MSCI quarterly index review (announcement date)

2010: The first-ever Youth Olympic Games held in Singapore.

FTSE 100	70	0.2	1.0
FTSE 250	78	0.2	0.7
S&P 500	56	0.0	1.0
NIKKEI	70	-0.4	1.2

Thu

15

1965: The Beatles play to nearly 60,000 fans at Shea Stadium in New York City, in an event later seen as marking the birth of stadium rock.

FTSE 100	60	0.1	1.2
FTSE 250	83	0.3	0.7
S&P 500	55	0.1	0.9
NIKKEI	60	0.7	1.6

Fri

16

1896: A gold rush is sparked when George Carmack discovers nuggets of gold in the Klondike River in Canada's Yukon.

FTSE 100	55	-0.1	1.1
FTSE 250	61	-0.1	1.1
S&P 500	59	0.1	0.8
NIKKEI	50	0.5	1.5

Sat 17

Sun 18

COMPANY NEWS

Interims Balfour Beatty, Bank of Georgia, Bank of Georgia Holdings, Bluecrest Allblue Fund, CRH, EnQuest, Eurasian Natural Resources Corporation, Henderson Group, Hikma Pharmaceuticals, Interserve, Menzies (John), Michael Page International, Petrofac, Resolution Ltd, Standard Life, Talvivaara Mining, Witan Investment Trust
Finals Rank Group

"The secret to life is honesty and fair dealing. If you can fake that, you've got it made."
Groucho Marx

MARKET BEHAVIOUR – BY WEEK

The two tables below list the historic ten best and worst weeks for the market.

The best week of the whole year – when the market has historically increased the most – is week 53, the last week of the year. In this week the market has risen 80% of recent years. The second best week is the week just before – week 52.

The week with the worst record is the second week. In only one year in four has the market increased in this week.

The performance figures below are ranked by the Up(%) – the percentage of years that the market has historically risen on the week.

10 strongest weeks in the year

Week	Up(%)	Avg Chng(%)	StdDev
53	80	-0.6	2.1
52	79	1	1.5
31	79	0.6	2.6
34	79	0.5	1.9
51	75	0.8	1.7
1	68	1.2	2.6
14	68	0.8	2
27	68	0.8	2.1
45	68	0.2	2.1
16	66	0.6	1.4

10 weakest weeks in the year

Week	Up(%)	Avg Chng(%)	StdDev
2	25	-0.5	1.8
25	34	-0.8	1.8
28	36	-0.6	2.5
37	39	-0.6	2.3
30	39	-0.4	2.4
22	41	0.3	1.9
36	43	-0.6	2.3
38	43	-0.2	3
13	43	0	1.9
21	45	-0.3	2.1

Note: The above best and worst weeks for the market are marked on the diary pages with a square around the arrow icon.

Analysis of Up-Weeks

Average Up(%)	55
Standard deviation	12

On average, for any particular week, the market can be expected to rise 55% of the time.

The standard deviation is 12, which means that:

- weeks that have an Up(%) over 67 (the average plus one standard deviation) can be considered **strong weeks**, and

- weeks that have an Up(%) under 43 (the average minus one standard deviation) can be considered **weak weeks**.

Mon

4th strongest market week

19

FTSE 100	45	-0.3	1.3
FTSE 250	63	-0.2	1.1
S&P 500	45	-0.2	0.9
NIKKEI	45	0.0	2.0

2011: Apple's worth shoots up to more than the combined market value of the 32 largest European banks.

Tue

20

FTSE 100	55	0.1	0.7
FTSE 250	56	0.1	0.7
S&P 500	59	0.3	0.9
NIKKEI	65	-0.2	1.4

1940: Winston Churchill makes the fourth of his famous wartime speeches, containing the line "Never was so much owed by so many to so few".

Wed

Full moon (market often strong this day)
MPC meeting minutes published
Cricket – England v Australia, 5th Ashes Test starts

21

FTSE 100	65	0.2	1.2
FTSE 250	67	0.1	1.0
S&P 500	49	0.0	1.0
NIKKEI	55	0.6	1.6

2012: The central bank of Germany, Bundesbank, opposes the European Central Bank's (ECB) idea of purchasing Italian and Spanish bonds in order to fight these nations' incremental borrowing costs.

Thu

22

FTSE 100	55	0.3	1.0
FTSE 250	56	0.4	1.0
S&P 500	59	0.0	0.7
NIKKEI	53	0.2	1.6

1864: The International Red Cross was founded by the Geneva Convention to assist the wounded and prisoners of war.

Fri

23

FTSE 100	50	0.0	0.8
FTSE 250	71	0.0	0.7
S&P 500	41	0.1	1.1
NIKKEI	35	0.0	1.7

1990: West Germany and East Germany announce that they will unite on 3 October.

Sat 24

Sun 25

COMPANY NEWS

Interims AMEC, Amlin, Antofagasta, AZ Electronic Materials SA, Berendsen, BH Global Ltd, Bovis Homes, Carillion, Derwent London, Dexion Absolute Ltd, Filtrona, Gem Diamonds, Glencore International, Hansteen Holdings, Hochschild Mining, IMI, John Wood Group, Jupiter Fund Management, Melrose, New World Resources, Persimmon, Phoenix Group, Premier Oil, Salamander Energy, Savills, Segro, SIG, SOCO International, Spirax-Sarco Engineering, UK Commercial Property Trust, WPP Group
Finals BHP Billiton, Diageo

"If no one ever took risks, Michelangelo would have painted the Sistine floor."
Neil Simon

SEPTEMBER MARKET

FTSE 100	46	-1.0	5.9
FTSE 250	42	-2.0	6.8
S&P 500	44	-0.6	4.5
NIKKEI	32	-1.8	6.0

Market performance this month

After the summer respite of July and August, the market often turns down again in September. This month is the third worst in the year. On average the market has fallen -1.0% in September and has only risen in 46% of years.

As can be seen in the chart below, the upside is fairly limited for this month; on the downside there is the potential for some large falls.

But, however bad the large caps are, the mid-cap cap stocks are even worse. On average, the FTSE 100 Index outperforms the FTSE 250 Index by almost a full percentage point in September – making September the worst month for mid-cap stocks relative to the large-caps.

Against the general market trend, this is the second strongest month for the Pharmaceuticals & Biotechnology sector relative to the FTSE 100 Index.

Summary: A tricky month.

Historic performance of the market in September

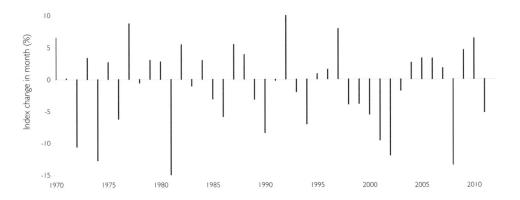

September summary

Month's performance ranking	10th
Average market change this month (standard deviation)	-1.0 (5.9)
First trading day: Up / average change	64.3% / 0.2%
Last trading day: Up / average change	46.4% / 0.0%
Main features of the month	The FTSE 100 is particularly strong relative to the FTSE 250 in September.
	The Pharma & Biotech sector is often strong in September.
	02 Sep: Start of the 7th weakest market week of the year
	09 Sep: 9th weakest market day of the year
	16 Sep: Start of the 8th weakest market week of the year
	27 Sep: 7th strongest market day of the year
	30 Sep: Last trading day in September is often weak
Significant dates	02 Sep: Labor Day (US) – NYSE closed
	05 September: MPC interest rate announcement at 12h00 (anticipated)
	06 Sep: US Nonfarm payroll report (anticipated)
	11 Sep: FTSE 100 Index quarterly review
	20 Sep: Triple Witching

Mon

Summer Bank Holiday (UK) – LSE closed
US Tennis Open (until 8th September)

26

2003: The US Congressional Budget Office predicts a federal deficit of $480 billion in 2004 and $5.8 trillion by 2013.

FTSE 100			
FTSE 250			
S&P 500	50	0.0	0.8
NIKKEI	60	-0.1	1.1

Tue

27

2003: Mars makes its closest approach to Earth in nearly 60,000 years, passing just 34,646,418 miles away.

FTSE 100	56	0.2	1.1
FTSE 250	67	0.0	0.8
S&P 500	55	-0.1	1.0
NIKKEI	55	0.0	2.0

Wed

28

1963: The fight for racial equality moves a step closer to victory as Martin Luther King tells thousands of Americans "I have a dream…" – 50th Anniversary

FTSE 100	50	-0.3	1.4
FTSE 250	50	-0.1	1.1
S&P 500	49	-0.1	0.9
NIKKEI	50	0.3	1.3

Thu

29

2005: Hurricane Katrina devastates much of the US Gulf Coast from Louisiana to the Florida Panhandle, killing more than 1,836 people and causing over $80 billion in damage.

FTSE 100	50	0.0	0.8
FTSE 250	50	0.1	0.7
S&P 500	55	0.1	0.9
NIKKEI	55	-0.1	1.5

Fri

30

1980: Striking Polish workers win a sweeping victory in a battle with their Communist rulers for the right to independent trade unions and the right to strike.

FTSE 100	75	0.4	1.0
FTSE 250	64	0.3	1.0
S&P 500	50	-0.1	0.9
NIKKEI	50	0.0	1.2

Sat 31

Sun 1

COMPANY NEWS

Interims Admiral Group, Aegis Group, Afren, BH Macro Ltd, Bunzl, Bwin.Party Digital Entertainment, Cairn Energy, Cape, Evraz, G4S, Heritage Oil Ltd, Hunting, International Public Partnership Ltd, IP Group, John Laing Infrastructure Fund, Kazakhmys, Kenmare Resources, Kentz Corporation Ltd, NMC Health, Perform Group, Petropavlovsk, Raven Russia, Regus, RusPetro, Serco Group, Yule Catto & Co
Finals Hays

"It's probably true that hard work never killed anyone, but I figure why take the chance?"
Ronald Reagan

DEFENSIVE STOCKS

September can be a dangerous time for stocks – the two worst months for the FTSE 100 Index since 2002 have been (in order of the worst performance) September 2008 and September 2002.

Since January 2002 the FTSE 100 Index has fallen in 46% of all months. The table below lists the ten worst performing months for the index since 2002.

Month	FTSE 100 Chng(%)
Sep-08	-13.0
Sep-02	-12.0
Oct-08	-10.7
Jan-03	-9.5
Jan-08	-8.9
Jul-02	-8.8
Jun-02	-8.4
Feb-09	-7.7
May-12	-7.3
Aug-11	-7.2

The average decrease for these ten worst months was -9.3% (the average change for all the months since 2002 was 0.15%).

Generally, when the market falls significantly all stocks go down. However, there are some stocks that (fairly) consistently outperform the index during these weak times. These stocks are often called *defensive stocks*.

The table below lists the 13 stocks that have performed the best during the ten worst monthly falls in the market since 2002 (as were shown in the table above). The table lists the stocks' percentage performance for each of the ten months and is ranked by the stocks' average monthly performance for the ten months.

Company	Sep 08	Sep 02	Oct 08	Jan 03	Jan 08	Jul 02	Jun 02	Feb 09	May 12	Aug 11	Avg
Randgold Resources Ltd	-8.3	24.1	-11.8	3.7	33.2	-10.7	7.7	0.5	-4.2	16.7	5.1
Next	-4	10.2	3.4	3.2	-13.6	-7.3	-6.7	-0.7	3.4	-0.6	-1.3
Smith & Nephew	-10.8	3.1	-3.7	-9.1	17.6	-7.7	-6.4	-0.2	-0.1	-2.4	-2.0
Carnival	-11.7	6.2	-18.4	-8.8	-2.3	5.5	-7.2	12.8	4.1	-5.1	-2.5
United Utilities Group	-2.8	-6.2	0.6	-7.9	-5.8	-5.6	-8.3	-6.2	6.2	2	-3.4
Severn Trent	-0.7	-11.2	1.2	-0.9	-6.8	-14	-7.1	-0.3	1.8	2.7	-3.5
Pennon Group	-4.6	-6.3	-8.3	-1.2	-2.4	-2	1.4	-4	-0.5	-10.7	-3.9
SSE	-1.4	2.2	-14.9	-10.7	-6.7	-0.6	-6.8	-3.8	0.2	-0.5	-4.3
Diageo	-7.1	0.9	0.6	-8	-6.3	-8.9	-0.9	-13.2	-0.3	-0.4	-4.4
GlaxoSmithKline	-6.6	1.2	-1.2	-4	-7.6	-12.3	1	-12.3	0.9	-3.9	-4.5
Reckitt Benckiser Group	-2.4	0.3	-3.7	-12.4	-10.1	-7.4	-2.9	0.7	-4	-5.3	-4.7
Unilever	3	-2	-8.3	-10.5	-12.5	-5.9	-4.8	-10.6	-2.9	6	-4.9
British Land Co	-2.7	-7.9	-17.3	-10	6.9	-1.6	-8.7	1.1	-1.3	-7.9	-4.9

Observations

1. All the stocks on average have outperformed the index (which has an average fall of -9.3%).

2. Only one stock out of the 100 in the index has a positive average performance – Randgold Resources.

3. Only three stocks rose in four or more months during the ten worst months: Randgold Resources, Next and Carnival.

Mon
2

Labor Day (US) – NYSE closed
3rd weakest market month
7th weakest market week
MSCI quarterly index review (effective date)
30th anniversary of the LSE flotation of Personal Assets Trust.

FTSE 100	50	0.0	1.0
FTSE 250	53	0.2	0.9
S&P 500			
NIKKEI	53	0.2	1.0

Tue
3

The FTSE 100 is particularly strong relative to the FTSE 250 in September and October.
The Pharma & Biotech sector is often strong in September.

1666: The Royal Exchange burns down in the Great Fire of London.

FTSE 100	55	0.0	1.5
FTSE 250	61	0.1	1.0
S&P 500	63	0.1	1.3
NIKKEI	45	-0.2	1.8

Wed
4

Beige Book published

1882: The Edison Electric Illuminating Company starts up its first electrical plant to distribute electricity in New York's shopping and financial district.

FTSE 100	60	0.0	1.0
FTSE 250	72	0.1	0.9
S&P 500	46	-0.2	1.0
NIKKEI	35	-0.2	1.3

Thu
5

New moon
MPC interest rate announcement at 12h00
ECB Governing Council meeting

1980: The St. Gotthard Tunnel opens in Switzerland as the world's longest highway tunnel at 10.14 miles (16.224 km), stretching from Göschenen to Airolo.

FTSE 100	50	-0.4	1.1
FTSE 250	56	-0.1	1.0
S&P 500	37	-0.1	0.9
NIKKEI	50	-0.2	1.3

Fri
6

Nonfarm payroll report (anticipated)

1991: The original name of Russia's second largest city, St. Petersburg, is restored after having been changed to Petrograd in 1914 and Leningrad in 1924.

FTSE 100	65	0.0	1.1
FTSE 250	50	-0.1	0.7
S&P 500	63	0.1	0.9
NIKKEI	30	-0.4	1.0

Sat 7

Sun 8

COMPANY NEWS

Interims Morrison (Wm) Supermarkets, Premier Farnell, Restaurant Group
Finals Dechra Pharmaceuticals, Genus, Go-Ahead Group, Hargreaves Lansdown, Murray Income Trust, Redrow, Wetherspoon (J D)

"The safest way to double your money is to fold it over and put it in your pocket."
Kin Hubbard

FTSE 100 REVIEWS – COMPANIES LEAVING THE INDEX

The charts below show the share prices of 12 companies that have left the FTSE 100 Index in the years 2011 and 2012. The time period for each chart is six months, starting from three months before the company joined the index. So it is possible to see the share price behaviour in the three months leading up to joining, and the three months after.

It can be seen that, in most cases, the share price falls in the period before the company leaves the FTSE 100 Index, and then rises afterwards.

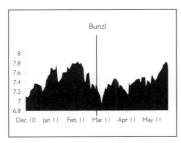

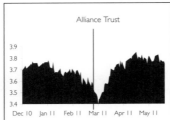

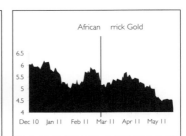

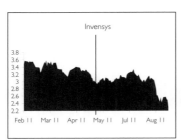

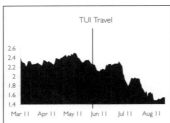

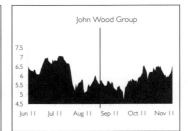

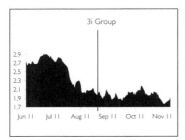

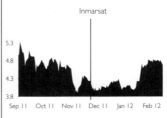

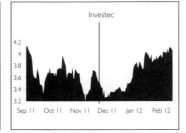

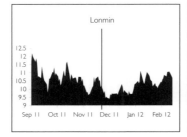

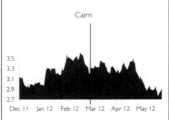

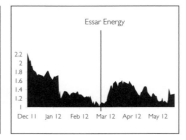

Mon 9

4th weakest market week
9th weakest market day
500th anniversary of the Battle of Flodden Field.

1850: A third of Texas's claimed territory is transferred to federal control, in return for the US federal government assuming $10 million of Texas's pre-annexation debt.

FTSE 100	30	-0.3	0.8
FTSE 250	37	-0.2	0.8
S&P 500	57	0.5	0.3
NIKKEI	45	0.3	1.2

Tue 10

1960: At the Summer Olympics in Rome, Abebe Bikila becomes the first sub-Saharan African to win a gold medal, winning the marathon in bare feet.

FTSE 100	40	-0.3	1.2
FTSE 250	44	-0.3	0.9
S&P 500	50	-0.1	0.8
NIKKEI	50	0.1	1.6

Wed 11

FTSE 100 quarterly review
Horse racing – St Leger Meeting (until 14th)

2001: The terrorist attacks on the World Trade Centre and the Pentagon in America cause approximately $40 billion in insurance losses, making September 11th one of the largest insured events ever.

FTSE 100	32	-0.1	0.9
FTSE 250	28	-0.2	1.0
S&P 500	52	0.0	1.1
NIKKEI	45	0.1	1.8

Thu 12

100th anniversary of the birth of Jesse Owens, the American athlete.

2008: 25 people are killed when a Metrolink commuter train crashes head-on into a Union Pacific freight train. Wrongful death lawsuits are expected to cause $500 million in losses for Metrolink.

FTSE 100	45	-0.3	1.2
FTSE 250	50	-0.2	1.0
S&P 500	51	0.0	0.9
NIKKEI	50	-0.9	1.9

Fri 13

Motor sport – Goodwood Revival (until 15th)

1898: Hannibal Goodwin patents the celluloid photographic film.

FTSE 100	50	0.1	0.9
FTSE 250	50	0.0	0.6
S&P 500	67	0.1	0.9
NIKKEI	80	-0.4	1.0

Sat 14

Sun 15

COMPANY NEWS

Interims Kingfisher, Merchants Trust, Next
Finals Ashmore Group, Barratt Developments, City of London Investment Trust, Dunelm Group, Galliford Try, Kier Group

"When it's a question of money, everybody is of the same religion."
Voltaire

MARKET BEHAVIOUR – BY MONTH

The table below ranks the 12 months by their historic performance since 1970.

The best month of the whole year – when the market has historically increased most often – is December. The proportion of years when the market has increased in December is 86%, rising an average of 2.6% in the month. Somewhat surprisingly, perhaps, the second strongest month is October; but note the very high standard deviation, indicating the volatility of the market in this month.

The month with the worst record is June. The market has only risen in June 41% of all years and the average market move for the month is 0.5% in this month.

The performance figures below are ranked by the Up(%) – the percentage of years that the market has historically risen on the month.

Ranking of monthly performance

Month	Up(%)	Avg Chng (%)	Std Dev
December	86	2.6	3
October	75	0.7	6.9
April	68	1.8	3.7
February	57	0.9	4.1
November	57	0.7	3.9
March	57	0.6	3.5
August	57	0.6	4.8
January	57	0.3	5.2
July	55	0.8	4.3
September	46	-1	5.9
May	45	-0.3	4.5
June	41	-0.7	3.5

The variation in performance between the months is statistically significant.

A big change in the ranking in the last five years is the performance of January. In 2007 January was ranked fourth with an average increase of 2.7%; but following a disastrous run of years from 2008 to 2011, it is now eighth, with an increase of just 0.3%.

Six-month effect

The chart below shows the average monthly performance of the FTSE 100 Index.

The strength of the market in the period November to April can be clearly seen in the chart – which gives rise to the six-month effect (as explained in week 17).

Mon 16

Respect for the Aged Day (Japan) – TSE closed
8th weakest market week

1992: The Pound Sterling is forced out of the European Exchange Rate Mechanism by currency speculators and is made to devalue against the Deutschmark.

FTSE 100	60	-0.1	1.2
FTSE 250	47	-0.3	1.1
S&P 500	66	0.4	0.8
NIKKEI			

Tue 17

60th anniversary of the LSE flotation of Murray Income Trust.

2008: Scottish banking group HBOS agrees to an emergency acquisition by its UK rival Lloyds TSB, after a major decline in its share prices.

FTSE 100	50	0.2	1.6
FTSE 250	44	0.0	1.5
S&P 500	52	-0.2	1.3
NIKKEI	58	-0.9	1.9

Wed 18

MPC meeting minutes published
ECB Governing Council Meeting

1882: The Pacific Stock Exchange opens.

FTSE 100	50	-0.1	1.4
FTSE 250	50	-0.1	1.3
S&P 500	49	0.1	1.0
NIKKEI	37	0.0	1.2

Thu 19

Full moon (market often strong this day)

2008: The US government announces a plan to purchase large amounts of illiquid, risky, mortgage backed securities from financial institutions, estimated to involve a minimum of $700 billion additional commitments.

FTSE 100	50	0.2	2.3
FTSE 250	22	0.1	2.2
S&P 500	45	0.0	1.2
NIKKEI	72	-0.4	1.4

Fri 20

Day following the Chinese Mid-Autumn Festival (HK) – HKSE closed
Triple Witching (market often strong on this day)

1873: The NYSE closes its doors for ten days to try and wait out the Panic of 1873, caused by the failure of the bank Jay Cooke & Company.

FTSE 100	50	-0.1	1.4
FTSE 250	50	-0.3	1.2
S&P 500	48	-0.1	0.9
NIKKEI	33	0.7	1.2

Sat 21

Sun 22   Autumn Equinox, also known as Mabon

COMPANY NEWS

Interims Alliance Trust, JD Sports Fashion, Mercantile Investment Trust, Ophir Energy
Finals Petra Diamonds Ltd

"A feast is made for laughter, and wine maketh merry: but money answereth all things."
The Bible, Ecclesiastes (Chapter 10, Verse 19)

MONTHLY SHARE MOMENTUM

Do shares exhibit a momentum effect from one month to the next?

If we selected the ten best performing FTSE 100 shares in one month and created an equally-weighted portfolio of those shares to hold for the following month, would that portfolio outperform the market index?

Or, more interestingly, if we did this systematically for a year (i.e. our portfolio each month is comprised of the ten best performing shares in the previous month), would that portfolio outperform the FTSE 100 Index?

The chart below shows the result of operating such a momentum portfolio in 2011. Each bar represents the outperformance of the portfolio over the FTSE 100 Index. For example, in February the ten-share portfolio would have increased 6.2% against a FTSE 100 increase of 2.2%, giving an outperformance of 4.0.

Over the year, the portfolio would have outperformed the index by an average 1.1 percentage points each month. At the end of the year the portfolio would have increased 10.3% on its starting value, while the FTSE 100 Index fell 3.1% over the same period.

The chart below illustrates the result of operating such a portfolio in 2010.

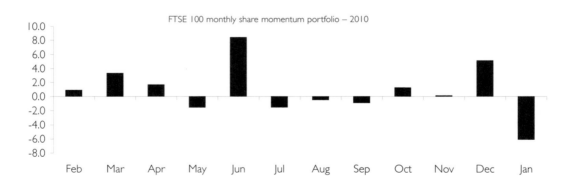

This time the average monthly outperformance of the portfolio over the FTSE 100 Index would have been 0.9%.

Note: An academic paper[1] published in 2001 looked at momentum trading strategies in the UK stock market. Although it identified several profitable strategies it found that momentum effects were not consistent and therefore the returns on the strategies were dependent on the period over which the strategies were applied.

---

[1] Hon, M., Tonks, I., 'Momentum in the UK Stock Market' (2001).

Mon
23
Autumnal equinox (Japan) – TSE closed

2002: The first public version of the web browser Mozilla Firefox (Phoenix 0.1) is released.

FTSE 100	35	-0.2	1.1
FTSE 250	37	-0.4	0.9
S&P 500	43	-0.1	1.0
NIKKEI			

Tue
24
1946: Cathay Pacific Airways is founded in Hong Kong.

FTSE 100	40	-0.1	1.3
FTSE 250	44	-0.1	1.1
S&P 500	43	-0.1	1.1
NIKKEI	75	-1.0	1.5

Wed
25
1906: In the presence of a great crowd, including the Spanish king, Leonardo Torres Quevedo successfully demonstrates the invention of the Telekino in the port of Bilbao, guiding a boat from the shore, in what is considered the birth of the remote control.

FTSE 100	45	-0.1	1.1
FTSE 250	50	0.0	0.9
S&P 500	47	-0.1	0.9
NIKKEI	45	0.4	1.4

Thu
26
2008: The Seattle-based bank holding company, Washington Mutal, declares bankruptcy. Its collapse is the largest American bank failure in history up to this point.

FTSE 100	55	0.3	1.4
FTSE 250	67	0.0	1.0
S&P 500	57	-0.2	1.3
NIKKEI	45	-0.4	1.6

Fri
27
7th strongest market day

2000: US President Clinton announces that there is a record-breaking government budget surplus of $230 billion.

FTSE 100	75	0.7	1.1
FTSE 250	65	0.3	0.8
S&P 500	53	0.0	0.9
NIKKEI	55	-0.1	1.5

Sat 28

Sun 29   100th anniversary of the birth of Trevor Howard, the English actor.

COMPANY NEWS

Interims Barr (A G), Polymetal International
Finals Close Brothers, Genesis Emerging Markets Fund Ltd, Smiths Group

"Money cannot buy health, but I'd settle for a diamond-studded wheelchair."
Dorothy Parker

OCTOBER MARKET

FTSE 100	75	0.7	6.9
FTSE 250	62	-0.5	8.1
S&P 500	60	0.8	5.6
NIKKEI	46	-1.0	7.4

Market performance this month

Despite its (deserved) reputation for large market falls, the long-term performance statistics for October are pretty good. October is the second best performing month in the year. On average, the market rises +0.7% in the month and the probability of a positive return in the month is a very high 75%.

Of course, a significant feature of the market is volatility. While the average change in the month is +0.7%, the standard deviation is very high at 6.9 (the highest of any month). And a glance at the chart below shows the magnitude of the occasional falls in this month.

As in September, mid-cap shares are often weak in this month relative to large-cap shares.

Six-month effect

A reminder to investors that the depressed six-month cycle (May to Oct) is ending this month and now is the time – history suggests – to start thinking about increasing a portfolio's weighting to equities.

Historic performance of the market in October

October summary

Month's performance ranking	2nd
Average market change this month (standard deviation)	0.7% (6.9)
First trading day: Up / average change	60.7% / 0.2%
Last trading day: Up / average change	75.0% / 0.6%
Main features of the month	Strong sectors in this fourth quarter are: Mobile Telecom, Tobacco, and Beverage.
	Weak sectors in this fourth quarter are: Real Estate Investment Trusts, Banks, and Forestry & Paper.
	The FTSE 100 is particularly strong relative to the FTSE 250 in this month.
	Small cap stocks are often weak in October.
	31 Oct: 4th strongest market day of the year
Significant dates	04 Oct: US Nonfarm payroll report (anticipated)
	10 Oct: MPC interest rate announcement at 12h00 (anticipated)
	30 Oct: FOMC monetary policy statement

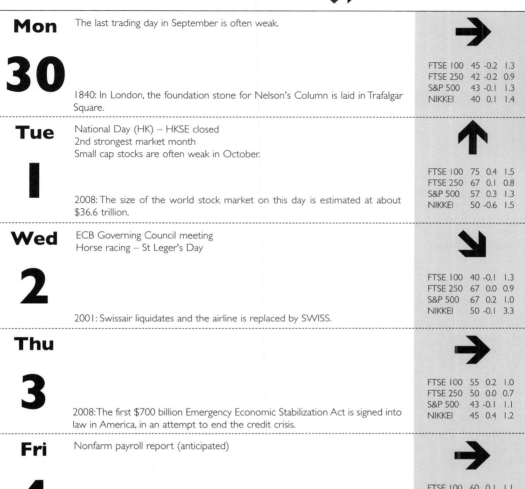

Mon

30

The last trading day in September is often weak.

→

FTSE 100	45	-0.2	1.3
FTSE 250	42	-0.2	0.9
S&P 500	43	-0.1	1.3
NIKKEI	40	0.1	1.4

1840: In London, the foundation stone for Nelson's Column is laid in Trafalgar Square.

Tue

1

National Day (HK) – HKSE closed
2nd strongest market month
Small cap stocks are often weak in October.

↑

FTSE 100	75	0.4	1.5
FTSE 250	67	0.1	0.8
S&P 500	57	0.3	1.3
NIKKEI	50	-0.6	1.5

2008: The size of the world stock market on this day is estimated at about $36.6 trillion.

Wed

2

ECB Governing Council meeting
Horse racing – St Leger's Day

↘

FTSE 100	40	-0.1	1.3
FTSE 250	67	0.0	0.9
S&P 500	67	0.2	1.0
NIKKEI	50	-0.1	3.3

2001: Swissair liquidates and the airline is replaced by SWISS.

Thu

3

→

FTSE 100	55	0.2	1.0
FTSE 250	50	0.0	0.7
S&P 500	43	-0.1	1.1
NIKKEI	45	0.4	1.2

2008: The first $700 billion Emergency Economic Stabilization Act is signed into law in America, in an attempt to end the credit crisis.

Fri

4

Nonfarm payroll report (anticipated)

→

FTSE 100	60	0.1	1.1
FTSE 250	61	0.0	1.1
S&P 500	59	0.1	0.8
NIKKEI	50	-0.1	1.3

1997: The second largest cash robbery in US history occurs at the Charlotte, North Carolina office of Loomis, Fargo and Company. $17.3 million is stolen.

Sat 5 New moon

Sun 6 Horse racing – Prix de l'Arc de Triomphe

COMPANY NEWS

Interims Fresnillo, Ted Baker, Tesco
Finals JPMorgan Emerging Markets Inv Trust, Wolseley

"October. This is one of the peculiarly dangerous months to speculate in stocks. Other dangerous months are July, January, September, April, November, May, March, June, December, August and February."
Mark Twain

SECTOR PERFORMANCE – FOURTH QUARTER

The table below shows the performance of FTSE 350 sectors in the fourth quarter (30 September to 31 December) of each year from 2002 to 2011. The table is ranked by the final column – the average performance for each sector over the ten years. For each year the top five performing sectors are highlighted in light grey, the bottom five in dark grey.

Sector	2002	2003	2004	2005	2006	2007	2008	2009	2010	2011	Avg
Mobile Telecom					15.3	6.7	12.8	3.3	5.4	9.3	8.8
Mining	15.5	18.3	-0.4	11.2	10.6	2.7	-31.5	24.1	22.8	8.5	8.2
Tobacco	-0.1	14.5	16.0	7.0	7.7	15.4	-0.9	4.5	3.7	12.0	8.0
Real Estate Inv & Srvs									6.8	8.8	7.8
Beverages	-11.5	14.1	10.7	1.5	8.5	3.4	3.8	16.3	9.0	11.0	6.7
Chemicals	4.0	5.5	10.7	9.2	9.1	9.2	-21.3	12.0	16.3	10.3	6.5
Fixed Line Telecoms	30.1	14.6	9.3	-8.2	12.6	-9.2	-13.7	2.5	18.7	5.9	6.3
Health Care Equip & Srvs	-0.4	26.7	4.4	13.3	6.3	3.2	-27.6	13.1	16.7	6.7	6.2
Food Producers	-2.0	4.1	15.0	-1.0	5.6	14.9	2.2	6.1	7.9	6.2	5.9
Oil & Gas Producers	2.8	10.3	-0.9	-5.6	-0.3	10.1	8.1	6.5	11.0	16.6	5.9
Oil Equip; Srvs & Dist					23.8	14.5	-38.3	3.6	15.9	14.0	5.6
Industrial Metals	-20.4	48.1	-1.0	14.6	36.7	10.0	-65.0	13.5	26.3	-9.6	5.3
Personal Goods	0.8	4.2	15.8	11.3	19.2	-1.8	-23.0	18.7	8.6	-1.3	5.3
Gas; Water & Multiutilities		9.4	6.0	6.2	9.9	4.3	-6.4	11.8	3.5	-1.1	4.8
Media	8.9	11.0	8.4	3.5	1.7	-4.7	-2.9	6.4	6.2	9.3	4.8
Nonlife Insurance	22.3	2.9	2.9	17.0	12.0	-4.8	3.5	-5.0	0.4	-3.4	4.8
Food & Drug Retailers	-3.2	8.2	11.2	7.6	10.2	2.7	-4.3	4.9	-1.1	7.5	4.4
Travel & Leisure	-8.1	13.9	12.3	11.5	16.6	-7.6	-13.6	0.9	10.0	6.9	4.3
Software & Comp Srvs	29.4	2.3	10.1	10.3	9.7	-9.5	-17.5	-1.1	2.0	3.6	3.9
Life Insurance	21.3	7.7	11.3	9.8	6.6	-4.8	-19.2	-1.1	-2.5	9.7	3.9
Support Services	2.8	2.9	6.9	8.0	10.3	-6.3	-5.7	4.3	6.5	8.0	3.8
Equity Inv Instruments	8.6	7.5	11.5	8.5	6.6	-1.7	-18.6	4.3	9.3	1.5	3.8
Construction & Materials	-5.6	6.5	8.2	13.7	4.5	-12.6	4.3	-8.4	16.3	8.0	3.5
Financial Services	5.3	4.0	19.4	10.2	10.6	0.3	-29.9	-2.7	19.0	-3.2	3.3
Aerospace & Defense	-11.9	1.6	3.4	11.5	5.4	4.4	-6.2	5.4	1.3	13.3	2.8
Industrial Engineering	-3.7	6.3	10.0	10.9	6.3	-18.8	-26.8	7.3	19.2	17.5	2.8
Electricity	2.0	6.3	4.1	-1.7	13.7	4.6	-14.8	-0.1	9.6	1.4	2.5
Pharm & Biotech	2.3	4.0	-3.5	3.7	-9.3	-4.7	8.9	6.2	-3.6	8.4	1.2
Industrial Transportation	-0.2	6.5	12.9	9.6	10.2	-5.3	-32.2	1.5	5.3	1.7	1.0
Electronic & Elect Equip	-12.4	-16.2	11.4	17.4	16.3	-15.7	-21.6	1.1	18.0	8.2	0.7
Household Goods					11.9	-7.9	-6.8	5.0	1.6	-0.5	0.6
General Retailers	-1.2	2.7	1.4	14.1	2.6	-12.1	-12.9	9.2	2.0	-1.0	0.5
Forestry & Paper	5.1	-1.8	4.5	9.8		-8.6	-21.0	8.4	-0.2	-3.9	-0.9
General Industrials					1.4	-13.2	-20.4	10.0	9.0	4.1	-1.5
Automobiles & Parts	-14.2	7.2	15.9	4.2	-3.2	-20.3	-50.4	2.9	31.2	4.0	-2.3
Technology Hard & Equip	-60.5	27.1	13.6	13.9	-8.1	-12.6	-22.2	12.5	5.0	5.9	-2.5
Banks	7.8	8.5	6.6	6.5	3.2	-10.3	-38.2	-9.2	-4.0	-0.3	-2.9
Real Estate Inv Trusts					11.0	-12.8	-33.6	4.7	7.6	-2.1	-4.2

Observations

1. The general clustering of light grey highlights at the top of the table, and dark grey at the bottom, suggests that certain sectors consistently perform well (or badly) in this quarter. This effect is the strongest in the first quarter.

2. **Strong sectors** in this quarter are: Mobile Telecom, Tobacco, and Beverages.

3. **Weak sectors** in this quarter are: Real Estate Investment Trusts, Banks, and Forestry & Paper.

Mon

7

1896: *The Wall Street Journal* begins publishing Dow's expanded list of stocks.

FTSE 100	50	0.0	0.7
FTSE 250	58	0.0	0.5
S&P 500	39	-0.1	1.4
NIKKEI	50	0.1	2.0

Tue

8

2003: Film star Arnold Schwarzenegger is elected governor of California.

FTSE 100	45	-0.3	1.5
FTSE 250	50	0.1	1.8
S&P 500	43	0.0	0.8
NIKKEI	44	0.0	2.8

Wed

9

2007: The Dow Jones Industrial Average jumps more than 120 points, ending at an all-time high of 14,164.53.

FTSE 100	45	-0.2	1.3
FTSE 250	50	-0.2	1.0
S&P 500	44	-0.3	1.7
NIKKEI	39	-0.7	1.1

Thu

10

MPC interest rate announcement at 12h00
200th anniversary of the birth of Giuseppe Verdi, the Italian composer.
50th anniversary of the premiere in the UK of *From Russia with Love*.

1582: Because of the implementation of the Gregorian calendar, this day does not exist in this year in Italy, Poland, Portugal and Spain.

FTSE 100	45	-0.3	2.2
FTSE 250	59	-0.3	1.7
S&P 500	45	0.1	1.3
NIKKEI	43	-0.4	3.8

Fri

11

1987: A huge sonar exploration of Loch Ness fails to find the world famous monster known affectionately as "Nessie".

FTSE 100	60	0.3	1.3
FTSE 250	61	0.3	1.0
S&P 500	52	0.2	1.0
NIKKEI	56	-1.4	1.9

Sat 12   30th anniversary of the LSE flotation of Oxford Instruments.

Sun 13

COMPANY NEWS

Interims Booker, Brown (N) Group, NB Global Floating Rate Income Fund
Finals Edinburgh Dragon Trust

"A group of lemmings looks like a pack of individuals compared with Wall Street when it gets a concept in its teeth."
Warren Buffett

VERY LARGE ONE-DAY MARKET FALLS

Analysis of the behaviour of the FTSE 100 Index for very large one-day falls.

26 years ago this week, on 20 October 1987, the FTSE 100 Index fell 12.2% in one day. This is the largest one-day fall in the index since its inception in 1984. The accompanying table shows the ten largest one-day falls in the index since 1984.

Judging by the table, it would seem that many of the largest one-day falls have occurred in recent years.

Is the FTSE 100 Index becoming increasingly volatile?

Since 1984 there have been 189 very large one-day falls, where "very large fall" is defined as a fall more than two standard deviations greater than the average daily change in the index. In other words, a very large fall is any decrease of more than -2.23%. These falls are plotted on the following chart.

Date	Change(%)
20 Oct 87	-12.2
10 Oct 08	-8.8
06 Oct 08	-7.9
15 Oct 08	-7.2
26 Oct 87	-6.2
19 Oct 87	-5.7
06 Nov 08	-5.7
22 Oct 87	-5.7
21 Jan 08	-5.5
15 Jul 02	-5.4

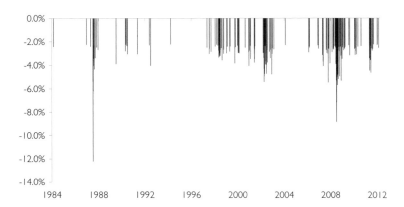

The chart does indeed show that the frequency of very large one-day falls has increased in recent years.

After the fall

The following chart shows how on average the index behaves in the days immediately following a very large fall. The Y-axis is the percentage move from the close of the index on the day of the large fall. For example, by day five the index has risen 0.8% above the index close on the day of the large fall.

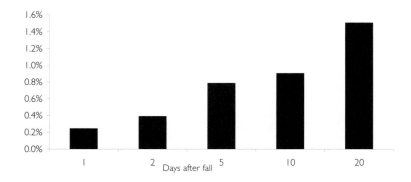

As can be seen, the index rises steadily in the days following a very large fall.

Note: An accompanying study on very large rises can be seen in week 47.

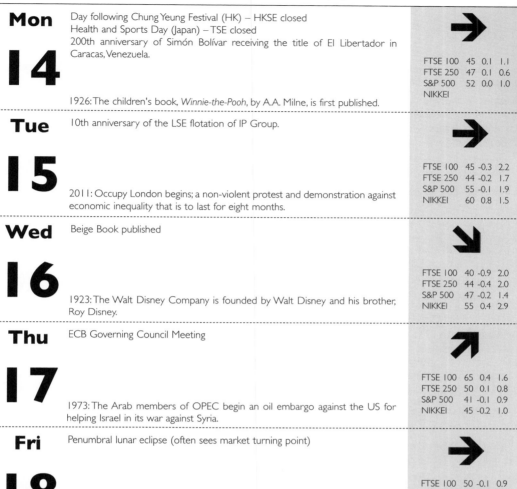

Mon 14	Day following Chung Yeung Festival (HK) – HKSE closed Health and Sports Day (Japan) – TSE closed 200th anniversary of Simón Bolívar receiving the title of El Libertador in Caracas, Venezuela. 1926: The children's book, *Winnie-the-Pooh*, by A.A. Milne, is first published.	→	FTSE 100 45 0.1 1.1 FTSE 250 47 0.1 0.6 S&P 500 52 0.0 1.0 NIKKEI
Tue 15	10th anniversary of the LSE flotation of IP Group. 2011: Occupy London begins; a non-violent protest and demonstration against economic inequality that is to last for eight months.	→	FTSE 100 45 -0.3 2.2 FTSE 250 44 -0.2 1.7 S&P 500 55 -0.1 1.9 NIKKEI 60 0.8 1.5
Wed 16	Beige Book published 1923: The Walt Disney Company is founded by Walt Disney and his brother, Roy Disney.	↘	FTSE 100 40 -0.9 2.0 FTSE 250 44 -0.4 2.0 S&P 500 47 -0.2 1.4 NIKKEI 55 0.4 2.9
Thu 17	ECB Governing Council Meeting 1973: The Arab members of OPEC begin an oil embargo against the US for helping Israel in its war against Syria.	↗	FTSE 100 65 0.4 1.6 FTSE 250 50 0.1 0.8 S&P 500 41 -0.1 0.9 NIKKEI 45 -0.2 1.0
Fri 18	Penumbral lunar eclipse (often sees market turning point) 2011: Apple surprises the market with weaker than expected earnings. The stock will not recover from a large loss for the rest of the month.	→	FTSE 100 50 -0.1 0.9 FTSE 250 56 -0.1 0.9 S&P 500 66 0.3 0.9 NIKKEI 45 0.2 1.3

Sat 19   200th anniversary of Battle of Leipzig – Napoleon is defeated (again).

Sun 20

COMPANY NEWS

Interims Home Retail Group, Whitbread
Finals Bellway, Debenhams, WHSmith

"You can't overestimate what happens when you encourage regulators to believe that the goal of regulation is not to regulate."
Joseph Stiglitz

SIX-MONTH STRATEGY WITH MACD

We have already looked at the six-month effect (the tendency for the November to April market to outperform the May to October market, see week 17) and how a portfolio based on this effect can outperform an index fund (see week 33). But it is not necessarily the case that the strong half of the year begins every year on exactly 1 November, nor that it ends exactly on 30 April. By tweaking the beginning and end dates it may be possible to enhance the (already impressive) returns of the six-month strategy.

This idea of finessing the entry/exit dates was first proposed by Sy Harding in his 1999 book, *Riding the Bear – How to Prosper in the Coming Bear Market*. Harding's system takes the six-month seasonal trading strategy and adds a timing element using the MACD indicator. First, by back-testing, Harding found that the optimal average days to enter and exit the market were in fact 16 October and 20 April. Then, using these dates, his system's rules are:

1. If the MACD already indicates that the market is in a bull phase on 16 October the system enters the market, otherwise the system waits until the MACD gives a buy signal.

2. If the MACD already indicates the market is in a bear phase on 20 April the system exits the market, otherwise the system waits until the MACD gives a sell signal.

Following such rules, the entry or exit dates of the strategy can be one or two months later than the standard 1 November and 30 April. Harding calls his system the Seasonal Timing Strategy (STS). Commenting on the STS, Mark Hulbert of Marketwatch.com said in April 2012,

> Harding's modification of the Halloween Indicator [six-month strategy] produced a 9.0% return (annualised) over the same period [2002-2012], or 2.0 percentage points per year more than a purely mechanical application of this seasonal pattern, and 3.6 percentage points ahead of a buy-and-hold.

Can such a strategy work in the UK market?

We found it difficult to replicate similar results for the UK market using Harding's STS system. One problem was that 1 November is such a good date for entering the market – it was difficult to consistently improve on it with any technical indicator. However, we did come up with one simple system that improved on the standard six-month strategy. Briefly, its rules are:

1. The system enters the market at close on 31 October.

2. The system exits the market on the first MACD sell signal after 1 April.

3. The parameters of the MACD indicator are increased from the usual default values to 24, 52, 18.

In effect, the standard entry date is unchanged, but the exit date is determined by the MACD. In some years, this can delay exit to June or later.

To illustrate the performance of this system the following chart shows the returns on three portfolios since 30 October 1999:

1. Portfolio 1: A portfolio tracking the FTSE All Share Index.

2. Portfolio 2: Employing the standard six-month strategy.

3. Portfolio 3: Employing the six-month strategy enhanced using MACD.

At the end of the 12-year period, with all the portfolios having a starting value of 1000, portfolio 1 (the market) was valued at 1027, portfolio 2 was valued at 1469 and portfolio 3 was valued at 1675.

It's quite possible that further tweaking of the parameters and system rules could additionally enhance the strategy's performance.

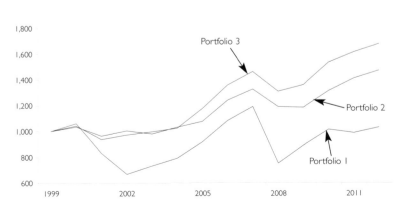

46, -0.8, 4.1 **Week 43**

Mon

21

1977: The European Patent Institute is founded.

FTSE 100	60	0.4	1.9
FTSE 250	63	0.4	1.2
S&P 500	45	0.2	1.7
NIKKEI	42	-0.3	1.3

Tue

22

1927: Nikola Tesla exposes his six new inventions, including a motor with one-phase electricity.

FTSE 100	35	-0.6	1.8
FTSE 250	50	-0.6	1.5
S&P 500	32	-0.4	1.3
NIKKEI	42	0.0	3.5

Wed

MPC meeting minutes published

23

1981: The US national debt breaks $1 trillion.

FTSE 100	60	-0.1	1.4
FTSE 250	44	-0.4	1.2
S&P 500	51	0.0	1.2
NIKKEI	45	0.1	2.1

Thu

24

1979: Exchange control restrictions are removed in the UK. Sterling and foreign currency can now be used for any purpose.

FTSE 100	45	-0.2	1.5
FTSE 250	44	-0.4	1.5
S&P 500	48	-0.1	1.0
NIKKEI	35	-0.5	2.3

Fri

25

1929: Black Friday – prices are sliding down in high volumes, but Wall Street manages to break the slide when a group of bankers begin placing higher than market bids on large stocks.

FTSE 100	35	-0.3	0.8
FTSE 250	44	0.0	0.6
S&P 500	34	-0.3	0.9
NIKKEI	35	-0.5	1.0

Sat 26

Sun 27   End of BST (clocks go back)

COMPANY NEWS

Interims

Finals

"I hesitate to deposit my money in a bank. I am afraid I shall never dare take it out again. When you go to confession and entrust your sins to the safe-keeping of a priest, do you ever come back for them?"
Jean Baurdillard

NOVEMBER MARKET

FTSE 100	57	0.7	3.9
FTSE 250	58	0.6	4.8
S&P 500	65	1.5	4.4
NIKKEI	57	0.3	6.6

Market performance this month

While market performance this month is nothing special – it is fifth in the ranking of months – November is worthy of note as being the first month in the six-month cycle (November to April) of strong market returns. In other words, investors should be increasing exposure to the market this month (if they haven't already done so in October).

On average, the market rises 0.7% this month and the probability of a positive return is 57%.

This is the best month in the year for the mining sector, which on average outperforms the FTSE 100 Index by 4.1 percentage points in the month.

Historic performance of the market in November

November summary

Month's performance ranking	5th
Average market change this month (standard deviation)	0.7% (3.9)
First trading day: Up / average change	64.3% / 0.1%
Last trading day: Up / average change	46.4% / -0.1%
Main features of the month	The mining sector is abnormally strong in November.
	04 Nov: Start of the 9th strongest market week of the year
	19 Nov: 10th weakest market day of the year
	29 Nov: Last trading day in November is often weak
Significant dates	01 Nov: US Nonfarm payroll report (anticipated)
	07 Nov: MPC interest rate announcement at 12h00 (anticipated)
	28 Nov: Thanksgiving Day (US) – NYSE closed

Mon

28

10th anniversary of the LSE flotation of Melrose.

1868: Thomas Edison applies for his first patent, the electric vote recorder.

FTSE 100	65	0.1	1.3
FTSE 250	68	-0.3	1.5
S&P 500	68	0.5	1.9
NIKKEI	55	-0.5	2.0

Tue

29

Two-day FOMC meeting starts

1929: The DJIA declines to 230, a 23.6% loss. This market crash sets in motion the financial elements that lead to the Great Depression.

FTSE 100	55	0.6	2.2
FTSE 250	61	0.5	1.5
S&P 500	59	0.3	1.3
NIKKEI	60	0.1	2.3

Wed

30

50th anniversary of Lamborghini starting to make cars.

1991: US President George Bush encourages Arabs and Israelis to "lay down the past" in his opening speech to the Middle East peace conference in Spain.

FTSE 100	65	0.4	1.4
FTSE 250	61	0.4	1.4
S&P 500	56	0.2	1.2
NIKKEI	30	0.6	2.7

Thu

31

Halloween
4th strongest market day
The last trading day in October is often strong.

1938: In an effort to restore investor confidence during the Great Depression, the New York Stock Exchange unveils a fifteen-point program aimed to upgrade protection for the investing public.

FTSE 100	80	0.5	1.0
FTSE 250	89	0.5	1.0
S&P 500	50	0.1	0.9
NIKKEI	60	0.4	1.5

Fri

1

Beginning of the strong half year (Six-month effect)
The mining sector is abnormally strong in November.
Nonfarm payroll report (anticipated)
40th anniversary of the LSE flotation of Rio Tinto.

1982: Honda becomes the first Asian automobile company to produce cars in the US with the opening of their factory in Marysville, Ohio. The Honda Accord is the first car produced there.

FTSE 100	55	-0.2	0.9
FTSE 250	56	-0.1	0.9
S&P 500	57	0.1	1.2
NIKKEI	40	-0.1	1.3

Sat 2   Lusophony Games (until 10th)

Sun 3   Diwali, New moon, Solar eclipse (annular/total)

COMPANY NEWS

Interims Scottish Mortgage Investment Trust, Stobart Group
Finals Imperial Tobacco

"If you think you're too small to make an impact, try going to bed with a mosquito in the room."
Dame Anita Roddick

SECTOR MONTHLY PERFORMANCE – MINING

Elsewhere in the *Almanac* we look at the quarterly performance of sectors; on this page we look in greater detail at the monthly performance of the mining sector. The FTSE 350 Mining sector is comprised of the following stocks:

African Barrick Gold [ABG]	Fresnillo [FRES]	Petropavlovsk [POG]
Anglo American [AAL]	Gem Diamonds [GEMD]	Polymetal Intl [POLY]
Antofagasta [ANTO]	Hochschild Mining [HOC]	Randgold Resources [RRS]
Aquarius Platinum [AQP]	Kazakhmys [KAZ]	Rio Tinto [RIO]
Avocet Mining [AVM]	Kenmare Resources [KMR]	Talvivaara [TALV]
BHP Billiton [BLT]	Lonmin [LMI]	Vedanta Resources [VED]
Centamin [CEY]	New World Resources [NWR]	Xstrata [XTA]
Eurasian Natural Res. [ENRC]	Petra Diamonds [PDL]	

The following table shows the outperformance of the FTSE 350 Mining sector over the FTSE 100 Index for every month since August 1999. For example, in January 2000 the Mining sector index fell -17.0% while the FTSE 100 Index fell -9.5%, giving an outperformance of the former over the latter of -7.5 percentage points. In months where the sector underperforms the FTSE 100 Index (i.e. the outperformance is negative) the cell is highlighted.

	Jan	Feb	Mar	Apr	May	Jun	Jul	Aug	Sep	Oct	Nov	Dec
1999								0.3	1.6	-6.0	9.4	11.6
2000	-7.5	-17.0	2.2	-5.5	2.0	10.9	-1.5	6.7	-3.3	5.8	-0.1	5.1
2001	6.6	14.2	-2.1	6.0	4.7	-4.0	-7.4	7.9	-7.2	2.3	14.5	0.8
2002	9.3	5.1	-5.2	-5.7	9.7	-1.3	-8.9	3.5	6.7	-2.1	6.9	4.0
2003	-1.9	10.7	-4.6	-7.5	0.2	-2.6	11.6	9.6	-4.9	8.7	-3.0	3.0
2004	0.2	2.7	-1.1	-12.7	4.1	0.7	6.2	2.1	5.6	-7.8	6.1	-3.5
2005	3.6	9.5	-4.8	-6.8	3.7	1.3	8.0	1.3	12.6	-3.2	5.7	6.4
2006	7.5	-3.5	6.2	4.5	0.4	-2.1	-1.6	0.2	-5.9	7.6	-1.1	-0.2
2007	-2.4	3.6	6.9	-0.9	10.6	3.5	3.4	-2.9	15.1	0.1	7.1	-4.4
2008	4.0	13.2	-5.0	5.5	4.8	7.0	-9.3	-6.2	-21.3	-11.3	-10.3	-3.3
2009	-1.8	6.6	22.4	7.2	5.2	-3.3	7.8	-4.5	2.2	2.1	13.1	2.3
2010	-5.0	2.4	10.2	-6.6	0.7	-3.5	2.5	-2.1	5.7	4.4	4.3	6.4
2011	-6.7	1.1	1.5	-2.2	-2.8	2.3	-2.5	-2.6	-14.7	5.7	0.1	-5.4
2012	11.6	-3.7	-7.4	2.8	-10.3	-1.6	-1.6					
average:	1.3	3.5	1.5	-1.7	2.5	0.6	0.5	1.0	-0.6	0.5	4.1	1.8

The following chart plots the average change in the sector index for each month.

Observations

1. There is only one month where the mining sector significantly underperforms the FTSE 100 Index – April.

2. Apart from April, the mining sector is strong relative to the FTSE 100 Index from November to May.

3. The mining sector is especially strong in February, May and November.

Mon

4

TSE closed
9th strongest market week

2008: Barack Obama becomes the first African-American to be elected President of the United States.

FTSE 100	40	0.4	1.6
FTSE 250	53	0.4	2.0
S&P 500	54	0.2	1.0
NIKKEI			

Tue

5

Guy Fawkes Night
100th anniversary of the birth of Vivien Leigh, the British actress.

2006: Saddam Hussein, former president of Iraq, and his co-defendants Barzan Ibrahim al-Tikriti and Awad Hamed al-Bandar are sentenced to death in the al-Dujail trial for their role in the massacre of the 148 Shi'as in 1982.

FTSE 100	65	-0.1	1.2
FTSE 250	61	0.0	0.6
S&P 500	68	0.3	1.3
NIKKEI	45	1.2	1.7

Wed

6

1851: Charles Dow, founder of Dow Jones & Company, *The Wall Street Journal* and the Dow Jones Industrial Average, is born.

FTSE 100	60	-0.2	1.4
FTSE 250	78	0.2	1.0
S&P 500	54	-0.2	1.2
NIKKEI	55	0.2	2.0

Thu

7

MPC interest rate announcement at 12h00
ECB Governing Council meeting
100th anniversary of the birth of Albert Camus, the French writer.

1665: *The London Gazette*, the oldest surviving journal, is first published.

FTSE 100	50	-0.1	1.0
FTSE 250	50	0.0	0.8
S&P 500	50	-0.1	1.0
NIKKEI	15	-0.2	1.4

Fri

8

2011: The Olympus Corporation admits that money has been used to cover losses on investments dating back to the 1990s. The scandal is one of the biggest and longest-running loss-hiding arrangements in Japanese corporate history.

FTSE 100	60	0.2	0.7
FTSE 250	50	0.1	0.8
S&P 500	51	0.1	0.7
NIKKEI	40	-0.9	1.2

Sat 9   20th anniversary of the LSE flotation of Dialight.

Sun 10

COMPANY NEWS

Interims 3i Group, 3i Infrastructure, Babcock International, BT, Cable & Wireless, Dairy Crest, Experian, FirstGroup, Great Portland Estates, Halfords, Invensys, Land Securities, Man Group, Marks & Spencer Group, Sainsbury (J), Shanks, SSE, Tate & Lyle, Vedanta Resources, Vodafone

Finals Dechra Pharmaceuticals, Edinburgh Dragon Trust, Genus

"With all due respect to Microsoft and Intel, there is no substitute for being in the right place at the right time."
Andrew S. Grove

FTSE 100/S&P 500 MONTHLY SWITCHING STRATEGY

In week 16 we saw how the FTSE 100 Index outperformed the S&P 500 Index in certain months of the year. On this page we will look at a strategy that exploits this feature.

The previous figures compared the FTSE 100 and S&P 500 in their domestic currencies. We will now look at comparing the performance of the FTSE 100 Index with a sterling-adjusted S&P 500 (i.e. the returns a UK investor would actually get from the S&P 500 Index taking into account fluctuations in the GBP/USD currency rate each month).

The following table shows the original monthly comparative performance figures we saw in week 16, and the new set of figures where the S&P 500 returns have been converted into sterling.

	Jan	Feb	Mar	Apr	May	Jun	Jul	Aug	Sep	Oct	Nov	Dec
FTSE 100 v S&P 500	-0.6	0.6	-0.5	0.4	-1.4	-0.7	0.3	0.8	-0.1	-0.1	-0.4	0.5
FTSE 100 v S&P 500(£)	-1.4	0.2	-0.1	1.2	-1.9	-0.6	1.2	0.0	-0.3	0.2	-0.7	0.8

One effect of adjusting for currency moves is to amplify the outperformance of the FTSE 100 Index in certain months (April, July and December). Conversely, the FTSE 100 underperformance is amplified in January, May and November. The currency-adjusted comparative performances for each month are shown in the following chart.

Whereas, before, the relatively strong FTSE 100 months were February, April, July, August and December, we can see that the currency-adjusted strong months are just April, July, and December.

The monthly switching strategy

The above results suggest a strategy of investing in the UK market (i.e. the FTSE 100 Index) in the months April, July and December and in the US market (i.e. the S&P 500 Index) for the rest of the year. In other words, a portfolio could be invested in the S&P 500 from January to March, at the end of March it switches out of the S&P 500 into the FTSE 100 for one month, then back into the S&P 500 for two months, into the FTSE 100 for July, back into the S&P 500 for four months, then back into the FTSE 100 for December, and finally back into the S&P 500 to start the next year.

The following chart shows the result of operating such a strategy every year from 1984. For comparison, the chart also includes the portfolio returns from continuous investments in the FTSE 100 and S&P 500.

The final result: the FTSE 100 portfolio would have grown 564%, the S&P 500 risen 751%, but the FTSE 100/S&P 500 monthly switching portfolio would have increased 1874%. Switching six times a year would have incurred some commission costs, but these would not have dented performance significantly.

Mon

11

2008: The RMS Queen Elizabeth 2 (QE2) sets sail on her final voyage to Dubai.

FTSE 100	55	0.1	1.5
FTSE 250	42	0.1	1.6
S&P 500	71	0.2	1.0
NIKKEI	50	0.0	1.5

Tue

12

1999: The Financial Services Modernisation Act is enacted in the US, opening the way for financial institutions to bundle financial services like insurance, banking and brokerage.

FTSE 100	60	0.3	1.3
FTSE 250	61	0.2	1.2
S&P 500	51	0.0	1.4
NIKKEI	47	-0.5	1.5

Wed

13

1998: TheGlobe.com, a little-known Web portal, breaks IPO records with a 606% first-day rise.

FTSE 100	45	-0.1	1.0
FTSE 250	28	-0.2	0.9
S&P 500	45	0.1	1.3
NIKKEI	30	-0.2	2.0

Thu

14

1922: The British Broadcasting Corporation (BBC) begins radio service in the UK.

FTSE 100	55	0.3	0.7
FTSE 250	56	0.1	0.6
S&P 500	50	0.1	1.1
NIKKEI	50	0.0	1.3

Fri

15

1867: Edward Calahan gives the financial world its first stock ticker by rebuilding a telegraph machine to print stock symbols.

FTSE 100	60	0.2	0.7
FTSE 250	72	0.2	0.7
S&P 500	45	-0.1	0.9
NIKKEI	45	0.1	1.5

Sat 16

Sun 17   Full moon

COMPANY NEWS

Interims Atkins (W S), AVEVA Group, British Land Co, BTG, Burberry Group, Cable & Wireless Worldwide, Cranswick, Electrocomponents, Fidelity China Special Situation, HICL, ICAP, Investec, London Stock Exchange, Oxford Instruments, SABMiller, Synergy Health, TalkTalk Telecom
Finals British Assets Trust, easyJet, Euromoney Institutional Investor, Lonmin

"The modern history of economic theory is a tale of evasions of reality."
Thomas Balogh

VERY LARGE ONE-DAY MARKET RISES

Analysis of the behaviour of the FTSE 100 Index for very large one-day rises.

Note: An accompanying study on *Very large one-day market falls* can be seen in week 42.

Five years ago this week, on 24 November 2008, the FTSE 100 Index rose 9.8% in one day. This is the largest one-day increase in the index since its inception in 1984. The accompanying table shows the ten largest one-day rises in the index since 1984.

As with very large one-day falls in the index, it would seem that the majority of the greatest one-day rises have occurred in recent years. Since 1984 there have been 159 very large one-day rises, where "very large rise" is defined as a rise more than two standard deviations greater than the average daily change in the index. In other words, a very large rise is any increase of mor than 2.29%. These rises have been plotted on the following chart.

Date	Change(%)
24 Nov 08	9.8
19 Sep 08	8.8
13 Oct 08	8.3
29 Oct 08	8.1
21 Oct 87	7.9
08 Dec 08	6.2
13 Mar 03	6.1
10 Apr 92	5.6
20 Oct 08	5.4
17 Oct 08	5.2

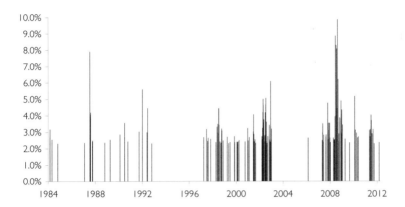

The chart does indeed show that the frequency of very large one-day rises has increased in recent years.

After the rise

The following chart shows how on average the index behaves in the days immediately following a very large rise. The Y-axis is the percentage move from the close of the index on the day of the large rise. For example, by day 5 the index has fallen 0.47% below the index close on the day of the large rise.

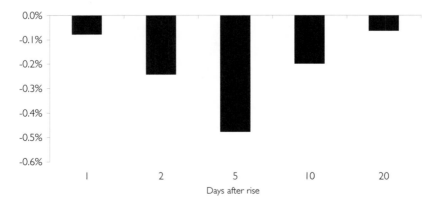

In the five days following the large market rise the index tends to fall back, losing its one-day gain. But, in contrast to the behaviour after large falls, the index then tends to recover and after 20 days has almost regained the level reached by the very large one-day rise.

In summary, in the 20 days after a very large *one-day fall* the market tends to steadily rise. But in the 20 days after a very large *one-day rise* the market tends to initially fall back but then recover and by day 20 has almost regained the close of the large one-day rise.

Mon

18

50th anniversary of the opening of the Dartford Tunnel.

FTSE 100	60	0.1	0.8
FTSE 250	53	0.1	0.7
S&P 500	48	0.0	1.0
NIKKEI	55	0.2	1.9

1967: The government announces it is lowering the exchange rate, so the pound will be worth $2.40, down from $2.80; a cut of just over 14%.

Tue

19

10th weakest market day

FTSE 100	30	0.6	1.5
FTSE 250	44	-0.6	1.4
S&P 500	45	-0.4	1.2
NIKKEI	50	0.3	1.5

1944: US President Franklin D. Roosevelt announces the Sixth War Loan Drive, aimed at selling $14 billion in war bonds to help pay for the war effort.

Wed

20

MPC meeting minutes published

FTSE 100	50	0.0	1.3
FTSE 250	50	-0.3	0.8
S&P 500	56	-0.1	1.4
NIKKEI	55	-0.5	2.1

1955: RCA offers a $35,00 contract for Elvis Presley.

Thu

21

ECB Governing Council Meeting

FTSE 100	50	-0.1	1.3
FTSE 250	33	-0.4	1.1
S&P 500	55	0.2	1.3
NIKKEI	50	0.1	1.3

2004: The Paris Club agrees to write off 80% (up to $100 billion) of Iraq's external debt.

Fri

22

100th anniversary of the birth of Benjamin Britten, the English composer.
50th anniversary of the release of The Beatles' second UK album, *With The Beatles*.
50th anniversary of the assassination of John F. Kennedy.

FTSE 100	45	-0.1	1.0
FTSE 250	56	-0.1	0.6
S&P 500	54	-0.1	1.0
NIKKEI	60	0.2	1.2

1995: *Toy Story* is released as the first feature-length film created completely using computer-generated imagery.

Sat 23   Labor Thanksgiving Day (Japan), 50th anniversary of the first episode of *Doctor Who*.

Sun 24

COMPANY NEWS

Interims Big Yellow Group, Caledonia Investments, De La Rue, Halma, Homeserve, Intermediate Capital, Johnson Matthey, KCOM, London & Stamford Property Ltd, MITIE Group, National Grid, PayPoint, Pennon, Perpetual Income & Growth Investment Trust, QinetiQ, Severn Trent, Telecom plus, Templeton Emerging Markets, TR Property Investment Trust

Finals Compass Group, Diploma, Grainger, Mitchells & Butlers, Paragon Group of Companies

"Economics is as much a study in fantasy and aspiration as in hard numbers — maybe more so."
Theordore Roszak

DECEMBER MARKET

FTSE 100	86	2.6	3.0
FTSE 250	77	2.8	4.0
S&P 500	76	1.7	3.2
NIKKEI	68	1.3	5.4

Market performance this month

The year ends with a flourish, with December being the best month for shares. On average, the market rises +2.6% this month, with a relatively low standard deviation of 3.0. The probability of positive returns in December is a very high 86%. In fact, the market has only fallen four times in the past 30 years.

The final two weeks of the month are especially strong – the strongest two-week period of the year. And these lead into the first week of the new year, which is also one of the strongest weeks in the year. December is also one of the three best months for the performance of the FTSE 100 Index relative to the S&P 500 Index.

One area that does suffer in December is the Pharmaceuticals & Biotechnology sector – December is the weakest month for this sector relative to the FTSE 100 Index.

Summary: Just look at the chart below – this is a great month for investors.

Historic performance of the market in December

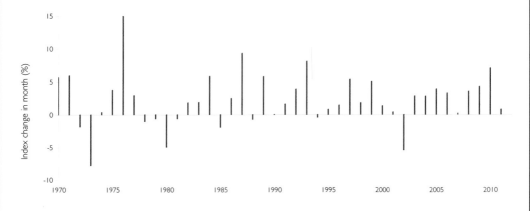

December summary

Month's performance ranking	1st
Average market change this month (standard deviation)	2.6% (3.0)
First trading day: Up / average change	46.4% / 0.0%
Last trading day: Up / average change	50.0% / 0.1%
Main features of the month	The FTSE 100 often outperforms the S&P 500 in December.
	The Pharma & Biotech sector is often weak in December.
	02 Dec: First trading day in December is often weak
	16 Dec: 9th strongest market day of the year
	16 Dec: Start of the strongest two-week period in the year
	23 Dec: 5th strongest market day of the year
	24 Dec: 6th strongest market day of the year
	27 Dec: Strongest market day of the year
	31 Dec: Start of the strongest market week of the year
Significant dates	05 Dec: MPC interest rate announcement at 12h00 (anticipated)
	06 Dec: US Nonfarm payroll report (anticipated)
	11 Dec: FTSE 100 Index quarterly review
	18 Dec: FOMC monetary policy statement
	20 Dec: Triple Witching
	25 Dec: Christmas Day – LSE closed
	26 Dec: Boxing day – LSE closed

Mon
25

1835: Andrew Carnegie is born in Scotland. The sale of his company, the Carnegie Steel Company, to US Steel will make Carnegie one of the world's richest men.

FTSE 100	60	0.0	1.0
FTSE 250	58	0.0	0.7
S&P 500	68	0.1	0.6
NIKKEI	70	-0.2	1.9

Tue
26

60th anniversary of the LSE flotation of PZ Cussons.

1983: The Brinks Mat robbery takes place in London, with 6,800 gold bars (worth nearly £26 million) being taken from the Brinks Mat vault at Heathrow Airport.

FTSE 100	50	-0.2	1.1
FTSE 250	61	-0.1	0.9
S&P 500	71	0.3	1.4
NIKKEI	55	0.4	1.4

Wed
27

2009: Dubai requests a debt deferment following its massive renovation and development projects. The announcement causes global stock markets to drop.

FTSE 100	60	0.2	0.8
FTSE 250	56	0.2	1.1
S&P 500	66	0.2	1.0
NIKKEI	55	0.3	1.5

Thu
28

Thanksgiving (US) – NYSE closed
Hanukkah

1814: *The Times* in London is printed for the first time by automatic, steam powered presses, signaling the beginning of the availability of newspapers to a mass audience.

FTSE 100	45	0.1	1.2
FTSE 250	56	0.3	1.2
S&P 500			
NIKKEI	53	0.4	1.5

Fri
29

NYSE closes early at 13h00
The last trading day in November is often weak.

1999: The Canadian Venture Exchange is created as a result of an agreement among the Vancouver, Alberta, Toronto and Montreal exchanges to restructure the Canadian capital markets.

FTSE 100	70	0.1	0.7
FTSE 250	53	0.1	0.7
S&P 500	48	0.0	0.7
NIKKEI	60	0.0	1.4

Sat 30   St Andrew's Day, Horse racing – Hennessy Gold Cup

Sun 1

COMPANY NEWS

Interims Daejan Holdings, Dixons Retail, Personal Assets Trust, RPC Group, United Utilities, Utilico Emerging Markets

Finals Britvic, ITE Group, Marston's, Sage Group, Shaftesbury

"What is robbing a bank compared with founding a bank?"
Bertolt Brecht

SHARE PERFORMANCE IN DECEMBER

Stocks that like December

The share prices of only 21 companies have risen nine times or more in the last ten years in the month of December. The table below shows these 21 companies and the percentage price change for the stock in the month of December for that year (for example, Aggreko increased 10.8% in December 2003).

Company	2002	2003	2004	2005	2006	2007	2008	2009	2010	2011	Avg
Aggreko	0.3	10.8	9.3	6.2	10.6	5	-0.4	26.3	1.2	6.7	7.6
Anglo-Eastern Plantations	19.6	6.8	-1.8	13.7	4.7	16.9	1.5	1	28	7	9.7
Anite	10.8	2.6	6.6	13.3	0.6	21.8	14.9	-8.6	10	17.4	8.9
Balfour Beatty	-12.5	0.7	4.5	6	6.5	1.9	7.6	1.2	14.3	5.5	3.6
BG Group	10.7	4.7	-2.5	6.3	1.2	13	4	1.7	11.6	1.3	5.2
British American Tobacco	7	5.6	2.1	3.2	-0.7	4.1	6	9.2	5.7	3.8	4.6
Compass Group	4.6	8.7	7.4	4.5	1	-3.2	12.3	3.3	4.6	3.7	4.7
Cranswick	1.4	2.7	9.5	-5.9	14.9	8.1	0.3	7.2	2.1	2.5	4.3
Diageo	0.8	1.4	1.5	0.9	2.7	-1.2	6	5.8	3.6	3.3	2.5
Domino Printing Sciences	3.1	-1.7	4.7	2	15	11.3	22.5	15.5	17.9	3.2	9.4
FirstGroup	2.6	1.3	3.2	16.9	4.5	14.8	-7.7	8.9	10.1	3.6	5.8
Hiscox Ltd	13.7	0.8	4.7	6.7	6	7.3	9.7	5.4	9.9	-6.2	5.8
Imperial Tobacco Group	15.6	3.3	4.7	0.8	7.5	7.8	14.3	10.9	4.3	6.4	7.6
National Grid	5.8	1.9	3.6	6.1	7.2	1.5	1.1	2.8	-2.6	0.1	2.8
Persimmon	2.9	15.2	11.7	13.8	4.5	0.1	6.4	13.5	23.1	-4.7	8.7
Prudential	-18	5.8	8.5	4.3	5.9	4.9	23.5	2.3	17.6	2.5	5.7
Robert Wiseman Dairies	6.8	1.8	-0.2	4.3	15.7	7.9	0.3	4.7	6.1	5.7	5.3
Senior	18.5	10.9	6.6	12.3	3.2	6.1	14.7	25	13.1	-2.6	10.8
SSE	9.8	3.1	6	3.4	6.8	3	10.3	3.9	9.4	-1.8	5.4
Unilever	3.2	3.1	6.8	1.8	4.8	5.9	5.8	11.8	10.5	1.2	5.5
William Hill	6	9.2	8.5	5.1	1	1.4	12.6	3.8	9.8	0.3	5.8
FTSE All Share:	-5.5	2.8	2.8	3.9	3.3	0.2	3.5	3.9	7.0	0.8	2.3

Only three companies, Unilever, William Hill and Imperial Tobacco, have risen in December in all ten of the years from 2002 to 2011. On average, the best performing companies in December have been Senior (average December increase of +10.8%), Anglo-Eastern Plantations (+9.7%) and Domino Printing Sciences (+9.4%).

A portfolio of these 21 companies would have outperformed the FTSE All Share Index in every December since 2002, with an average outperformance of 3.9% each December over the Index.

Stocks that don't like December

Traditionally December is a strong month for the market; however, the seven stocks below have distinguished themselves by falling in at least eight of the past ten Decembers.

Company	2002	2003	2004	2005	2006	2007	2008	2009	2010	2011	Avg
CML Microsystems	-8.5	2.3	-0.8	-4.9	-16.8	-2.8	-15.1	4	-1.8	-6	-5.0
HMV Group	-6.7	-0.4	8.8	-3.3	-14.9	5.3	-9.1	-16.1	-30.4	-3.5	-7.0
Quarto Group (The) Inc	-1.1	-0.9	0.8	-2.4	-1.7	-2.8	-28.6	-12.6	-1.5	3.7	-4.7
Rank Group (The)	-5.5	-3.7	-13	-1.1	-15.9	-9.2	13.4	8.2	-2	-15.4	-4.4
SkyePharma	-7.8	-0.3	-2.3	0.5	20.9	-5.8	-4.5	-5.4	-10	-20.6	-3.5
Thorntons	-1.1	-3.3	-3.6	-3.1	-7.7	-2.2	13.6	-6.4	-3	-46.3	-6.3
Wincanton	-22.7	-1.2	-0.6	-4.2	-4.8	-8	-2.3	-7.5	1.2	2	-4.8
FTSE All Share:	-5.5	2.8	2.8	3.9	3.3	0.2	3.5	3.9	7.0	0.8	2.3

Wincanton has the distinction of being the only listed company to have fallen in nine Decembers over the past ten years. A portfolio of these seven stocks would have underperformed the FTSE All Share Index in every December since 2002, with an average underperformance of 7.4% each December.

Mon 2

Strongest market month
The first trading day in December is often weak.
The FTSE 100 often outperforms the S&P 500 in December.
The Pharma & Biotech sector is often weak in December.

1930: President Herbert Hoover goes before the United States Congress to ask for a $150 million public works program to help generate jobs and stimulate the economy.

FTSE 100	50	0.1	0.9
FTSE 250	74	0.3	0.8
S&P 500	48	0.1	1.0
NIKKEI	60	0.7	1.9

Tue 3

New moon

1937: *The Dandy*, the world's longest-running comic, is first published.

FTSE 100	50	0.1	0.8
FTSE 250	56	-0.1	0.7
S&P 500	50	-0.1	1.1
NIKKEI	45	-0.1	1.5

Wed 4

Beige Book published

2003: The US withdraws a punitive tax on imported steel, to avoid a damaging trade war between America and Europe.

FTSE 100	35	-0.1	0.7
FTSE 250	50	-0.2	0.8
S&P 500	67	0.2	1.0
NIKKEI	60	0.0	1.3

Thu 5

MPC interest rate announcement at 12h00
ECB Governing Council meeting

1958: Subscriber Trunk Dialling is inaugurated by Queen Elizabeth II when she speaks to Lord Provost on a call from Bristol to Edinburgh.

FTSE 100	55	0.3	1.2
FTSE 250	61	0.2	1.1
S&P 500	48	0.2	1.2
NIKKEI	60	-0.1	1.0

Fri 6

Nonfarm payroll report (anticipated)

2006: NASA reveals photographs taken by Mars Global Surveyor suggesting the presence of liquid water on Mars.

FTSE 100	50	-0.1	0.8
FTSE 250	44	0.0	0.8
S&P 500	57	0.2	0.9
NIKKEI	55	0.3	1.4

Sat 7

Sun 8

COMPANY NEWS

Interims Anite, Ashtead Group, Berkeley Group Holdings, Greene King, Micro Focus International, Monks Investment Trust, Smith (DS), Stagecoach

Finals Aberdeen Asset Management, Brewin Dolphin Holdings, Electra Private Equity, Scottish Investment Trust, TUI Travel, Victrex

"If you want to understand entrepreneurs, you have to study the psychology of the juvenile delinquent. They don't have the same anxiety triggers that we have."
Abraham Zaleznik

BOUNCEBACK STOCKS

There is a theory that stocks that have fallen greatly in a year tend to bounce back the first three months of the following year.

Is this true?

The accompanying table shows the ten stocks in the FTSE 350 Index that fell the most in 2011 and their performance for January to March 2012.

The results look encouraging. The ten stocks all fell more than 50% in 2011 and yet increased by an average of 27% in the first three months of 2012. Over the same three-month period the FTSE 350 Index rose just 4.9%, giving this *2011 Bounceback Portfolio* an outperformance of 22.1 points.

Was this a one-off, or does the Bounceback Effect happen in many years?

The chart below shows the results of testing this Bounceback Effect for the ten years from 2002 to 2011. Each year the ten worst performing stocks in the FTSE 350 Index are put into an equally-weighted portfolio, the performance of which is measured for January to March of the following year. In the chart, the Bounceback Portfolio is shown with black bars and the FTSE 350 Portfolio is shown with white bars.

Company	2011(%)	Jan-Mar 2012(%)
Essar Energy	-70.4	-9.4
Ocado Group	-69.5	110.5
Talvivaara Mining Company Ltd	-66.4	20.4
Lloyds Banking Group	-60.6	29.7
Vedanta Resources	-59.7	21.0
Man Group	-57.5	7.2
Dixons Retail	-57.2	90.0
Heritage Oil Ltd	-57.1	-27.2
Home Retail Group	-55.8	36.7
Aquarius Platinum Ltd	-55.5	-9.4
average change:		27.0
FTSE 350:		4.9
difference:		22.1

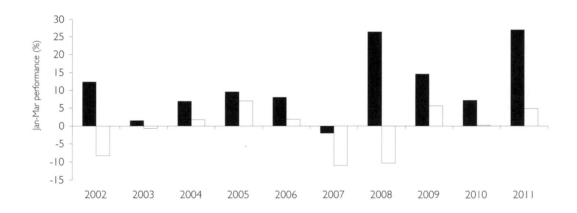

Observations

1. The Bounceback Portfolio has outperformed the FTSE 350 Index every year since 2002. Impressive!

2. The FTSE 350 has fallen in four years in the January to March period since 2002; whereas the Bounceback Portfolio has fallen just once (the 2007 bounceback portfolio fell 2% in January to March 2008).

3. The Bounceback Portfolio has outperformed the FTSE 350 Index by an average of 12.0 percentage points each year since 2002.

Mon

9

1999: The shares of VA Linux jump from $35 to over $235 on the first day of trading.

FTSE 100	50	0.1	0.9
FTSE 250	63	0.1	1.0
S&P 500	57	0.0	0.8
NIKKEI	55	-0.2	1.4

Tue

10

10th anniversary of the LSE flotation of Vedanta Resources.

1968: Japan's biggest heist, the still-unsolved "300 million yen robbery", is carried out in Tokyo.

FTSE 100	35	-0.2	0.7
FTSE 250	50	0.0	0.7
S&P 500	55	0.1	0.9
NIKKEI	45	0.3	1.4

Wed

11

FTSE 100 Index quarterly review

2008: Bank of America says it is cutting 35,000 jobs after forcing through a $50 billion all-stock takeover of Merrill Lynch. The takeover occurs as Merrill Lynch comes within days of collapse.

FTSE 100	40	-0.2	1.0
FTSE 250	50	0.0	0.8
S&P 500	44	-0.2	0.9
NIKKEI	45	-0.1	1.4

Thu

12

1985: GE announces a $6.3 billion dollar purchase of RCA.

FTSE 100	45	-0.3	0.9
FTSE 250	44	-0.4	0.9
S&P 500	52	0.0	0.7
NIKKEI	65	-0.1	1.7

Fri

13

2007: Billions of dollars are injected into the markets in a joint-action by British, American, Canadian and Swiss central banks and the European Central Bank.

FTSE 100	70	0.1	1.0
FTSE 250	67	0.0	0.9
S&P 500	55	0.0	0.6
NIKKEI	50	0.2	1.7

Sat 14

Sun 15   20th anniversary of the LSE flotation of BlackRock World Mining Trust.

COMPANY NEWS

Interims Betfair, Carpetright, Imagination Technologies, Polar Capital Technology Trust, Sports Direct International

Finals Domino Printing Sciences

"Techniques shrouded in mystery clearly have value to the purveyor of investment advice. After all, what witch doctor has ever achieved fame and fortune by simply advising 'Take two aspirins'?"
Warren Buffett

TRADING AROUND CHRISTMAS & NEW YEAR – FTSE 100

The analysis on this page looks at the historical behaviour of the FTSE 100 Index since 1984 around Christmas and New Year. The days studied were:

- **Days 1-3**: The three trading days leading up to Christmas. (For example, in 2011: day 1 was 21 Dec, day 2 was 22 Dec and day 3 was 23 Dec.)

- **Days 4-6**: The three trading days between Christmas and New Year. (In year 2011: day 4 was 28 Dec, day 5 was 29 Dec, and day 5 was 30 Dec.)

- **Days 7-9**: The first three trading days of the year. (In year 2012: day 7 was 3 Jan, day 8 was 4 Jan, and day 9 was 5 Jan.)

The table shows the results of the analysis where:

1. *Up days(%)*: the percentage of all days that the market has risen on this day.
2. *Average change on day(%)*: the average change of the market for this day.
3. *Standard deviation*: the standard deviation of the changes for this day.

	1	2	3	4	5	6	7	8	9
Up days(%)	58	69	77	81	69	54	58	62	46
Average change on day(%)	0.12	0.27	0.20	0.36	0.20	0.06	0.07	0.12	0.14
Standard deviation	0.80	0.67	0.49	1.20	0.76	0.94	1.13	1.09	0.91

The average change on the days is illustrated in the chart below.

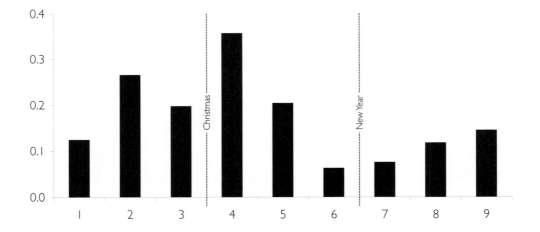

Analysis

1. The average daily change of the FTSE 100 Index from 1984 for all days is 0.03%, so it can be seen that all nine days around Christmas and New Year are stronger than average.

2. The strongest days are historically the two days leading up to Christmas and the two immediately following it.

3. Generally, the market is strong on the fourth day (the trading day immediately after Christmas) – this is the strongest day of the whole period, when the markets increases 81% of years since 1984 with an average rise of 0.36%. Although it should be noted that the standard deviation is the highest on this day, meaning that the volatility of returns is greatest (the index actually fell 3% on this day in 1987 and 2002).

4. The weakest day in the period is the final trading day of the year – this is perhaps not surprising with traders closing positions for the year end.

5. The new year generally starts strongly, but not as strong as those days of a week before and after Christmas.

Mon

16

Start of the strongest two-week period
5th strongest week
9th strongest market day

1835: A fire ravages Wall Street. The inside of the Merchants' Exchange building is nearly destroyed, leaving the New York Stock and Exchange Board without a home.

⬆

FTSE 100	75	0.6	0.8
FTSE 250	74	0.4	0.6
S&P 500	68	0.4	1.0
NIKKEI	55	0.2	0.9

Tue

17

Full moon (market often strong this day)
Two-day FOMC meeting starts

2010: Mohamed Bouazizi sets himself on fire. This act is the catalyst for the Tunisian Revolution and the wider Arab Spring.

➡

FTSE 100	45	-0.1	1.0
FTSE 250	44	0.1	0.6
S&P 500	50	0.1	1.0
NIKKEI	50	0.0	1.2

Wed

18

MPC meeting minutes published
ECB Governing Council Meeting

1989: The Labour Party abandons its policy on trade union closed shops in line with European legislation.

↗

FTSE 100	65	0.2	0.9
FTSE 250	67	0.3	0.7
S&P 500	58	0.2	1.2
NIKKEI	45	0.1	1.0

Thu

19

1843: Charles Dickens' *A Christmas Carol* goes on sale. It is priced at five shillings (equal to £20.79 today) and the first run of 6,000 copies sells out by Christmas Eve.

➡

FTSE 100	55	-0.1	0.9
FTSE 250	50	-0.1	0.6
S&P 500	43	0.0	0.7
NIKKEI	45	-0.1	1.8

Fri

20

Triple Witching (market often strong on this day)

2004: A gang of thieves steal £26.5 million worth of currency from the Donegall Square West headquarters of Northern Bank in Belfast, Northern Ireland – one of the largest bank robberies in UK history.

↗

FTSE 100	65	0.1	0.9
FTSE 250	67	0.2	0.6
S&P 500	34	-0.1	0.9
NIKKEI	60	-0.5	1.2

Sat 21   100th anniversary of the first publication of a "word-cross" (crossword).

Sun 22   Winter Solstice, also known as Yule

COMPANY NEWS

Interims
Finals Carnival, JPMorgan Asian Investment Trust

"Foul cankering rust the hidden treasure frets, but gold that's put to use more gold begets."
William Shakespeare

TRADING AROUND CHRISTMAS & NEW YEAR – FTSE 250

In week 51 we looked at the performance of large cap stocks around Christmas and New Year. This week looks at the performance of mid-cap stocks over the same period, with an analysis of the FTSE 250 Index.

Note: Refer to week 51 for an explanation of the terms used in the table below.

	1	2	3	4	5	6	7	8	9
Up days(%)	62	85	85	88	81	65	69	73	69
Average change on day(%)	0.17	0.37	0.27	0.38	0.39	0.07	0.66	0.33	0.24
Standard deviation	0.60	0.44	0.36	0.79	0.56	0.64	1.07	0.93	0.93

The average change on the days is illustrated in the chart below.

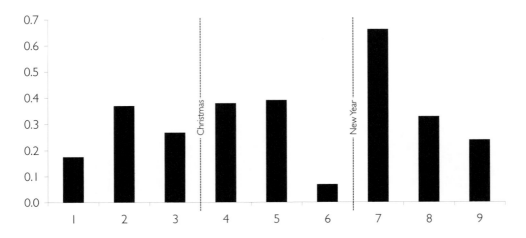

Analysis

1. The average daily change of the FTSE 250 Index from 1984 for all days is 0.04%, so it can be seen that – as with the FTSE 100 Index – all nine days around Christmas and New Year are stronger than average for mid-cap stocks.

2. The two trading days before and after Christmas are significantly strong – all four days see increases in over 80% of years. But the strongest day by the average change is first trading of the year.

3. Again, as for the FTSE 100 Index, the weakest day in the period is the last trading day of the year (day 6).

4. In the new year, the FTSE 250 Index gets off to a much stronger start than the FTSE 100.

Mon 23

Emperor's Birthday (Japan) – TSE closed
2nd strongest week
5th strongest market day
100th anniversary of the creation of The Federal Reserve by Woodrow Wilson.

1986: Voyager, piloted by Dick Rutan and Jeana Yeager, becomes the first aircraft to fly non-stop around the world without aerial or ground refueling.

FTSE 100	80	0.4	0.6
FTSE 250	89	0.4	0.4
S&P 500	48	0.0	0.8
NIKKEI			

Tue 24

Christmas Eve
LSE closes early at 12h30, NYSE closes early at 13h00
6th strongest market day

1968: The crew of Apollo 8 enters into orbit around the Moon, becoming the first humans to do so. They perform ten lunar orbits and broadcast live TV pictures that become the famous Christmas Eve Broadcast; one of the most watched programs in history.

FTSE 100	80	0.2	0.6
FTSE 250	76	0.2	0.4
S&P 500	65	0.2	0.5
NIKKEI	47	-0.1	1.2

Wed 25

UK Holiday: Christmas Day (Western Christianity)
LSE, NYSE, HKEX closed

1643: Christmas Island is found and named by Captain William Mynors of the East India Company vessel, the Royal Mary.

FTSE 100			
FTSE 250			
S&P 500	65	0.2	0.5
NIKKEI	47	-0.2	1.4

Thu 26

UK Holiday: Boxing Day
LSE, HKEX closed

1945: The CFP franc and CFA franc are created.

FTSE 100			
FTSE 250			
S&P 500	85	0.2	0.5
NIKKEI	78	0.5	1.5

Fri 27

Strongest market day

1977: Thousands of people flock to UK cinemas to watch the popular blockbuster *Star Wars*.

FTSE 100	83	0.5	1.2
FTSE 250	89	0.4	0.4
S&P 500	57	0.1	0.8
NIKKEI	55	0.5	0.8

Sat 28

Sun 29

COMPANY NEWS

Interims
Finals

"You might merge with another organisation, but two drunks don't make a sensible person."
Gary Hamel

MONTHLY PERFORMANCE OF THE FTSE 100 INDEX

The table below shows the monthly percentage performance of the FTSE 100 Index from 1980. The months where the index fell are highlighted. By scanning the columns it is possible to get a feel for how the market moves in certain months.

Monthly percentage changes for the FTSE 100 Index

Year	Jan	Feb	Mar	Apr	May	Jun	Jul	Aug	Sep	Oct	Nov	Dec
1980	9.2	4.9	-9.2	3.4	-2.3	11.2	3.7	0.7	3.2	5.9	0.6	-5.3
1981	-1.5	4.3	0.4	6.9	-5.0	1.9	0.4	5.0	-16.6	3.2	10.5	-1.1
1982	4.5	-4.9	3.5	1.1	3.4	-4.3	3.6	2.9	6.1	2.0	0.9	1.7
1983	3.1	0.6	1.8	8.1	0.2	2.8	-2.1	2.6	-2.6	-3.4	5.7	1.9
1984	6.3	-2.1	6.9	2.3	-10.3	2.0	-3.0	9.3	3.3	0.9	2.6	4.3
1985	3.9	-1.6	1.4	1.1	1.7	-5.9	2.2	6.3	-3.8	6.8	4.5	-1.8
1986	1.6	7.6	8.1	-0.5	-3.5	2.9	-5.6	6.6	-6.3	4.9	0.3	2.6
1987	7.7	9.5	0.9	2.6	7.4	3.7	3.4	-4.7	5.2	-26.0	-9.7	8.4
1988	4.6	-1.2	-1.5	3.4	-1.0	4.1	-0.2	-5.4	4.2	1.4	-3.2	0.0
1989	14.4	-2.4	3.6	2.1	-0.2	1.7	6.8	4.0	-3.7	-6.8	6.3	6.4
1990	-3.5	-3.5	-0.3	-6.4	11.5	1.3	-2.0	-7.0	-8.0	3.0	4.8	-0.3
1991	1.3	9.7	3.2	1.2	0.5	-3.4	7.2	2.2	-0.9	-2.1	-5.7	3.0
1992	3.1	-0.4	-4.8	8.8	2.0	-6.9	-4.8	-3.6	10.4	4.1	4.5	2.4
1993	-1.4	2.2	0.4	-2.3	1.0	2.1	0.9	5.9	-2.0	4.4	-0.1	7.9
1994	2.1	-4.7	-7.3	1.3	-5.0	-1.7	5.6	5.5	-6.9	2.3	-0.5	-0.5
1995	-2.4	0.6	4.3	2.5	3.2	-0.1	4.5	0.4	0.9	0.6	3.8	0.7
1996	1.9	-0.8	-0.7	3.2	-1.8	-1.0	-0.2	4.4	2.2	0.6	2.0	1.5
1997	3.8	0.8	0.1	2.9	4.2	-0.4	6.6	-1.8	8.9	-7.7	-0.2	6.3
1998	6.3	5.7	2.9	-0.1	-1.0	-0.7	0.1	-10.1	-3.5	7.4	5.6	2.4
1999	0.2	4.7	1.9	4.1	-5.0	1.5	-1.4	0.2	-3.5	3.7	5.5	5.0
2000	-9.5	-0.6	4.9	-3.3	0.5	-0.7	0.8	4.8	-5.7	2.3	-4.6	1.3
2001	1.2	-6.0	-4.8	5.9	-2.9	-2.7	-2.0	-3.3	-8.3	2.8	3.3	0.3
2002	-1.0	-1.2	3.3	-2.0	-1.6	-8.4	-8.8	-0.4	-12.0	8.5	3.2	-5.5
2003	-9.5	2.5	-1.2	8.7	3.1	-0.4	3.1	0.1	-1.7	4.8	1.3	3.1
2004	-1.9	2.3	-2.4	2.4	-1.3	0.8	-1.1	1.0	2.5	1.2	1.7	2.4
2005	0.8	2.4	-1.5	-1.9	3.4	3.0	3.3	0.3	3.4	-2.9	2.0	3.6
2006	2.5	0.5	3.0	1.0	-5.0	1.9	1.6	-0.4	0.9	2.8	-1.3	2.8
2007	-0.3	-0.5	2.2	2.2	2.7	-0.2	-3.8	-0.9	2.6	3.9	-4.3	0.4
2008	-8.9	0.1	-3.1	6.8	-0.6	-7.1	-3.8	4.2	-13.0	-10.7	-2.0	3.4
2009	-6.4	-7.7	2.5	8.1	4.1	-3.8	8.5	6.5	4.6	-1.7	2.9	4.3
2010	-4.1	3.2	6.1	-2.2	-6.6	-5.2	6.9	-0.6	6.2	2.3	-2.6	6.7
2011	-0.6	2.2	-1.4	2.7	-1.3	-0.7	-2.2	-7.2	-4.9	8.1	-0.7	1.2
2012	2.0	3.3	-1.8	-0.5	-7.3	4.7	1.2					

Observations

1. In recent years the index has been weak in January, May, November and June; and strong in February, April(ish) and December.

2. In the last 20 years it can clearly be seen that the strongest month has been December (only down four times in 30 years). By contrast, in the 70s and 80s the strongest month was April (which increased every year from 1971 to 1985).

3. Looking across the table, it can be seen that the longest period of consecutive down months was April 2002 to September 2002, while the longest period of consecutive up months was July 1982 to June 1983 (the only time the FTSE 100 Index has risen 12 months without a break).

Mon

30

6th strongest market week

FTSE 100	60	0.2	0.9
FTSE 250	68	0.3	0.6
S&P 500	64	0.2	0.7
NIKKEI	50	0.2	1.5

1924: Edwin Hubble announces the existence of other galaxies.

Tue

31

New Year's Eve
LSE closes early at 12h30
TSE closed
60th anniversary of the LSE flotation of Barclays.

FTSE 100	56	0.1	1.1
FTSE 250	69	0.0	0.7
S&P 500	68	0.1	0.6
NIKKEI			

1975: The first public index mutual fund is launched. It is called the First Index Investment Trust; it tracks the S&P 500 and starts with just $11 million in assets.

Wed

1

UK Holiday: New Year's Day
LSE, NYSE, HKEX, TSE closed

1377: The English parliament convenes and imposes the poll tax.

Thu

2

TSE closed

FTSE 100	56	0.3	1.1
FTSE 250	73	0.5	1.1
S&P 500	62	0.3	1.3
NIKKEI			

1987: Rate support grant settlements impose cuts of up to 30% on rates proposed by 20 UK local authorities.

Fri

3

TSE closed
Nonfarm payroll report (anticipated)

FTSE 100	69	0.3	1.2
FTSE 250	67	0.4	1.1
S&P 500	50	0.3	1.2
NIKKEI			

1977: Apple Computer is incorporated.

Sat 4

Sun 5

COMPANY NEWS

Interims RIT Capital Partners
Finals JPMorgan Indian Investment Trust

"I'm spending a year dead for tax reasons."
Douglas Adams

2

REFERENCE

CONTENTS

MARKET INDICES

COMPARATIVE PERFORMANCE OF UK INDICES

The table below gives the year-end closing values for eight UK stock indices.

Year end closing values of UK indices

Name	EPIC	2002	2003	2004	2005	2006	2007	2008	2009	2010	2011
FTSE 100	UKX	3940.40	4476.90	4814.3	5618.8	6220.8	6456.9	4434.17	5412.88	5899.94	5572.28
FTSE 250	MCX	4319.30	5802.30	6936.8	8794.3	11177.8	10657.8	6360.85	9306.89	11558.8	10102.9
FTSE All Share	ASX	1893.73	2207.38	2410.75	2847.02	3221.42	3286.67	2209.29	2760.8	3062.85	2857.88
FTSE Fledgling	NSX	1676.60	2624.20	3170.4	3748.8	4389.4	4022.3	2321.76	4035.39	4789.69	4081.64
FTSE Small Cap	SMX	1820.60	2475.10	2758.1	3305.5	3905.6	3420.3	1854.2	2780.2	3228.6	2748.8
FTSE TechMARK 100	TIX	648.78	1015.00	1196.43	1431.72	1512.38	1641.1	1217	1704.8	2040	2064.1
FTSE4Good UK 50	4UK5	3480.60	3918.64	4199.54	4802.23	5267.43	5428.6	3787.4	4577.9	4852.9	4529.8
FTSE AIM	AXX	602.90	835.40	1005.6	1046.1	1054	1049.1	394.32	653.24	933.63	693.18

The table below gives the annual percentage performance of the eight indices. The light grey cells highlight the best performing index in the year, the dark grey cells highlight the worst performing.

Annual percentage performance of UK indices

Name	EPIC	2002	2003	2004	2005	2006	2007	2008	2009	2010	2011
FTSE 100	UKX	-24.5	13.6	7.5	16.7	10.7	3.8	-31.3	22.1	9.0	-5.6
FTSE 250	MCX	-27.3	34.3	19.6	26.8	27.1	-4.7	-40.3	46.3	24.2	-12.6
FTSE AIM	AXX	-32.8	38.6	20.4	4.0	0.8	-0.5	-62.4	65.7	42.9	-25.8
FTSE All-Share	ASX	-25.0	16.6	9.2	18.1	13.2	2.0	-32.8	25.0	10.9	-6.7
FTSE Fledgling	NSX	-18.4	56.5	20.8	18.2	17.1	-8.4	-42.3	73.8	18.7	-14.8
FTSE Small Cap	SMX	-29.4	35.9	11.4	19.8	18.2	-12.4	-45.8	49.9	16.1	-14.9
FTSE TechMARK 100	TIX	-55.9	56.4	17.9	19.7	5.6	8.5	-25.8	40.1	19.7	1.2
FTSE4Good UK 50	4UK5	-25.3	12.6	7.2	14.4	9.7	3.1	-30.2	20.9	6.0	-6.7

The FTSE Fledgling and FTSE TechMARK 100 indices have been the best performing indices in the year the most number of times, while the FTSE AIM and FTSE 4Good UK 50 indices are at the bottom of the class, having been the worst performing index in the year the most number of times.

The following chart shows the relative performance of the FTSE 100, FTSE 250, FTSE AIM and FTSE Fledgling indices.

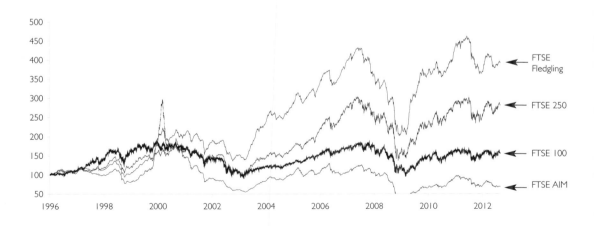

PRICE HISTORY PROFILE OF THE FTSE ALL SHARE INDEX

The FTSE All Share Index is the aggregation of the FTSE 100, FTSE 250 and FTSE Small Cap indices. Effectively, all those LSE listed companies with a market capitalisation above the lower limit for inclusion in the FTSE Small Cap Index. The FTSE All Share Index is the standard benchmark for measuring the performance of the broad UK market.

Yearly data

Data starts	1899 (112 years)
Largest one year rise	136.3% (1975)
Largest one year fall	-55.3% (1974
Average annual change (Standard deviation)	5,73% (20.59)
Number of times the index has risen 5 years in a row (last time)	15 (2003-2007)
Number of times the index has risen 8 years in a row (last time)	6 (1983-1989)
Number of times the index has risen 10 years in a row (last time)	4 (1980-1989)
Most number of consecutive years risen	13 (1977-1989)
Number of times the index has fallen 3 years in a row (last time)	8 (2000-2002)
Number of times the index has fallen 4 years in a row (last time)	2 (1912-1915)
Number of times the index has fallen 5 years in a row	0

Monthly data

Data starts	1946 (799 months)
Largest one month rise	52.7% (Jan 1975)
Largest one month fall	-26.6% (Oct 1987)
Average monthly change (Standard deviation)	0.67% (5.15)
Number of times the index has risen 6 months in a row (last time)	52 (Nov 05-Apr 06)
Number of times the index has risen 8 months in a row (last time)	16 (Dec 86-Jul 87)
Number of times the index has risen 10 months in a row (last time)	6 (Oct 86-Jul 87)
Most number of consecutive months risen	12 (Jun 53-May 54)
Number of times the index has fallen 4 months in a row (last time)	20 (Jun 11-Sep 11)
Number of times the index has fallen 6 months in a row (last time)	3 (Apr 02-Sep 02)
Number of times the index has fallen 7 months in a row	0

Daily data

Data starts	2 Jan 1969 (11,021 days)
Largest one day rise	9.4% (24 Jan 75)
Largest one day fall	-11.2% (20 Oct 87)
Average daily change (Standard deviation)	0.03% (1.08)
Number of times the index has risen 5 days in a row	559
Number of times the index has risen 8 days in a row (last time)	92 (24 Jun 11-5 Jul 11)
Number of times the index has risen 10 days in a row (last time)	28 (14 Jul 09-27 Jul 09)
Most number of consecutive days risen	18 (19/12/86-16/01/87)
Number of times the index has fallen 5 days in a row	295
Number of times the index has fallen 8 days in a row (last time)	25 (15 Nov 11-24 Nov 11)
Number of times the index has fallen 10 days in a row (last time)	7 (14 Jan 03-27 Jan 03)
Most number of consecutive days fallen	13 (6 Jun 74-24 Jun 74)

DAY OF THE WEEK PERFORMANCE

Is the performance of the FTSE 100 Index affected by the day of week?

The table below shows the results of analysis on daily data for the FTSE 100 Index since January 2007. The columns in the table are explained below:

- Column B: number of weeks where the index increased on the day (%)
- Column C: average index change for the day (%)
- Column D: standard deviation of the average in column C

Day	Up(%)	Avg Chg(%)	StdDev
A	B	C	D
Monday	50.4	0.01	1.79
Tuesday	52.3	0.12	1.41
Wednesday	47.9	-0.05	1.49
Thursday	50.5	-0.05	1.40
Friday	52.3	0.00	1.44

The proportion of days where the index rose (column B) is displayed in the chart below.

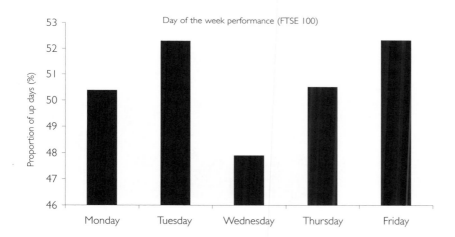

Day of the week performance (FTSE 100)

Observations

1. The weakest day of the week can be quite clearly seen as Wednesday. The market is only up on 47.9% of Wednesdays – the only day with the proportion of Up days under 50%.

2. The strongest days are Tuesday and Friday (both up 52.3% of all weeks); although Tuesday has the higher average increase each week.

3. The day of the week behaviour has changed over time. Analysing data from 1984 to the present day shows Monday as the weakest day (with negative average returns) and Friday easily the strongest. This longer-term result regarding Friday/Monday performance (sometimes called the weekend effect) is in accordance with numerous academic papers on the topic; the first of which was Osborne (1962)[1].

---

[1] Osborne, M. F. M., 'Periodic structure in the Brownian motion of stock returns', *Operations Research* 10 (1962), 345–379.

MARKET FALLS ON CONSECUTIVE DAYS

Later in this Reference section we look at market momentum for days, weeks, months and years. On this page we look in some more detail at the behaviour of the market when the market falls for several consecutive days.

The following table shows the results of analysis on the daily FTSE All Share Index from 1969.

The first column is the number of consecutive days the markets falls. For example Down(4) is the market falls four days in a row.

The second column is the frequency of such behaviour. For example, since 1969 there have been 11,021 market days and on 612 occasions the market has fallen four consecutive days (that's 6% of the total).

The third column is the average performance of the market on the day following the consecutive day fall. For example, after the market has fallen for four consecutive days, on average the market increases 0.01% on the fifth day.

The fourth column is the average performance of the market over the five days following the consecutive day fall. For example, after the market has fallen for four consecutive days, on average the market has increased 0.19% by the fifth day after the fall.

The fifth column is as per the previous column, except this measures the average performance 20 days after the fall.

From 1969

Down days	Frequency(%)	After 1 day(%)	After 5 days(%)	After 20 days(%)
Down(2)	24	-0.05	0.09	0.51
Down(3)	12	0.00	0.18	0.65
Down(4)	6	0.01	0.19	0.85
Down(5)	3	0.02	0.07	0.86

As can be seen, after multiple-day consecutive falls, the market tends to bounce back fairly quickly. And the longer the fall, the greater the bounce back. The exception is with a 2-day fall when the market tends to fall again on the third day.

Since 1969 the market has fallen for 5 consecutive days on 296 occasions (3% of the total). The following chart plots the frequency of these falls.

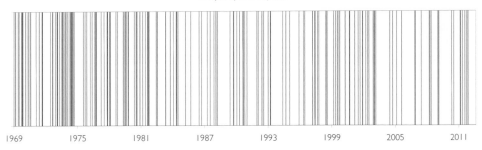

Frequency of 5-day falls

1969	1975	1981	1987	1993	1999	2005	2011

The greatest frequency of 5-day falls was in the early 70s and in the years around the millennium. In recent years there have been relatively fewer occasions when the market has fallen 5 days in a row.

To see if the behaviour of the market following falls has changed in recent years the data was also analysed for the period since 2000. The table below shows the results. Generally, the bounce back after 1 and 5 days has been stronger recently.

From 2000

Down days	Frequency(%)	After 1 day(%)	After 5 days(%)	After 20 days(%)
Down(2)	23%	0.10	0.22	0.44
Down(3)	10%	0.21	0.30	0.60
Down(4)	4%	0.09	0.35	0.83
Down(5)	2%	-0.03	0.11	0.92

FTSE 100 – DAILY CHANGE MAP

One day while writing this Almanac the FTSE 100 Index fell 1.5% and we wondered how many times the index had fallen by that amount or more. Or, to put it another way, is a fall of 1.5% unusual or quite ordinary? So we created the chart on this page to act as a quick guide to answer such questions.

The FTSE 100 daily change map

1. The chart plots the 7,177 daily changes of the FTSE 100 Index since the index started in 1984.

2. The changes are ordered on the X-axis by size (not by date). So, all the falls in the market are on the left side of the chart, the increases on the right side. The 7,177 daily changes are divided into percentage deciles on the X-axis.

3. The Y-axis has been truncated at +/- 3% to enable easier reading of smaller values. Daily changes of over 3% or under -3% have occurred in less than 1% of days.

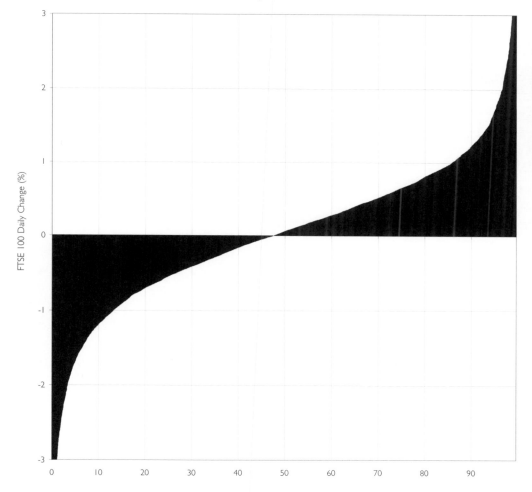

Reading the map

1. If the FTSE 100 Index increases one day by 1%, looking this up on the chart gives a reading of around 86%. This tells us that since 1984 the index has increased by less than 1% on 86% of all days, and increased by more than 1% on 14% of all days.

2. Looking up a daily change of -1.5% (the fall that prompted this exercise), the chart gives a value of around 5%. This means that the market has fallen 1.5% or more on 5% of all days. Or, in a year of roughly 250 trading days, we can expect the market to fall 1.5% or more on 4 days in the year.

MARKET MOMENTUM (UP) ANALYSIS

The table below displays the results of analysis on market momentum – the tendency of the market to increase in one period having also risen in the previous period(s). Notes on the analysis–

1. The index analysed was the FTSE All Share. The number of observations to August 2012 (for each frequency) is indicated in column 0. For example, 11,021 days to August 2012 (from Jan 1969) was the sample data for the "Daily" analysis.

2. The first rows ("Total") of the columns display the number of consecutive periods that the index rose for that frequency. For example, the market rose 5819 days (out of the total 11,021); 3262 times it rose on 2 consecutive days; and 304 times it rose 6 days in a row. The second rows ("% Total") express the first row as a percentage of the total sample. For example, the market rose 6 days in a row 2.8% of the whole period (11,021 days).

3. The rows "% 1 up" expresses the proportion of times that the market rose for n consecutive periods following the market rising for 1 period (expressed as a percentage of the number of times the market rose once). For example: after the market had risen for 1 day, the market rose for a second day in 56.1% of all cases; after the market had risen for 1 day, the market went on to rise 6 days consecutively in 5.2% of all cases.

4. The subsequent rows display the tendency of the market to rise following n consecutive increases. For example: after the market has risen 4 days consecutively, the market rose for a 5th day in 55.6% of all cases; after the market had risen 3 years in a row, the market rose again the following year in 72.4% of all cases.

Frequency		0	1	2	3	4	5	6
Daily	Total	11,021	5819	3262	1801	1005	559	304
	% Total		52.8	29.6	16.3	9.1	5.1	2.8
	% 1 up			56.1	31.0	17.3	9.6	5.2
	% 2 up				55.2	30.8	17.1	9.3
	% 3 up					55.8	31.0	16.9
	% 4 up						55.6	30.2
	% 5 up							54.4
Weekly	Total	2484	1370	757	430	246	146	81
	% Total		55.2	30.5	17.3	9.9	5.9	3.3
	% 1 up			55.3	31.4	18.0	10.7	5.9
	% 2 up				56.8	32.5	19.3	10.7
	% 3 up					57.2	34.0	18.8
	% 4 up						59.3	32.9
	% 5 up							55.5
Monthly	Total	799	485	302	187	118	79	52
	% Total		60.7	37.8	23.4	14.8	9.9	6.5
	% 1 up			62.3	38.6	24.3	16.3	10.7
	% 2 up				61.9	39.1	26.2	17.2
	% 3 up					63.1	42.2	27.8
	% 4 up						66.9	44.1
	% 5 up							65.8
Yearly	Total	112	68	45	29	21	15	10
	% Total		60.7	40.2	25.9	18.8	13.4	8.9
	% 1 up			66.2	42.6	30.9	22.1	14.7
	% 2 up				64.4	46.7	33.3	22.2
	% 3 up					72.4	51.7	34.5
	% 4 up						71.4	47.6
	% 5 up							66.7

Observations

The market would appear to display a degree of fractal behaviour – where its properties are similar whatever time-frame one looks at. Trends do seem to become more established the longer they last. For example, the probability of the market rising in a week increases the longer the period of previous consecutive up weeks. Although this trend falls off after 5 consecutive up periods.

The market displays greater momentum for longer frequencies. For example, the market only rose 6 days consecutively 2.8% of the time, whereas it rose 6 years consecutively 8.9% of the time. In addition, the market rose for a 6th year (after 5 years of consecutive increases) 66.7% of the time, against just 54.4% for daily increases.

MARKET MOMENTUM (DOWN) ANALYSIS

The table on the previous page looked at market momentum for the market going up. The table below shows the results of analysis of market momentum when the market falls.

The structure of the table is similar to that on the previous page (where an explanation of the figures is given).

Frequency		0	1	2	3	4	5	6
Daily	Total	11021	5185	2629	1304	621	295	138
	% Total		47.0	23.9	11.8	5.6	2.7	1.3
	% 1 down		50.7	25.1	12.0	5.7	2.7	
	% 2 down			49.6	23.6	11.2	5.2	
	% 3 down				47.6	22.6	10.6	
	% 4 down					47.5	22.2	
	% 5 down						46.8	
Weekly	Total	2484	1111	497	242	123	58	32
	% Total		44.7	20.0	9.7	5.0	2.3	1.3
	% 1 down		44.7	21.8	11.1	5.2	2.9	
	% 2 down			48.7	24.7	11.7	6.4	
	% 3 down				50.8	24.0	13.2	
	% 4 down					47.2	26.0	
	% 5 down						55.2	
Monthly	Total	799	312	131	54	20	10	3
	% Total		39.0	16.4	6.8	2.5	1.3	0.4
	% 1 down		42.0	17.3	6.4	3.2	1.0	
	% 2 down			41.2	15.3	7.6	2.3	
	% 3 down				37.0	18.5	5.6	
	% 4 down					50.0	15.0	
	% 5 down						30.0	
Yearly	Total	112	44	20	8	2	0	0
	% Total		39.3	17.9	7.1	1.8	0.0	0.0
	% 1 down		45.5	18.2	4.5	0.0	0.0	
	% 2 down			40.0	10.0	0.0	0.0	
	% 3 down				25.0	0.0	0.0	
	% 4 down					0.0	0.0	
	% 5 down						0.0	

Observations

1. Since 1969, the market has fallen on 6 consecutive days on 138 occasions (the last time was November 2011 – when, in fact, the market fell for 9 straight days). The most consecutive days the market has fallen is 13, which it has done once (in June 1974).

2. Since 1946 the market has only fallen 4 consecutive months on 20 occasions (2.5%). Random chance would suggest 6.3%.

3. Since 1900, the market has never fallen for 5 consecutive years. The market has fallen for 3 consecutive years on 8 occasions, but having done so the market continued to fall for a 4th year only twice.

4. As with up markets (previous page), down markets appear to display a degree of fractal behaviour, where their properties are similar whatever time-frame one looks at.

5. Down markets display far less momentum tendency than that seen for up markets. For example, if the market rises for 3 consecutive months, there's a 63.1% probability that the market will continue to rise for a 4th month as well. However, if the market falls 3 consecutive months, there's only a 37.0% probability that the market will fall for a 4th month as well.

INTRA-DAY VOLATILITY

Since 1985, the average daily Hi-Lo range of the FTSE 100 Index has been 1.3%. This means that when the index is at, say, 6000, the average daily difference between the high and low levels of the index is 78 points. The standard deviation of this daily range is 0.9. We could define a very volatile day as one where the day's Hi-Lo range is 2 standard deviations above the average. This would be 3.1%.

The chart below plots the Hi-Lo range (as a percentage of the close) for the 277 days since 1985 when the range has been over 3.1%.

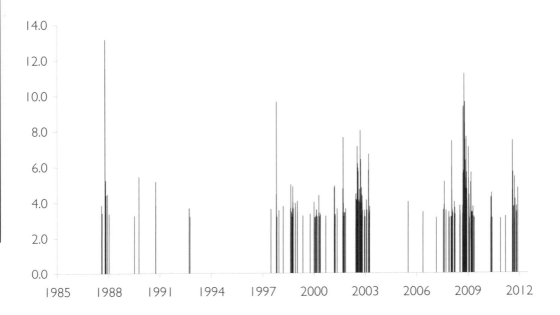

As we can see, the intra-day volatility of the index seems to be increasing. Although the record for the greatest Hi-Lo range in a day is still 13.1%; seen on 20 October 1987.

Hi-Lo-Close

The table below shows the frequency with which the index closes within a certain percentage of the high (or low) of the day. For example, since 1985 the FTSE 100 Index has closed within 10% of its daily high 21.4% of all days, and it has closed within 1% of its low 5.7% of all days.

	10%	5%	1%
Top	21.4	15.9	10.2
Bottom	15.0	9.9	5.7

Continuing this analysis of where the index closes in relation to the Hi-Lo range of the day, the table below shows the performance of the FTSE 100 Index on the following day. For example, on the days when the index closes within 10% of its low for the day, on average the index increases 0.004% the following day. When the index closes within 1% of its high for the day, on average the index increases 0.184% the following day.

	10%	5%	1%
Top	0.122	0.144	0.184
Bottom	0.004	-0.003	0.008

INDEX PROFILES – COMPANY FINANCIALS

The table below presents a range of company financials characteristics for the six main stock market indices in the UK. For example, the average turnover for the 248 companies in the FTSE Small Cap Index is £241m.

	FTSE 100	FTSE 250	Small Cap	Fledgling	AIM	techMARK
Number of companies in index	100	250	248	128	1,120	69
Turnover, average (£m)	14,979	946	241	75	44	2,336
Turnover growth last five years, average (%)	91	115	68	34	201	93
Turnover to capitalisation ratio, average	1.0	1.3	3.0	13.0	4.8	2.0
Number of companies making a profit	97	180	102	48	433	54
Number of companies making a profit (%)	97	72	41	38	39	78
Profit, average (£m)	2,218.9	61.1	1.5	-13.7	3.7	477.1
Profit growth last five years, average (%)	101	108	46	37	162	144
Profit / turnover, average (%)	22	11	9	-11	-146	-171
Current ratio, average	1.3	2.4	1.1	1.6	7.6	2.2
Net cash, average (£m)	5,699	250	27	7	11	349
Net cash, sum total (£m)	552,799	60,832	6,654	857	11,108	23,730
Price to net cash ratio, average	24	25	31	21	15	18
Net borrowings, average (£m)	3,263	217	108	51	7	731
Net borrowings, sum total (£m)	274,133	40,237	14,320	4,132	6,705	49,721
Net gearing, average	143	26	-3	-18	7	-84
Interest cover, average	31	118			-14	94
Dividend cover, average	3	2	2	2	3	3
ROCE, average (%)	174	62	60	14	74	66
ROCE, standard deviation	1,156	276	211	55	3,123	257

Notes and observations

1. Care should be taken with some of the figures above – especially those of indices with few companies (such as the FTSE Fledgling and techMARK) – as the averages can be significantly affected by one or two outlier numbers. In addition, the techMARK Index is very non-homogenous, combining, as it does, very large and very small companies in the same index.

2. Only 39% of AIM companies, and 41% of Small Caps reported a profit for 2011.

3. On average, FTSE 100 companies have £5,699m net cash (2007: £1,647m), while FTSE 250 companies have net cash of £250m (2007: £114m).

Data compiled August 2012

INDEX PROFILES – SHARE PRICES

The table below presents a range of share price-related characteristics for six stock market indices in the UK. For example, the average market capitalisation of the 1,120 companies in the AIM index is £54m.

	FTSE 100	FTSE 250	Small Cap	Fledgling	AIM	techMARK
Number of companies in index	100	250	248	128	1,120	69
Market capitalisation, average (£m)	15,756	1,003	171	27	54	4,105
Market capitalisation, standard deviation	22,821	599	90	19	138	14,266
Share price, average (£)	11.07	6.23	3.01	3.35	0.73	4.71
Number of companies paying a dividend	97	208	189	76	236	48
Number of companies paying a dividend (%)	97	83	76	59	21	70
Dividend yield, average (%)	3.6	3.4	3.9	4.5	4.3	3.1
Dividend yield, standard deviation	2.4	2.1	2.8	3.0	10.3	2.6
PE ratio, average	15.4	29.8	38.4	53.3	28.7	20.5
PE ratio, standard deviation	8.0	53.5	75.3	117.5	65.9	15.4
PEG, average	2.1	1.3	1.2	1.3	1.0	1.8
Correlation (FTSE100), average	0.5	0.4	0.3	0.2	0.1	0.2
Correlation (FTSE100), standard deviation	0.1	0.2	0.2	0.1	0.1	0.1
Beta (FTSE100), average	1.0	0.7	0.5	0.3	0.2	0.6
Beta (FTSE100), standard deviation	0.5	0.4	0.3	0.2	0.3	0.3

Notes and observations

1. As for the accompanying table "Index profiles – company financials", care should be taken with some of the figures above – especially those of indices with few companies (such as the FTSE Fledgling and techMARK) – as the averages can be significantly affected by one or two outlier numbers. In addition, the techMARK Index is very non-homogenous, combining, as it does, very large and very small companies in the same index.

2. Just 21% of AIM companies pay a dividend. The figures for all the indices have changed very little from 2007. (NB. The average dividend yield is an average for the companies that pay a dividend – not all the companies in the index.)

3. The average PE for the FTSE 100 companies is 15.4 with the PE values fairly tightly clustered around this average level; but the PEs for companies in the other indices have a very wide range around the average.

4. Correlation is calculated relative to the FTSE 100 index. (Note: the averages calculated here are equally weighted, not market capitalisation weighted.)

5. Beta is calculated relative to the FTSE 100 index.

Data compiled August 2012

INDEX PROFILES – INDUSTRY

The pie charts below show the profiles of the major UK stock market indices by industry. The size of the respective sectors in these charts is determined by the number of companies in the sector and not their market capitalisations.

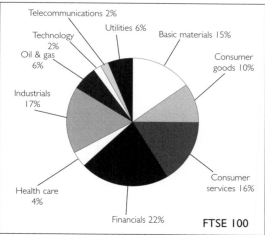

FTSE 100

Telecommunications 2%
Utilities 6%
Basic materials 15%
Technology 2%
Consumer goods 10%
Oil & gas 6%
Consumer services 16%
Industrials 17%
Health care 4%
Financials 22%

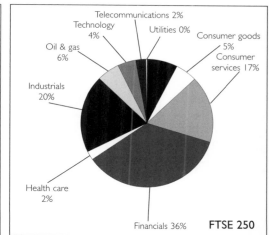

FTSE 250

Telecommunications 2%
Technology 4%
Utilities 0%
Consumer goods 5%
Oil & gas 6%
Consumer services 17%
Industrials 20%
Health care 2%
Financials 36%

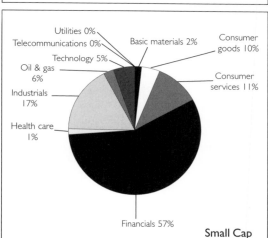

Small Cap

Utilities 0%
Telecommunications 0%
Basic materials 2%
Consumer goods 10%
Technology 5%
Oil & gas 6%
Consumer services 11%
Industrials 17%
Health care 1%
Financials 57%

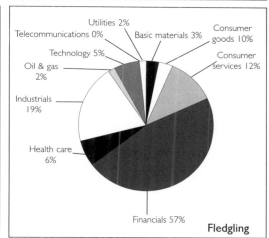

Fledgling

Utilities 2%
Telecommunications 0%
Basic materials 3%
Consumer goods 10%
Technology 5%
Oil & gas 2%
Consumer services 12%
Industrials 19%
Health care 6%
Financials 57%

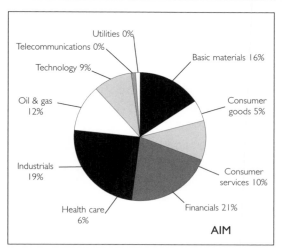

AIM

Utilities 0%
Telecommunications 0%
Basic materials 16%
Technology 9%
Consumer goods 5%
Oil & gas 12%
Consumer services 10%
Industrials 19%
Financials 21%
Health care 6%

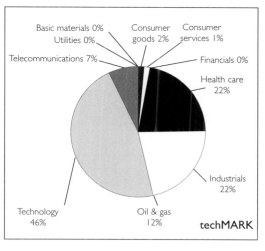

techMARK

Basic materials 0%
Consumer goods 2%
Consumer services 1%
Utilities 0%
Financials 0%
Telecommunications 7%
Health care 22%
Industrials 22%
Oil & gas 12%
Technology 46%

No.	Company	TIDM	Turnover (£m)	Profit (£m)	Profit Margin (%)	Capital (£m)	Weighting (%)	Cumulative Weighting (%)
1	Royal Dutch Shell	RDSB	302,500	35,815	11.2	145,230	8.9	8.9
2	HSBC Holdings	HSBA		14,074		107,010	6.5	15.4
3	Vodafone Group	VOD	46,420	9,549	13.4	86,479	5.3	20.7
4	BP	BP.	241,600	24,988	8.3	85,706	5.2	25.9
5	GlaxoSmithKline	GSK	27,390	7,698	30.0	70,326	4.3	30.2
6	British American Tobacco	BATS	15,400	4,931	35.5	61,351	3.7	33.9
7	Rio Tinto	RIO	38,950	8,503	37.3	46,304	2.8	36.7
8	BG Group	BG.	13,560	4,858	38.1	44,247	2.7	39.4
9	SABMiller	SAB	13,620	3,507	19.5	43,306	2.6	42.1
10	BHP Billiton	BLT	46,050	14,678		43,276	2.6	44.7
11	Diageo	DGE	10,760	3,121	29.5	42,186	2.6	47.3
12	Standard Chartered	STAN		4,359		36,044	2.2	49.5
13	AstraZeneca	AZN	21,610	7,958	36.1	36,037	2.2	51.7
14	Xstrata	XTA	21,800	5,243	24.0	31,844	1.9	53.6
15	Anglo American	AAL	19,680	6,938	31.2	28,978	1.8	55.4
16	Unilever	ULVR	38,810	5,216	15.0	28,814	1.8	57.2
17	Lloyds Banking Group	LLOY		-3,542		28,144	1.7	58.9
18	Barclays	BARC		5,879		28,031	1.7	60.6
19	Tesco	TSCO	64,540	3,835	4.9	27,814	1.7	62.3
20	Glencore International	GLEN	119,800	2,576	1.9	26,227	1.6	63.9
21	Reckitt Benckiser Group	RB.	9,485	2,376	26.1	25,796	1.6	65.5
22	National Grid	NG.	13,830	2,559	26.9	24,902	1.5	67.0
23	Imperial Tobacco Group	IMT	29,220	2,153	9.5	22,794	1.4	68.4
24	Prudential	PRU		1,943		21,834	1.3	69.7
25	BT Group	BT.A	18,900	2,445	14.2	18,350	1.1	70.8
26	Centrica	CNA	22,820	1,268	8.2	17,268	1.1	71.9
27	Royal Bank of Scotland Group	RBS		-766		16,788	1.0	72.9
28	Rolls-Royce Group	RR.	11,120	1,105	9.1	16,560	1.0	73.9
29	Fresnillo	FRES	1,411	987	69.7	13,411	0.8	74.7
30	SSE	SSE	31,720	269	2.1	13,226	0.8	75.5
31	Tullow Oil	TLW	1,483	690	54.2	13,208	0.8	76.3
32	Antofagasta	ANTO	3,910	1,979	54.6	13,151	0.8	77.1
33	Compass Group	CPG	15,830	958	6.5	13,120	0.8	77.9
34	British Sky Broadcasting Group	BSY	6,791	1,189		11,950	0.7	78.7
35	BAE Systems	BA.	17,770	1,466	9.2	11,275	0.7	79.3
36	WPP Group	WPP	10,020	1,008	11.6	10,910	0.7	80.0
37	Shire	SHP	2,743	703	27.4	10,699	0.7	80.7
38	Aviva	AV.		813		10,597	0.6	81.3
39	Experian	EXPN	2,808	431	17.2	10,409	0.6	81.9
40	Associated British Foods	ABF	11,070	757	7.2	10,094	0.6	82.6
41	Pearson	PSON	5,862	1,155	12.9	9,714	0.6	83.2
42	CRH	CRH	15,100	594	5.5	9,231	0.6	83.7
43	Old Mutual	OML		994		8,626	0.5	84.2
44	Legal & General Group	LGEN		956		8,142	0.5	84.7
45	Wolseley	WOS	13,560	391	3.8	8,048	0.5	85.2
46	ARM Holdings	ARM	492	157	30.6	8,026	0.5	85.7
47	Reed Elsevier	REL	3,175	390	16.6	7,372	0.4	86.2
48	Morrison (Wm) Supermarkets	MRW	17,660	947	5.5	7,109	0.4	86.6
49	Randgold Resources Ltd	RRS	725	312	43.1	6,815	0.4	87.0
50	Standard Life	SL.		595		6,675	0.4	87.4
51	Kingfisher	KGF	10,830	797	7.1	6,590	0.4	87.8
52	Sainsbury (J)	SBRY	22,290	799	3.4	6,438	0.4	88.2
53	Aggreko	AGK	1,396	324	24.2	6,394	0.4	88.6
54	Land Securities Group	LAND	672	516	70.7	6,208	0.4	89.0
55	Smith & Nephew	SN.	2,748	546	21.8	6,205	0.4	89.4

No.	Company	TIDM	Turnover (£m)	Profit (£m)	Profit Margin (%)	Capital (£m)	Weighting (%)	Cumulative Weighting (%)
56	Marks & Spencer Group	MKS	9,934	658	8.8	5,988	0.4	89.7
57	Petrofac Ltd	PFC	3,733	438	11.7	5,766	0.4	90.1
58	Next	NXT	3,441	580	17.5	5,538	0.3	90.4
59	Johnson Matthey	JMAT	12,020	409	3.7	5,273	0.3	90.7
60	Carnival	CCL	10,040	1,216	14.3	4,908	0.3	91.0
61	British Land Co	BLND	332	479	28.9	4,869	0.3	91.3
62	Burberry Group	BRBY	1,857	366	20.1	4,831	0.3	91.6
63	Capita Group (The)	CPI	2,930	303	11.9	4,817	0.3	91.9
64	InterContinental Hotels Group	IHG	1,138	342	32.2	4,788	0.3	92.2
65	Eurasian Natural Resources	ENRC	4,958	1,773	36.4	4,677	0.3	92.5
66	United Utilities Group	UU.	1,565	280	35.5	4,657	0.3	92.8
67	Intertek Group	ITRK	1,749	213	14.5	4,370	0.3	93.1
68	RSA Insurance Group	RSA		613		4,316	0.3	93.3
69	Schroders	SDR	1,502	407	25.3	4,254	0.3	93.6
70	Smiths Group	SMIN	2,842	398	17.3	4,154	0.3	93.8
71	Polymetal International	POLY	854	263	34.0	4,137	0.3	94.1
72	Whitbread	WTB	1,778	306	18.4	4,105	0.3	94.3
73	Kazakhmys	KAZ	2,293	1,044	30.7	4,048	0.2	94.6
74	Severn Trent	SVT	1,771	157	23.6	4,016	0.2	94.8
75	Evraz	EVR	10,550	562	11.2	3,935	0.2	95.1
76	Sage Group (The)	SGE	1,334	331	25.7	3,926	0.2	95.3
77	Weir Group	WEIR	2,292	392	17.6	3,878	0.2	95.5
78	GKN	GKN	5,746	351	6.2	3,865	0.2	95.8
79	Rexam	REX	4,734	431	11.7	3,793	0.2	96.0
80	G4S	GFS	7,522	279	5.2	3,682	0.2	96.2
81	Bunzl	BNZL	5,110	194	5.7	3,663	0.2	96.5
82	AMEC	AMEC	3,261	259	7.5	3,604	0.2	96.7
83	Aberdeen Asset Management	ADN	784	224	30.5	3,486	0.2	96.9
84	ITV	ITV	2,140	327	18.4	3,407	0.2	97.1
85	Hammerson	HMSO	344	346	77.0	3,327	0.2	97.3
86	Babcock International Group	BAB	2,848	173	7.3	3,320	0.2	97.5
87	Croda International	CRDA	1,068	242	23.6	3,280	0.2	97.7
88	Meggitt	MGGT	1,455	226	18.9	3,218	0.2	97.9
89	Resolution Ltd	RSL		-268		3,115	0.2	98.1
90	IMI	IMI	2,131	301	15.9	3,110	0.2	98.3
91	Hargreaves Lansdown	HL.	239	153		3,062	0.2	98.5
92	Admiral Group	ADM		299		3,054	0.2	98.7
93	Capital Shopping Centres Group	CSCG	516	36	17.3	3,031	0.2	98.8
94	Tate & Lyle	TATE	3,088	379	11.0	3,011	0.2	99.0
95	International Consolidated Airlines	IAG	13,450	453	4.5	2,970	0.2	99.2
96	Serco Group	SRP	4,646	238	6.0	2,921	0.2	99.4
97	Vedanta Resources	VED	8,765	1,092	16.3	2,897	0.2	99.6
98	Pennon Group	PNN	1,233	201	16.4	2,658	0.2	99.7
99	Ashmore Group	ASHM	334	243		2,319	0.1	99.9
100	ICAP	IAP	1,681	217	19.9	2,267	0.1	100.0

Notes to the table

1. The *Weighting* column expresses a company's market capitalisation as a percentage of the total capitalisation of all companies in the FTSE 100 Index. The table is ranked (in descending order) by this column.

2. Figures accurate as of September 2012.

Observations

- The 5 largest companies in the FTSE 100 Index account for 30% of the total market capitalisation. (In 2004 the comparable figure was 36% – the biggest companies are getting relatively smaller.)

- The 13 largest companies in the index account for just over half of total capitalisation. (2004: 10 companies)

- The 25 smallest companies in the index account for only roughly 5% of total capitalisation. In other words, the individual movements of these 25 companies has very little impact on the value of the index.

- The aggregate capitalisation of all 100 companies in the index is £1,640bn (2006: £1,397bn). When the index started in 1984 the aggregate capitalisation was £100 billion.

FTSE 100 INDEX QUARTERLY REVIEWS

To keep the FTSE 100 Index in accordance with its purpose, the constituents of the index are periodically reviewed. The reviews take place on the Wednesday after the first Friday of the month in March, June, September and December. If any changes are to be made (i.e. companies ejected and introduced) these are announced sometime after the market has closed on the day of the review.

The review dates for 2013 are: 6 March, 12 June, 11 September and 11 December.

Since the index's inception in 1984, the company that has danced in and out of the index the most is Tate & Lyle, which has been added 6 times (and ejected 5 times).

A table of companies entering and exiting the FTSE 100 Index since January 2008, as a result of the FTSE quarterly reviews, is shown below.

Company	In	Out
3i Group	Jun 09	Mar 09, Sep 11
Aberdeen Asset Management	Mar 12	
African Barrick Gold	Jun 10	Mar 11
Aggreko	Dec 09	
Alliance & Leicester		Jun 08
Alliance Trust		Mar 11
Amlin	Dec 08	Jun 09
Ashmore Group	Sep 11	
Autonomy Corporation	Sep 08	
Babcock International Group	Jun 12	
Balfour Beatty		Sep 09
Bunzl	Apr 08, Sep 11	Mar 11
Cable and Wireless Worldwide		Sep 10
Cairn Energy		Mar 12
Carphone Warehouse Group		Sep 08
Cobham	Mar 08	Dec 10
CRH	Dec 11	
Croda International	Mar 12	
Drax Group	Jun 08	Jun 09
Enterprise Inns		Sep 08
Essar Energy	Jun 10	Mar 12
Evraz	Dec 11	
Ferrexpo	Jun 08	Sep 08
First Group		Mar 09
Foreign & Col Inv Trust	Mar 09	Sep 09
Fresnillo	Sep 08, Mar 09	Dec 08
Glencore	May 11	
Hargreaves Lansdown	Mar 11	
Home Retail Group	Dec 08	Jun 08, Sep 10
IMI	Dec 10	
Inmarsat	Sep 08	Dec 11
Intertek Group	Mar 09	
Invensys	Jun 08	May 11
Investec	Mar 10	Dec 11
ITV	Mar 11	Sep 08
London Stock Exchange Group	Jun 09	Mar 09, Jun 10
Lonmin	Mar 09	Dec 08, Dec 11
Man Group		Jun 12
Pennon Group		Sep 09
Persimmon		Jun 08
Petrofac	Jun 08, Mar 09	Dec 08

Company	In	Out
Polymetal International	Dec 11	
Randgold Resources	Dec 08	
Rentokil Initial	Sep 09	Mar 08, Dec 09
Resolution	Sep 10	Apr 08, Mar 10
Scottish & Newcastle		Apr 08
Segro	Sep 09	Sep 10
Serco Group	Dec 08	
Stagecoach Group	Sep 08	Dec 08
Tate & Lyle	Mar 08, Dec 08, Jun 11	Jun 08, Mar 09
Taylor Wimpey		Mar 08
Thomas Cook Group		Jun 10
Tomkins	Sep 10	
TUI Travel		Jun 11
Weir Group	Sep 10	
Whitbread	Sep 09	Jun 09
Wolseley	Jun 09	Mar 09
Wood Group (John)	Apr 08, Mar 11	Dec 08, Sep 11
Yell Group		Mar 08

Source: FTSE International

SECTORS

SECTOR ANNUAL PERFORMANCE

The table below shows the year-on-year percentage performance of the FTSE 350 sectors. The three best [worst] performing sectors in each year are highlighted in light grey [dark grey].

Sector performance 2002-2011 (percentage change YoY)

Sector	2002	2003	2004	2005	2006	2007	2008	2009	2010	2011
Aerospace & Defense	-36.8	23.3	31.9	54.3	6.0	20.4	-27.6	15.8	7.7	1.1
Alternative Energy									-52.3	128.2
Automobiles & Parts	-16.0	44.4	9.1	25.0	-3.5	1.4	-65.6	78.7	89.9	-17.6
Banks	-22.1	17.8	6.8	7.3	10.0	-21.3	-56.8	23.8	-0.1	-29.6
Beverages	-11.8	8.6	12.4	19.7	16.5	14.4	-11.6	28.9	15.6	9.3
Chemicals	-15.9	-1.4	14.3	32.1	33.6	41.3	-37.8	43.8	58.5	-7.8
Construction & Materials	-19.4	45.8	22.6	35.1	29.0	4.5	-35.7	-0.7	19.6	-13.1
Electricity	-4.1	3.5	21.0	33.4	41.2	6.5	-16.2	-1.0	14.0	8.5
Electronic & Electrical Equipment	-57.4	-30.8	-5.3	35.7	23.4	-5.5	-31.4	23.0	81.2	-6.6
Equity Investment Instruments	-28.3	20.7	12.1	30.8	12.4	6.5	-36.1	31.3	18.5	-10.9
Financial Services	-37.5	28.2	7.3	25.9	37.9	2.0	-55.4	39.7	21.5	-28.5
Fixed Line Telecommunications	-38.9	22.2	4.9	-1.1	32.9	-5.4	-44.5	-1.7	19.8	-5.2
Food & Drug Retailers	-20.8	26.2	12.1	3.8	23.6	20.2	-22.5	12.5	1.8	-3.6
Food Producers	-0.8	-5.2	10.7	12.1	9.8	12.9	-19.9	25.1	6.3	7.8
Forestry & Paper	-7.0	11.7	2.8	6.6		-49.7	-52.1	64.4	53.3	-11.4
Gas; Water & Multiutilities			24.8	13.9	31.0	7.3	-17.8	-0.6	7.9	2.8
General Industrials						-13.1	-30.0	23.2	37.6	-12.3
General Retailers	-19.4	21.9	14.2	3.3	16.6	-25.9	-47.8	75.2	-2.5	-11.7
Health Care Equipment & Services	-19.3	29.6	5.8	4.0	-2.9	18.6	-36.3	47.0	7.5	-7.2
Household Goods						-15.0	-28.6	30.9	1.0	-5.2
Industrial Engineering	-29.0	37.1	14.4	27.6	19.8	-7.2	-31.1	83.1	78.2	3.2
Industrial Metals	-62.2	639.9	68.3	16.8	79.8	-56.6	-83.9	307.3	72.4	-54.0
Industrial Transportation	-15.5	23.6	15.3	25.7	49.9	-20.8	-61.2	52.3	25.7	-12.2
Leisure Goods	3.7	70.9	13.4	-12.8						
Life Insurance	-41.1	7.4	17.9	17.1	18.5	-10.1	-43.3	26.5	2.0	-4.6
Media	-32.5	15.7	4.9	6.0	4.0	0.2	-34.1	28.3	21.5	-1.9
Mining	-7.7	33.5	8.6	63.0	22.9	50.4	-55.7	108.5	27.8	-29.7
Mobile Telecommunications						32.9	-25.7	4.6	14.7	8.6
Nonlife Insurance	-56.4	-9.0	-5.4	44.6	28.6	-6.2	1.2	-1.7	17.6	-12.3
Oil & Gas Producers	-16.8	4.9	12.5	25.6	-2.0	19.3	-16.0	13.3	0.5	4.8
Oil Equipment; Services & Distribution						38.1	-45.7	87.8	56.3	-10.4
Personal Goods	20.9	5.5	24.2	20.9	40.7	2.2	-42.9	105.8	76.1	-1.6
Pharmaceuticals & Biotechnology	-31.2	12.9	-12.1	28.7	-5.1	-9.5	8.0	4.2	-1.2	14.5
Real Estate Investment & Services									-2.0	-1.3
Real Estate Investment Trusts						33.8	-36.5	-44.7	6.2	2.7	-12.6
Software & Computer Services	-61.1	42.9	-6.1	16.7	-2.9	-7.5	-26.2	63.9	23.7	2.1
Support Services	-40.0	12.1	-0.9	17.5	20.4	-9.7	-27.2	28.7	19.7	-2.4
Technology Hardware & Equipment	-89.1	172.2	-9.9	5.5	-10.4	-1.2	-43.3	131.6	70.4	21.6
Tobacco	20.5	12.1	23.4	31.0	14.8	34.0	-14.6	9.9	15.0	23.9
Travel & Leisure	-24.7	46.9	29.8	18.5	27.6	-15.9	-40.8	22.5	24.2	-15.9

Observations

1. No sector has been in the top three best or worst performing sectors for more than two consecutive years.
2. The most volatile sector has been Industrial Metals which has been one of the top three best or worst performing sectors in eight years since 2002.

SECTOR TRADING VALUE

The table on this page shows the trading value by sector from January-August 2012. For example, over this period the companies in the Media sector traded a total value of £19.7bn.

The final three columns show the proportion of each sector's trade that was from companies in the three respective indices. In the case of the Media sector, 81% of the total trade of £19.7bn was attributable to companies in the FTSE 100 Index.

Sector Code	Sector	Total FTSE All Share (£m)	FTSE 100 (%)	FTSE 250 (%)	FTSE Small Cap (%)
1770	Mining	85,978.9	95	5	0
530	Oil & Gas Producers	53,632.5	91	9	0
8350	Banks	45,903.9	100	0	0
4570	Pharmaceuticals & Biotechnology	29,045.0	98	2	0
2790	Support Services	20,179.5	68	31	1
5550	Media	19,708.6	81	19	0
6570	Mobile Telecommunications	18,970.0	95	5	0
7570	Gas, Water & Multiutilities	18,394.6	96	4	0
3780	Tobacco	17,572.6	100	0	0
5750	Travel & Leisure	16,874.2	62	36	2
8570	Life Insurance	14,984.2	99	1	0
3530	Beverages	14,316.2	97	3	0
5330	Food & Drug Retailers	13,687.7	96	4	0
8770	General Financial	11,040.4	50	49	1
3570	Food Producers	10,564.0	96	2	2
5370	General Retailers	10,345.6	72	27	1
2710	Aerospace & Defence	9,767.7	81	18	0
3720	Household Goods	9,715.6	71	29	0
8670	Real Estate Investment Trusts	7,576.9	72	27	1
2750	Industrial Engineering	7,456.2	69	30	0
6530	Fixed Line Telecommunications	5,928.0	80	20	0
9530	Software & Computer Services	5,767.0	24	74	2
570	Oil Equipment, Services & Distribution	5,455.6	67	32	1
9570	Technology Hardware & Equipment	4,942.5	79	19	2
8530	Nonlife Insurance	4,490.3	58	41	1
7530	Electricity	4,422.9	81	19	0
2350	Construction & Materials	4,176.4	80	18	1
2720	General Industrials	4,101.3	64	36	0
1350	Chemicals	3,920.7	68	32	0
8980	Equity Investment Instruments	3,459.1	0	79	21
3760	Personal Goods	3,292.9	92	7	1
1750	Industrial Metals	1,935.2	67	33	0
4530	Health Care Equipment & Services	1,788.8	95	3	1
2730	Electronic & Electrical Equipment	1,717.9	0	94	6
3350	Automobiles & Parts	1,489.3	100	0	0
1730	Forestry & Paper	784.6	0	100	0
8630	Real Estate Investment & Services	643.2	0	71	29
2770	Industrial Transportation	196.9	0	86	14
3740	Leisure Goods	5.3	0	0	100
580	Alternative Energy	3.3	0	0	100

The data in the table is illustrated in the bar chart on the opposite page.

Chart: trading value on LSE by sector (Jan-Aug 2012)

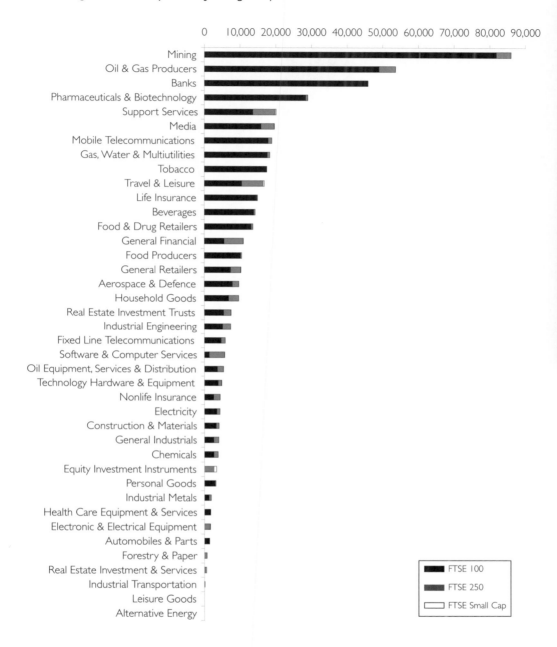

SECTOR PROFILES OF THE FTSE 100 & FTSE 250 INDICES

The chart below shows the sector weightings in the FTSE 100 and FTSE 250 indices. The figures in the chart show the weighting of sectors in the FTSE 100 Index.

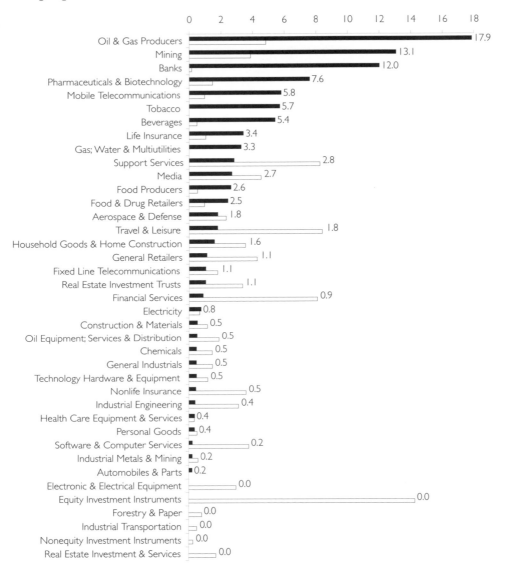

Note: Figures as of August 2012

Observations

1. The top four FTSE sectors (oil and gas producers, mining, banks and pharmaceuticals) together account for 50.6% of the total market capitalisation of the index. (In 2006, the top sectors accounted for 55% of the index capitalisation.)

2. In 1935 the FT30 Index was dominated by engineering and machinery companies. Today, the sector isn't represented at all in the FTSE 100 Index.

3. The FTSE 100 Index is still dominated by the old industries of oil, mining and banks, while the FTSE 250 has, proportionately, a greater representation of service (support, financial and computer) companies.

COMPANIES

COMPANY RANKINGS

On the following pages are tables with companies ranked according to various criteria. The tables are grouped into the following categories:

1. FTSE 350
2. FTSE 100
3. AIM
4. Investment Trusts

Table index

A summary of the tables is given below.

1. 10 largest companies by **market capitalisation**
2. 10 companies with largest average **daily trade value**
3. 5-year **share performance** 2007-2012 [FTSE 350]
4. 5-year **share performance** 2002-2007 [FTSE 350]
5. 10 companies with highest **turnover**
6. 10 companies with greatest **turnover growth** in 5 years to 2012 [FTSE 350]
7. 10 companies with greatest **turnover growth** in 5 years to 2007 [FTSE 350]
8. 10 companies with highest **ROCE** [FTSE 350]
9. 10 companies with highest **profits**
10. 10 companies with greatest **profit growth** in the 5 years to 2012 [FTSE 350]
11. 10 companies with highest **operating margins** [FTSE 350]
12. 10 companies with highest **EPS growth** in the 5 years to 2012 [FTSE 350]
13. 10 companies with highest **dividend growth** in the 5 years to 2012 [FTSE 350]
14. 10 companies with highest **dividend growth** in the 5 years to 2007 [FTSE 350]
15. 10 companies paying the most **tax** in last year
16. Best value **CEO** (best pay for performance)
17. Worst value **CEO** (highest excess remuneration)
18. 10 companies with largest **market capitalisation** [AIM]
19. 10 companies with largest **market capitalisation** (2007) [AIM]
20. 10 companies with largest **profits** [AIM]
21. 10 companies with largest **profits** (2007) [AIM]
22. 5-year **share performance** 2007-2012 [AIM]
23. 5-year **share performance** 2002-2007 [AIM]
24. 10 largest investment trusts by **capitalisation**
25. 10 **best performing** investment trusts 2007-2012
26. 10 investment trusts with highest **dividend growth** in the last 5 years

Note: All figures accurate as of 31 August 2012.

FTSE 350

Size, volume and performance

Table 1: 10 largest companies by market capitalisation

Rank	Rank (2007)	Company	EPIC	Capital (£m)
1	6	Royal Dutch Shell	RDSB	141,652
2	2	HSBC Holdings	HSBA	99,875
3	3	Vodafone Group	VOD	89,250
4	1	BP	BP.	84,016
5	4	GlaxoSmithKline	GSK	70,895
6	13	British American Tobacco	BATS	64,172
7	25	SABMiller	SAB	44,305
8	17	BG Group	BG.	43,754
9	18	Diageo	DGE	43,234
10	12	BHP Billiton	BLT	38,778

Table 2: 10 companies with largest average daily trade value

Rank	Company	EPIC	Average daily trade value (£m)
1	Rio Tinto	RIO	163
2	Vodafone Group	VOD	137
3	BHP Billiton	BLT	125
4	HSBC Holdings	HSBA	120
5	BP	BP.	116
6	GlaxoSmithKline	GSK	111
7	Barclays	BARC	96
8	Xstrata	XTA	95
9	British American Tobacco	BATS	83
10	AstraZeneca	AZN	81

Table 3: 5-year share performance 2007-2012 [FTSE 350]

Rank	Company	EPIC	5-yr change (%)
1	Dialight	DIA	581
2	Oxford Instruments	OXIG	466
3	Randgold Resources Ltd	RRS	431
4	Telecom plus	TEP	361
5	Imagination Technologies Group	IMG	352
6	Aggreko	AGK	327
7	Booker Group	BOK	311
8	ARM Holdings	ARM	290
9	Croda International	CRDA	257
10	Devro	DVO	255

Table 4: 5-year share performance 2002-2007 [FTSE 350]

Rank	Company	EPIC	5-yr change (%)
1	JKX Oil & Gas	JKX	1697.3
2	Datamonitor	DTM	1243.2
3	SOCO International	SIA	675.1
4	AVEVA Group	AVV	585.2
5	Axon Group	AXO	573.2
6	Charter	CHTR	551.9
7	Savills	SVS	548.8
8	Chemring Group	CHG	539.3
9	Detica Group	DCA	481.2
10	ITE Group	ITE	477.8

Turnover

Table 5: 10 companies with highest turnover

Rank	Rank (2007)	Company	EPIC	Turnover (£m)
1	1	Royal Dutch Shell	RDSB	302,500
2	2	BP	BP.	241,600
3		Glencore International	GLEN	119,800
4	3	Tesco	TSCO	64,540
5	4	Vodafone Group	VOD	46,420
6	9	BHP Billiton	BLT	46,050
7	18	Rio Tinto	RIO	38,950
8	6	Unilever	ULVR	38,810
9	17	SSE	SSE	31,720
10	60	Imperial Tobacco Group	IMT	29,220

Table 6: 10 companies with greatest turnover growth in 5 years to 2012 [FTSE 350]

Rank	Company	EPIC	Turnover 5-yr growth(%)
1	Booker Group	BOK	1000+
2	Stobart Group Ltd	STOB	1000+
3	International Public Partnership Ltd	INPP	1000+
4	Salamander Energy	SMDR	1000+
5	Centamin	CEY	1000+
6	Petra Diamonds Ltd	PDL	1000+
7	Raven Russia Ltd	RUS	1000+
8	Petropavlovsk	POG	911
9	Imperial Tobacco Group	IMT	824
10	Hochschild Mining	HOC	491

Table 7: 10 companies with greatest turnover growth in 5 years to 2007 [FTSE 350]

Rank	Company	EPIC	Turnover 5-yr growth(%)
1	Xstrata	XTA	1000+
2	Venture Production	VPC	1000+
3	CSR	CSR	1000+
4	Dana Petroleum	DNX	708
5	Tullow Oil	TLW	655
6	Tullett Prebon	TLPR	534
7	Big Yellow Group	BYG	510
8	Mouchel Parkman	MCHL	423
9	Helphire Group	HHR	389
10	Detica Group	DCA	375

Table 8: 10 companies with highest ROCE [FTSE 350]

Rank	Company	EPIC	ROCE(%)
1	Imperial Tobacco Group	IMT	10,300
2	Atkins (W S)	ATK	3,530
3	Carillion	CLLN	939
4	Sage Group (The)	SGE	556
5	Dixons Retail	DXNS	368
6	Aegis Group	AGS	285
7	Rightmove	RMV	270
8	William Hill	WMH	249
9	Capita Group (The)	CPI	175
10	London Stock Exchange Group	LSE	\155

Profits

Table 9: 10 companies with highest profits

Rank	Rank (2007)	Company	EPIC	Profit (£m)
1	1	Royal Dutch Shell	RDSB	35,815
2	2	BP	BP.	24,988
3	6	BHP Billiton	BLT	14,678
4	3	HSBC Holdings	HSBA	14,074
5	348	Vodafone Group	VOD	9,549
6	9	Rio Tinto	RIO	8,503
7	11	AstraZeneca	AZN	7,958
8	5	GlaxoSmithKline	GSK	7,698
9	10	Anglo American	AAL	6,938
10	7	Barclays	BARC	5,879

Table 10: 10 companies with greatest profit growth in the 5 years to 2012 [FTSE 350]

Rank	Company	EPIC	5-yr profit growth(%)
1	Croda International	CRDA	1000+
2	Hargreaves Lansdown	HL.	1000+
3	Centamin	CEY	1000+
4	Melrose	MRO	1000+
5	Oxford Instruments	OXIG	1000+
6	Ferrexpo	FXPO	981
7	Petropavlovsk	POG	912
8	BTG	BTG	785
9	Randgold Resources Ltd	RRS	729
10	Hochschild Mining	HOC	721

Table 11: 10 companies with highest operating margins [FTSE 350]

Rank	Company	EPIC	Operating margin (%)
1	John Laing Infrastructure Fund Ltd	JLIF	197
2	Derwent London	DLN	79
3	Hammerson	HMSO	77
4	Segro	SGRO	75
5	Ashmore Group	ASHM	72
6	Land Securities Group	LAND	71
7	Fresnillo	FRES	70
8	SOCO International	SIA	68
9	Great Portland Estates	GPOR	68
10	Rightmove	RMV	65

Table 12: 10 companies with highest EPS growth in the 5 years to 2012 [FTSE 350]

Rank	Company	EPIC	EPS 5-Yr Growth%
1	Centamin	CEY	1000+
2	Ferrexpo	FXPO	1000+
3	Melrose	MRO	895
4	Whitbread	WTB	799
5	Shire	SHP	659
6	Randgold Resources Ltd	RRS	654
7	Petrofac Ltd	PFC	592
8	Worldwide Healthcare Trust	WWH	561
9	Spirent Communications	SPT	515
10	Fresnillo	FRES	480

Dividends

Table 13: 10 companies with highest dividend growth in the 5 years to 2012 [FTSE 350]

Rank	Company	EPIC	5-yr Div Growth(%)
1	Edinburgh Dragon Trust	EFM	1000+
2	Hochschild Mining	HOC	886
3	RIT Capital Partners	RCP	803
4	Petrofac Ltd	PFC	700
5	Worldwide Healthcare Trust	WWH	483
6	BlackRock World Mining Trust	BRWM	460
7	Randgold Resources Ltd	RRS	409
8	Fidelity European Values	FEV	405
9	AVEVA Group	AVV	402
10	Regus	RGU	383

Table 14: 10 companies with highest dividend growth in the 5 years to 2007 [FTSE 350]

Rank	Company	EPIC	5-yr Div Growth(%)
1	Mouchel Parkman	MCHL	1000+
2	Topps Tiles	TPT	885
3	Sage Group (The)	SGE	735
4	BT Group	BT.A	655
5	ITE Group	ITE	600
6	Enterprise Inns	ETI	447
7	Vodafone Group	VOD	360
8	Aquarius Platinum Ltd	AQP	357
9	Capital & Regional	CAL	333
10	London Stock Exchange Group	LSE	329

Tax

Table 15: 10 companies paying the most tax in last year

Rank	Company	EPIC	Tax paid (£m)
1	Royal Dutch Shell	RDSB	15,700
2	BP	BP.	8,200
3	Rio Tinto	RIO	4,140
4	Vodafone Group	VOD	2,550
5	HSBC Holdings	HSBA	2,530
6	GlaxoSmithKline	GSK	2,240
7	BG Group	BG.	2,080
8	Barclays	BARC	1,930
9	Anglo American	AAL	1,840
10	British American Tobacco	BATS	1,550

FTSE 100

Table 16: Best value CEO (best pay for performance)

Rank	Company	EPIC	Excess remuneration (%)
1	Admiral	ADM	-93%
2	Hargreaves Lansdown	HL.	-89%
3	Vedanta Resources	VED	-85%
4	Severn Trent	SVT	-73%
5	Wolseley	WOS	-73%
6	Petrofac	PFC	-68%
7	GKN	GKN	-62%
8	IMI	IMI	-62%
9	Inmarsat	ISAT	-57%
10	Intertek	ITRK	-54%

Source: Obermatt

Table 17: Worst value CEO (highest excess remuneration)

Rank	Company	EPIC	Excess remuneration (%)
1	Reckitt Benckiser	RB.	1199%
2	Xstrata	XTA	391%
3	ICAP	IAP	388%
4	BG Group	BG.	322%
5	Tullow Oil	TLW	310%
6	Tesco	TSCO	226%
7	BHP Billiton	BLT	210%
8	GlaxoSmithKline	GSK	208%
9	Schroders	SDR	181%
10	Vodafone	VOD	102%

Source: Obermatt

AIM

Table 18: 10 companies with largest market capitalisation [AIM]

Rank	Name	EPIC	Capital (£m)
1	Indus Gas Ltd	INDI	1,838
2	Gulf Keystone Petroleum	GKP	1,801
3	ASOS	ASC	1,492
4	Energy XXI	EXXI	1,474
5	Cove Energy	COV	1,220
6	Coastal Energy Company	CEO	1,088
7	African Minerals Ltd	AMI	835
8	Abcam	ABC	808
9	Mulberry Group	MUL	794
10	Songbird Estates	SBD	782

Table 19: 10 companies with largest market capitalisation (2007) [AIM]

Rank	Name	EPIC	Capital (£m)
1	Sibir Energy	SBE	1,616
2	Mecom Group	MEC	1,389
3	Nikanor	NKR	1,270
4	Clipper Windpower	CWP	898
5	Central African Mining & Exploration	CFM	811
6	Playtech Ltd	PTEC	810
7	Climate Exchange	CLE	793
8	Lamprell	LAM	783
9	Peter Hambro Mining	POG	769
10	Monsoon	MSN	701

Table 20: 10 companies with largest profits [AIM]

Rank	Name	EPIC	Profit (£m)
1	SacOil Holding Ltd	SAC	5,510
2	Energy XXI	EXXI	374
3	Asian Citrus Holdings Ltd	ACHL	108
4	Asian Growth Properties Ltd	AGP	101
5	Datatec Ltd	DTC	86
6	Douglasbay Capital	DBAY	86
7	Highland Gold Mining Ltd	HGM	85
8	Valiant Petroleum	VPP	83
9	Coastal Energy Company	CEO	69
10	Origin Enterprises	OGN	63

Table 21: 10 companies with largest profits (2007) [AIM]

Rank	Name	EPIC	Profit (£m)
1	R.G.I International Ltd	RGI	88.4
2	Dawnay; Day Treveria	DTR	87.7
3	Songbird Estates	SBDB	77.2
4	Sportingbet	SBT	71.5
5	Sibir Energy	SBE	58.3
6	NETeller	NLR	56.8
7	Monsoon	MSN	53.5
8	Hotel Corporation (The)	HCP	51.2
9	RAB Capital	RAB	50.3
10	Abbey	ABBY	47.1

Table 22: 5-year share performance 2007-2012 [AIM]

Rank	Name	EPIC	5-yr share price (%)
1	ASOS	ASC	1,471
2	Sirius Petroleum	SRSP	1,233
3	Cove Energy	COV	1,099
4	Lo-Q	LOQ	917
5	Coastal Energy Company	CEO	808
6	Berkeley Mineral Resources	BMR	782
7	Judges Scientific	JDG	733
8	Abcam	ABC	551
9	Amerisur Resources	AMER	458
10	Mulberry Group	MUL	411

Table 23: 5-year share performance 2002-2007 [AIM]

Rank	Name	EPIC	5-yr share price (%)
1	Group NBT	NBT	3,353
2	Griffin Mining	GFM	2,847
3	Just Car Clinics Group	JCR	2,250
4	TMN Group	TMN	1,678
5	Cape	CIU	1,514
6	CPL Resources	CPS	1,464
7	Northern Petroleum	NOP	1,322
8	Stanley Gibbons Group (The) Ltd	SGI	1,321
9	Petroceltic International	PCI	1,150
10	Your Space	YSP	1,148

Investment Trusts

Table 24: 10 largest investment trusts by capitalisation

Rank	Rank (2007)	Investmet Trust	EPIC	Capital (£m)
1	1	Alliance Trust	ATST	2,044
2	5	RIT Capital Partners	RCP	1,810
3	3	Templeton Emerging Markets Investment Trust	TEM	1,779
4	2	Foreign & Colonial Investment Trust	FRCL	1,753
5	4	Scottish Mortgage Investment Trust	SMT	1,717
6	79	BH Macro Ltd	BHMU	1,274
7	28	Murray International Trust	MYI	1,176
8	22	3i Infrastructure Ltd	3IN	1,109
9	68	HICL Infrastructure Company Ltd	HICL	1,089
10	10	Edinburgh Investment Trust (The)	EDIN	990

Table 25: 10 best performing investment trusts 2007-2012

Rank	Investment Trust	EPIC	5-yr price change (%)
1	Biotech Growth Trust (The)	BIOG	170
2	Aberdeen Asian Smaller Companies Inv Tr	AAS	154
3	Aberdeen New Thai Investment Trust	ANW	95
4	Aberdeen Asian Income Fund Ltd	AAIF	93
5	Scottish Oriental Smaller Co's Tr (The)	SST	92
6	Standard Life UK Smaller Companies Trust	SLS	81
7	Ruffer Investment Company Ltd	RICA	76
8	Polar Capital Technology Trust	PCT	75
9	F&C US Smaller Companies	FSC	74
10	Worldwide Healthcare Trust	WWH	72

Table 26: 10 investment trusts with highest dividend growth in the last 5 years

Rank	Investment Trust	EPIC	5-yr div growth (%)
1	Edinburgh Dragon Trust	EFM	1000+
2	RIT Capital Partners	RCP	803
3	Henderson European Investment Trust	HEFT	788
4	European Investment Trust	EUT	606
5	Worldwide Healthcare Trust	WWH	483
6	BlackRock World Mining Trust	BRWM	460
7	Jupiter Primadona Growth Trust	JPG	422
8	Fidelity European Values	FEV	405
9	Impax Environmental Markets	IEM	350
10	BlackRock Latin American Investment Trust	BRLA	312

TEN BAGGERS

The term *ten bagger* was coined by Peter Lynch, the legendary manager of the Fidelity Magellan fund, in his book *One Up on Wall Street*. The phrase *ten bagger* comes from baseball and Lynch used it to describe stocks that rise ten times in value.

The table below shows the UK stocks that rose ten times or more from August 2002 to August 2012.

UK ten baggers August 2002 – August 2012

Company	TIDM	Price increase (%)	Capital (£m)	PE	Sector
Domino's Pizza UK & IRL	DOM	1,999	889	28.7	Travel & Leisure
Randgold Resources	RRS	1,741	5,707	23.6	Mining
Regus	RGU	1,667	966	24.6	Support Services
Carclo	CAR	1,577	326	51.2	Chemicals
AVEVA Group	AVV	1,576	1,264	31.0	Software & Computer Services
Tullow Oil	TLW	1,538	12,480	24.1	Oil & Gas Producers
Aggreko	AGK	1,489	6,118	23.8	Support Services
Imagination Technologies	IMG	1,334	1,440	73.7	Technology Hardware & Equipment
Cape	CIU	1,142	233	4.7	Oil Equipment; Services & Distribution
Goodwin	GDWN	1,124	93	10.4	Industrial Engineering
Antofagasta	ANTO	1,055	10,973	11.9	Mining
SDL	SDL	1,050	534	21.0	Software & Computer Services
Dialight	DIA	1,002	349	34.2	Electronic & Electrical Equipment

Observations

1. The table above does not include those companies that rose ten times in the interim only to see their share prices fall back again. Of course, in the run up to the credit crunch this included quite a few companies.

2. Jim Slater's comment that "elephants don't gallop" would seem to hold true. Many of the above ten baggers are small companies – even after rising ten times in value. As Peter Lynch says, "The very best way to make money in a market is in a small growth company that has been profitable for a couple of years and simply goes on growing."

3. It can be seen that the ten baggers come from quite a wide range of sectors. In other words, it's not necessary to look for ten baggers in just a few glamour sectors.

LONG TERM

BUY AND HOLD

The last decade or so has not been the best for buy-and-hold investors. On 2 March 1998 the FTSE 100 Index closed at 5820; at the time of writing, in September 2012, the index is trading at 5793. The question is being asked: is buy and hold is dead?

Such thinking inspired Richard Bernstein to write a paper[1] in July 2012 called, appropriately, "Is buy and hold dead?" In the paper, which advocates longer-term investing, Bernstein says-

> There are sound economic reasons why extending one's time horizon can benefit investment returns. Changes within the economy tend to be very gradual, and significant adjustments rarely happen within a short period of time. Certainly, there is plenty of daily news, but how much of that news is actually important and worth acting on? The data suggest very little of that information is meaningful and valuable. Most of it is simply noise.

He also writes-

> investment returns can be significantly hurt by strategies based on short-term, noise-driven strategies. The data clearly and consistently showed that extending one's investment time horizon was a simple method for improving investment returns.

In the paper he presents a chart showing the probability of sustaining a loss over different time horizons for an investment in the S&P 500 Index.

The chart on this page does the same for the FTSE All Share Index. The analysis was carried out on daily data for the FTSE All Share Index from 1970 to 2012.

Probability of a loss for the FTSE All Share Index (1970-2012)

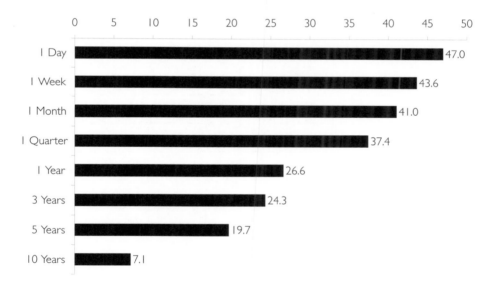

The analysis found that if an investment was made in the index on any day since 1970, the chance of the index being lower one week later (i.e. 5 trading days later) was 43.6%. Similarly, since 1970, in 41.0% of cases the index was lower than a month (20 trading days) previously.

As can be seen, the longer the time horizon of an investment, the lower the chance of loss. Conversely, the shorter the time horizon, the closer the probability of loss tends to 50/50 (i.e. the closer it becomes to a simple coin toss).

Finally, the paper makes the interesting point that while longer time horizons tend to progessively improve investment returns in many financial assets (e.g. shares), this is not necessarily the case for real assets such as gold and other commodities.

---

[1] www.rbadvisors.com

THE MARKET'S DECENNIAL CYCLE

The following table shows the annual performance of the FTSE All Share Index since 1801. The table is arranged to easily compare the performance of the market for the same year in each decade.

For example, in the third year of the 1801-1810 decade (1803), the market fell 21.9%, while in the third year of the 1811-1820 decade (1813), the market fell 0.2%. Years in which the market fell are highlighted.

At the bottom of the table is some summary analysis of the data.

Decades	1st	2nd	3rd	4th	5th	6th	7th	8th	9th	10th
1801-1810	11.0	1.4	-21.9	10.3	8.5	0.7	3.5	4.7	10.4	-9.2
1811-1820	-14.6	-7.5	-0.2	2.4	-6.2	-12.2	32.6	5.5	-8.3	3.2
1821-1830	4.5	9.4	9.2	90.7	-22.7	-20.1	4.6	-14.5	3.3	-14.8
1831-1840	-15.7	2.2	16.5	-9.3	5.0	5.2	-8.5	-3.6	-12.7	3.1
1841-1850	-9.7	7.1	12.3	16.5	-2.1	-1.8	-13.9	-13.5	-7.3	14.4
1851-1860	-0.2	9.6	-6.8	-3.2	-3.4	5.4	-5.9	6.5	-2.0	11.1
1861-1870	3.1	16.6	12.8	5.0	1.4	-22.4	-2.2	6.8	7.4	8.6
1871-1880	18.9	4.0	3.6	-5.2	-7.9	-2.4	-9.6	-11.0	12.1	4.9
1881-1890	-0.6	-6.3	-5.0	-2.1	0.2	0.6	-3.6	5.8	13.1	-6.2
1891-1900	0.7	-0.1	1.6	6.0	11.2	22.0	5.2	0.3	-2.0	-0.9
1901-1910	-4.9	-1.3	-5.6	2.5	6.2	-0.4	-14.7	8.1	4.8	-2.5
1911-1920	0.3	-0.9	-6.7	-6.9	-5.1	0.5	-10.5	11.0	2.4	-13.3
1921-1930	-5.4	17.6	2.0	9.5	4.4	2.4	8.3	8.1	-7.4	-19.4
1931-1940	-23.5	5.6	27.2	8.3	7.8	13.9	-19.3	-14.3	0.8	-13.0
1941-1950	22.6	18.6	8.1	10.7	-0.6	18.1	-2.7	-4.0	-13.9	6.4
1951-1960	2.4	-5.1	16.0	34.5	1.6	-9.0	-3.3	33.2	43.4	-4.7
1961-1970	-2.5	-1.8	10.6	-10.0	6.7	-9.3	29.0	43.4	-15.2	-7.5
1971-1980	41.9	12.8	-31.4	-55.3	136.3	-3.9	41.2	2.7	4.3	27.1
1981-1990	7.2	22.1	23.1	26.0	15.2	22.3	4.2	6.5	30.0	-14.3
1991-2000	15.1	14.8	23.3	-9.6	18.5	11.7	19.7	10.9	21.2	-8.0
2001-2010	-15.4	-25.0	16.6	9.2	18.1	13.2	2.0	-32.8	25.0	10.9
Since 1810										
up years:	11	13	14	13	14	12	10	14	13	9
average(%):	1.7	4.5	5.0	6.2	9.2	1.6	2.7	2.9	5.2	-1.2
Since 1921										
up years:	5	6	8	6	8	6	6	6	6	3
average(%):	4.7	6.6	10.6	2.6	23.1	6.6	8.8	6.0	9.8	-2.5
Since 1951										
up years:	4	3	5	3	6	3	5	5	5	2
average(%):	8.1	3.0	9.7	-0.9	32.7	4.2	15.5	10.6	18.1	0.6

Observations

1. Since 1801 the strongest years have been the 3rd, 5th and 8th years in the decades. The markets have risen 14 out of the 21 decades in these years. But the single year champion has got to be the 5th year in each decade, which has risen an average of 9.2%.

2. The stand-out weakest year in the decade since 1801 has been the 10th – this is the only year to have risen below 10 times in the 21 decades and also the only year to have a negative average change (-1.2%).

3. Generally, performance in the more recent decades has not changed too much from the long-term picture. In the six decades since 1951, the strong years are still the 3rd, 5th and 8th years, although now also joined by the 7th and 9th years. The dominance of the 5th year is greater than ever – the only year to rise in every decade since 1951. And the 10th year continues to be weakest, increasing only twice in the past six decades.

SHARES, INTEREST RATES, STERLING & GOLD SINCE WWII

FTSE All Share Index

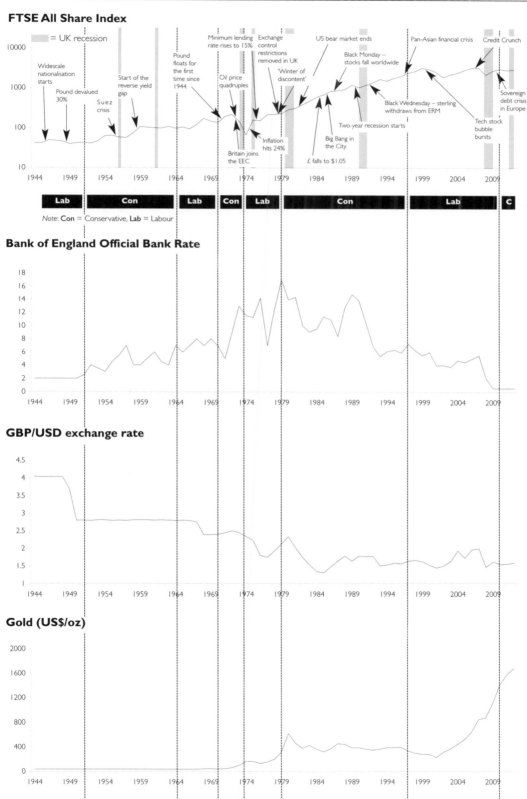

= UK recession

10000

1000

100

10

Widescale
nationalisation
starts

Pound devalued
30%

Suez
crisis

Start of the
reverse yield
gap

Pound
floats for
the first
time since
1944

Oil price
quadruples

Britain joins
the EEC

Minimum lending
rate rises to 15%

Exchange
control
restrictions
removed in UK

'Winter of
discontent'

Inflation
hits 24%

£ falls to $1.05

US bear market ends

Black Monday –
stocks fall worldwide

Big Bang in
the City

Two-year recession starts

Black Wednesday – sterling
withdraws from ERM

Pan-Asian financial crisis

Tech stock
bubble
bursts

Credit Crunch

Sovereign
debt crisis
in Europe

1944   1949   1954   1959   1964   1969   1974   1979   1984   1989   1994   1999   2004   2009

| Lab | Con | Lab | Con | Lab | Con | Lab | C |

Note: **Con** = Conservative, **Lab** = Labour

Bank of England Official Bank Rate

18
16
14
12
10
8
6
4
2
0

1944   1949   1954   1959   1964   1969   1974   1979   1984   1989   1994   1999   2004   2009

GBP/USD exchange rate

4.5
4
3.5
3
2.5
2
1.5
1

1944   1949   1954   1959   1964   1969   1974   1979   1984   1989   1994   1999   2004   2009

Gold (US$/oz)

2000
1600
1200
800
400
0

1944   1949   1954   1959   1964   1969   1974   1979   1984   1989   1994   1999   2004   2009

CORRELATION BETWEEN UK AND US MARKETS

It's generally well known that the UK market closely follows the movements of the US market. But it hasn't always been like this – as the charts below show.

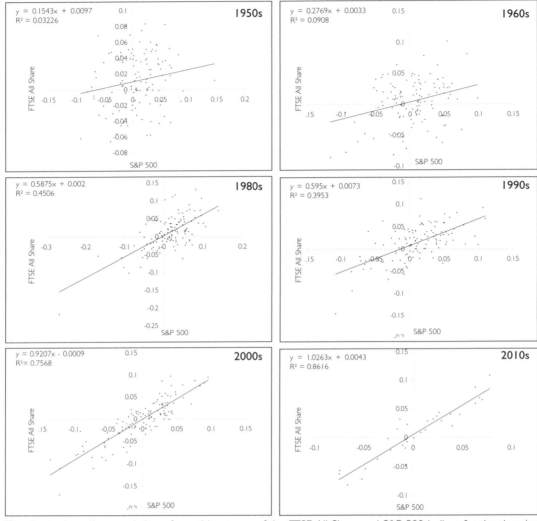

The charts show the correlation of monthly returns of the FTSE All Share and S&P 500 indices for the decades since 1950 (except the 1970s).

Analysis

In the 1950s and 1960s there was negligible correlation between the UK and US markets on a monthly basis. The US market might rise one month and the UK would respond by rising or falling – there was no connection. In the 1970s some evidence of correlation can be seen for the first time – although it was still very weak. It was not until the 1980s that the correlation became statistically significant. There could be many reasons for this increase in correlation, but one contributing factor was undoubtedly the increasing presence of computers in trading rooms. And, of course, the October crash in 1987 would have alerted many for the first time to the scale of the inter-connectedness of worldwide markets.

Correlation stayed at a similar level in the 1990s to that reached in the previous decade. But it has been in recent years that the level of correlation has soared – to almost double the level seen in the 1990s. This can be clearly seen in the last two charts, where the points are closely aligned along the line of best fit. The level of correlation between the UK and US market is now so high that the usefulness of independent analysis of the larger-cap UK market indices is pretty much moot.

ULTIMATE DEATH CROSS

In July 2012 Albert Edwards, a renowned bearish analyst at Société Générale, published a note warning that the S&P 500 Index was nearing an ultimate death cross.

What's an ultimate death cross?

Good question. Apparently it's when the 50-month moving average moves down through the 200-month moving average. At the time the *Financial Times* commented on the note, "it is, of course, very easy to scoff at this sort of thing", but they did quote Edwards as saying-

> Japan suffered a monthly death cross in 1998 and 14 years later we are still in the firm embrace of the bear.

As the combination of 50 and 200-month moving averages is an unusual configuration to see in a chart, we thought it might be interesting to see what they reveal for the UK market.

The chart below plots the FTSE All Share Index from 1945 with 50-month and 200-month simple moving averages (MAV). The Y-axis is logarithmic due to the long time period.

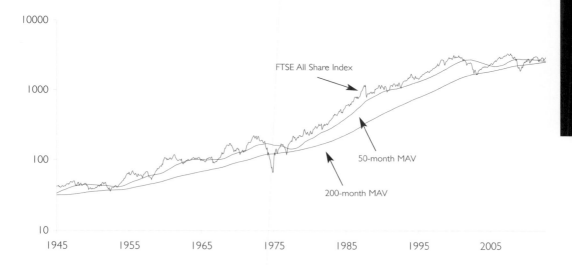

Since 1945 the closest the 50-month MAV has come to crossing the 200-month MAV was in June 1953 and then August 1977. The table below compares the difference between the moving averages for those two times with the situation today.

Date	Diff (50M-200M)	Diff(%)
Jun 1953	3.9	0.10
Aug 1977	11.4	0.06
Aug 2012	101.9	0.03

Although the difference in index points between the two moving averages was far narrower in 1953 and 1977, the percentage difference was larger than today.

So, it does indeed look like we are approaching new territory since 1945 for the index.

If the 50-month average *does* fall below the 200-month average will that signal lost decade(s) for the UK market as in Japan?

On the other hand, the closing, but then ultimate failure, of the two moving averages to cross in 1953 and 1977 could be seen as fantastic buy signals for the massive bull markets that followed soon after.

FT 30 INDEX 1935 – WHERE ARE THEY NOW?

The FT 30 Index was started by the *Financial Times* on 1 July 1935. Today the most widely followed index is the FTSE 100, but for many years the FT 30 (originally called the *FT Ordinaries*) was the measure everyone knew. The table below lists the original companies in the FT 30 Index in 1935 – a time when brokers wore bowler hats and share certificates were printed on something called paper. It's interesting to see what became of the stalwarts of UK PLC from over 70 years ago.

Company	Notes
Associated Portland Cement	The name was changed to Blue Circle Industries in 1978, and then left the index in 2001 when it was bought by Lafarge.
Austin Motor	Left the index in 1947. In 1952 Austin merged with rival Morris Motors Limited to form The British Motor Corporation Limited (BMC). In 1966 BMC bought Jaguar and two years later merged with Leyland Motors Limited to form British Leyland Motor Corporation. In 1973 British Leyland produced the Austin-badged Allegro... (the story is too painful to continue).
Bass	Left the index in 1947. In 1967 merged with Charrington United Breweries to form Bass Charrington, In 2000 its brewing operations were sold to Interbrew (which was then instructed by the Competition Commission to dispose parts to Coors), while the hotel and pub holdings were renamed Six Continents. In 2003 Six Continents was split into a pubs business (Mitchells & Butlers) and a hotels and soft drinks business (InterContinental Hotels Group).
Bolsover Colliery	Left the index in 1947. The mines were acquired by the National Coal Board on nationalisation in 1947. Bolsover Colliery closed in 1993.
Callenders Cables & Construction	Left the index in 1947. Merged with British Insulated Cables in 1945 to form British Insulated Callender's Cables, which was renamed BICC Ltd in 1975. In 2000, having sold its cable operations, it renamed its contruction business Balfour Beatty.
Coats (J & P)	Left the index in 1959. Traded as Coats Patons Ltd after the takeover of Patons & Baldwins, then as Coats Viyella, finally as Coats plc. Finally taken over by Guinness Peat Group in 2004.
Courtaulds	Demerged its chemical and textile interests in the 1980s, with the former eventually being bought by Akzo Nobel and the latter by Sara Lee. Left the index in 1998.
Distillers	Purchased by Guinness in the infamous bid battle of 1986 when it left the index.
Dorman Long	Left the index in 1947. Joined British Steel following nationalisation in 1967.
Dunlop Rubber	Left the index in 1983 and was bought in 1985 by BTR (which became Invensys).
Electrical & Musical Industries	In 1971 changed its name to EMI and later that year merged with THORN Electrical Industries to form Thorn EMI but then de-merged in 1996. In 2007 EMI Group plc was taken over by Terra Firma Capital Partners but following financial difficulties ownership passed to Citigroup in 2011.
Fine Spinners and Doublers	Fell out of the index in 1938, and was later bought by Courtaulds in 1963.
General Electric	General Electric was re-named Marconi in 1999, suffered disastrous losses in the dot-com crash and was bought by Ericsson in 2006.
Guest Keen & Nettlefolds	Guest Keen is better known as GKN and is still in the FT 30 today.
Harrods	Left the index in 1959 when it was bought by House of Fraser, and then later by Mohamed Al Fayed.
Hawker Siddeley	Left the index in 1991, and was then bought in 1992 by BTR (which became Invensys).
Imperial Chemical Industries	Spun out Zeneca in 1993, and the rump (called ICI) was sold to Akzo Nobel in 2007.
Imperial Tobacco	Still going strong.
International Tea Co Stores	Fell out of the index in 1947, was acquired by BAT Industries in 1972 and ended up as Somerfield in 1994.
London Brick	Replaced in the index by Hanson which bought it in 1984.
Murex	Left the index in 1967 due to "poor share performance". Acquired by BOC Group in 1967.
Patons & Baldwins	Left the index in 1960 when bought by J&P Coats.
Pinchin Johnson & Associates	Left the index in 1960 when bought by Courtaulds.

Company	Notes
Rolls-Royce	In 1971 RR was taken into state ownership, the motor car business was floated separately in 1973, and RR returned to the private sector in 1987.
Tate & Lyle	Still going strong, although its sugar refining and golden syrup business was sold to American Sugar Refining in 2010.
Turner & Newall	Left the index in 1982. The company was heavily involved with asbestos production, so it is not surprising that things ended badly. In 1998 the business was acquired by Federal-Mogul, which soon after filed for Chapter 11 protection as a result of asbestos claims.
United Steel	Left the index in 1951. The iron and steel works on nationalisation became part of British Steel Corporation (and now part of Tata Steel); while the mining interests passed to the National Coal Board (now closed).
Vickers	Left the index in 1986. Bought by Rolls-Royce in 1999.
Watney Combe & Reid	Left the index in 1972 when it was bought by Grand Metropolitan, which itself became part of Diageo.
Woolworth (FW)	Left the index in 1971. Bought by the forerunner of Kingfisher in 1982, and then de-merged and re-listed in 2001. But the remaining Woolworths stores all closed by January 2009.

Of the 30 companies only four exist today as listed companies: GKN, Imperial Tobacco, Rolls-Royce and Tate & Lyle (all of which are in the FTSE 100 Index). And only GKN and Tate & Lyle are in today's FT30.

The star performer from the original line-up has been Imperial Tobacco.

It's interesting to note the complete lack of representation of the four sectors that dominate the UK market today – no banks, telecom, oil or drug companies.

FTSE 100 INDEX – 1984

The FTSE 100 Index was started on 3 January 1984 with a base level of 1000. The table below shows the original companies in the index. Of the initial 100 companies only 18 remain in the index today (indicated in bold in the table, and with their new names in brackets) – a sign of the great changes in UK PLC in under 30 years.

Allied – Lyons	Ferranti	Plessey Co.
Associated British Foods	Fisons	**Prudential Corporation [Prudential]**
Associated Dairies Group	General Accident Fire & Life	RMC Group
Barclays Bank [Barclays]	General Electric	Racal Electronics
Barratt Developments	Glaxo Holdings	Rank Organisation
Bass	Globe Investment Trust	**Reckitt & Colman [Reckitt Benckiser Group]**
BAT Industries	Grand Metropolitan	Redland
Beecham Group	**Great Universal Stores [Experian]**	**Reed International [Reed Elsevier]**
Berisford (S. & W.)	Guardian Royal Exchange	**Rio Tinto – Zinc Corporation [Rio Tinto]**
BICC	Guest Keen & Nettlefolds	Rowntree Mackintosh
Blue Circle Industries	Hambro Life Assurance	**Royal Bank of Scotland Group**
BOC Group	Hammerson Prop.Inv. & Dev. 'A'	Royal Insurance
Boots Co.	Hanson Trust Harrisons & Crossfield	**Sainsbury (J.)**
Bowater Corporation	Hawker Siddeley Group	Scottish & Newcastle Breweries
BPB Industries	House of Fraser	Sears Holdings
British & Commonwealth	Imperial Chemical Industries	Sedgwick Group
British Aerospace	Imperial Cont. Gas Association	**Shell Trans. & Trad. Co. [Royal Dutch Shell]**
British Elect. Traction Co.	Imperial Group	Smith & Nephew Associated Co's.
British Home Stores	Johnson Matthey	Standard Chartered Bank
British Petroleum [BP]	Ladbroke Group	Standard Telephones & Cables
Britoil	**Land Securities**	Sun Alliance & London Insurance
BTR	**Legal & General Group**	Sun Life Assurance Society
Burton Group	**Lloyds Bank [Lloyds Banking Group]**	THORN EMI
Cable & Wireless	Lonrho	Tarmac
Cadbury Schweppes	MEPC	**Tesco**
Commercial Union Assurance [Aviva]	MFI Furniture Group	Trafalgar House
Consolidated Gold Fields	**Marks & Spencer**	Trusthouse Forte
Courtaulds	Midland Bank	Ultramar
Dalgety Distillers Co.	National Westminster Bank	**Unilever**
CJ Rothschild	Northern Foods	United Biscuits
Edinburgh Investment Trust	P & O Steam Navigation Co.	Whitbread & Co. 'A'
English China Clays	**Pearson (S.) & Son [Pearson]**	Wimpey (George)
Exco International	Pilkington Brothers	

The following table compares the market capitalisations of the top five largest companies in the index in 1984 and today.

	Rank (1984)	Capital (£m)	Rank (2012)	Capital (£m)
1	British Petroleum Co.	7,401	Royal Dutch Shell	141,652
2	Shell Trans. & Trad. Co.	6,365	HSBC Holdings	99,875
3	General Electric Co.	4,915	Vodafone Group	89,250
4	Imperial Chemical Industries	3,917	BP	84,016
5	Marks & Spencer	2,829	GlaxoSmithKline	70,895

Oil is still there today, but industrial, chemical and retail have been replaced by bank, telecom and pharmaceutical.

In 1984 the total market capitalisation of the index was £100,145 million; in 2012 the total market capitalisation is £1,639,594 million. It's interesting to note that Shell's market cap. today is 40% larger than the whole FTSE 100 Index in 1984.

GOLD AND THE STOCK MARKET

UK stock market shares are priced in sterling. But what would the market look like if shares were priced in gold? Gold is a solid asset, unlike sterling which is a fiat currency with a woolly relationship to the laws of supply and demand.

The chart on this page plots the daily value of the FTSE All Share Index divided by the daily gold fixing price in sterling. The resulting chart is effectively the market index priced in gold. For reference, UK recessions are shaded grey.

Daily FTSE All Share Index / gold (GBP) [1970-2012]

The steep fall in the chart from 1970 to 1975 reflects the fall in the stock market and rise in the gold price during the 1970s oil crisis. Then from 1975 to 1980 the chart is flat-ish as both shares and gold rose.

From 1980 to 2000 was the great equity bull market, during which gold took a back seat and did little. Since then stocks have generally been weak and gold very strong – hence the fall in the chart over this period.

Some key levels for the chart are shown in the following table.

Event	Date	FTSE All Share/gold
1974 low	Dec 74	0.79
1980 low	Jan 80	0.68
Today	Aug 12	2.96

For the moment, the trend of the chart is decisively down, towards the lows seen in 1974 and 1980. To return to the low of 1980 the chart must fall 77%, which could happen by:

1. the FTSE All Share Index falling from its level today of 3042 to 699, while the gold price stays steady, or

2. the gold price increasing from 1028 (in sterling today) to 4473 while the equity index stays where it is, or

3. a combination of the above.

THE LONG, LONG TERM

The chart below plots a composite UK stock market index from 1693 to 2012. Yes, that's 1693 – a 319-year chart. To put the starting date of the chart in some context,

1. just seven years before this date Sir Isaac Newton had presented his law of universal gravitation,
2. eight years later the seed drill was invented by Jethro Tull, and
3. the English and French were fighting.

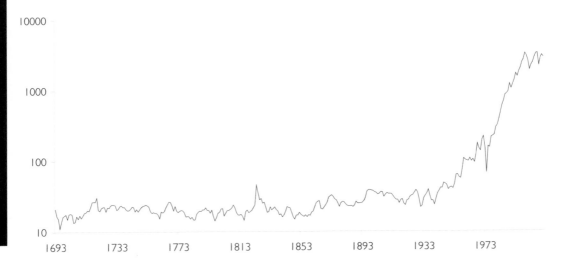

What can one do with data going back such a long way? Two academics used the data history to check the persistency of monthly seasonality effects in the (very) long term. Their paper[1] has some interesting findings-

*   Many months have under- or outperformed for long periods but none have done so persistently over the whole 300 years.
*   Of all the months, July and October displayed the greatest persistency of underperformance.
*   December has the strongest record of outperforming the market. Before 1830 there was a very strong December effect, but this weakened (possibly as the January effect grew). Other strong months have been January, April and August.
*   From having lower returns, after the 1850s January displayed stronger returns, which is attributed to the beginning of the celebration of Christmas as a public holiday from around 1835. The authors support this theory by their finding that stock markets in Christmas-celebrating countries significantly outperform stock markets in non-Christmas-celebrating countries around the turn of the year.
*   In contrast to the monthly seasonality effects above, the six-month effect ("Sell in May…") has shown robustness over the whole 300-year period and has been significantly strong since the 1950s.
*   They attribute this six-month effect to vacation behaviour.
*   They found that the stock market in the summer period underperformed the risk-free rate.
*   A strategy based on the six-month effect beats the market more than 80% of the time over a 5-year time horizon and over 90% of the time for a 10-year time horizon.

---

[1] Zhang, Cherry Yi and Jacobsen, Ben, 'Are Monthly Seasonals Real? A Three Century Perspective', *The Review of Finance* (6 September 2012).

THE LONG TERM FORMULA

The chart below plots the FTSE All Share Index from 1920 to the present day. Notes:

1. The Y-scale is logarithmic, which presents percentage (rather than absolute) changes better over long periods, and so is more suitable for long-term charts.

2. The straight line is a line of best fit calculated by regression analysis.

$$y = 3.0584e^{0.0002x}$$
$$R^2 = 0.9206$$

Observations

The R^2 for the line of best fit is 0.92, which is fairly high (i.e. the line of best fit fairly accurately approximates the real data points).

The FTSE All Share Index traded below the long-term trend line (line of best fit) from 1938 to 1984, and then traded above the trend line until 2008 (having only just stayed above it in 2003).

Forecasts

The equation of the line of best fit in the chart above is-

$$y = 3.058400662e^{0.000167346x}$$

The equation allows us to make forecasts for the FTSE All Share Index. It is, in effect, the Holy Grail, the key to the stock market – as simple as that!

For example, at the time of writing the FTSE All Share Index is 2991; while the above equation forecasts a value today (according to the long-term trend line) of 2996 (accurate to within 0.2%). Admittedly, that is something of a fluke. As can be seen in the above chart the index can spend long periods trading above or below the long-term trend line; it just happens that at the moment it is trading close to the trend line.

But, if we think that the trend of the market in the last 90 years will broadly continue, then we can use the equation to forecast the level of the FTSE All Share Index in the future. And this is what has been done in the table. Forecasts for the FTSE 100 Index have also been given.

Date	FTSE All Share Forecast	FTSE 100 Forecast	Chng(%)
Dec 2018	4,410	8473	+48
Dec 2023	5,986	11,501	+101
Dec 2033	11,031	21,195	+271
Dec 2063	69,015	132,603	+2,222

- The equation estimates that the FTSE 100 will be at 8473 in December 2018 (48% above the current level).

- Looking forward 10 years, to 2023, the forecast is for a FTSE 100 level of 11,501 (+101%).

- And in 50 year's time (well, why not?) the FTSE 100 is forecast to be 132,603 (+2222%).

Now's the time to place those 50-year spread bets.

Definition of statistics-

> The science of producing unreliable facts from reliable figures.
> Evan Esar

MARGINAL UTILITY

COMPANY ADDRESSES

We can put the 100 companies of the FTSE 100 Index into four groups:

1. *City Slickers* – companies with their registered address in London (52 companies)
2. *Provincial Hayseeds* – companies with their registered address in the provinces (38 companies)
3. *Dodgy Islanders* – companies with their registered address in the Channel Islands (9 companies)
4. *Una Paloma Blanca* – companies with their registered address in a café in Madrid (International Consolidated Airlines)

The table below lists companies and the group in which they belong.

City Slickers	Provincial Hayseeds	Dodgy Islanders
Anglo American, Antofagasta, Ashmore Group, Associated British Foods, AstraZeneca, Aviva, Babcock International Group, BAE Systems, Barclays, BHP Billiton, BP, British American Tobacco, British Land Co, BT Group, Bunzl, Burberry Group, Capita Group, Capital Shopping Centres Group, Carnival, Diageo, Eurasian Natural Resources Corporation, Evraz, Fresnillo, Hammerson, HSBC Holdings, ICAP, Intertek Group, ITV, Johnson Matthey, Kazakhmys, Kingfisher, Land Securities Group, Legal & General Group, Marks & Spencer Group, National Grid, Old Mutual, Pearson, Prudential, Reed Elsevier, Rexam, Rio Tinto, Rolls-Royce Group, Royal Dutch Shell, RSA Insurance Group, Sainsbury (J), Schroders, Smith & Nephew, Smiths Group, Standard Chartered, Tate & Lyle, Tullow Oil, Vedanta Resources, Xstrata	Aberdeen Asset Management, Admiral Group, Aggreko, AMEC, ARM Holdings, BG Group, British Sky Broadcasting Group, Centrica, Compass Group, CRH, Croda International, G4S, GKN, GlaxoSmithKline, Hargreaves Lansdown, IMI, Imperial Tobacco Group, InterContinental Hotels Group, Lloyds Banking Group, Meggitt, Morrison (Wm) Supermarkets, Next, Pennon Group, Reckitt Benckiser Group, Royal Bank of Scotland Group, SABMiller, Sage Group, Serco Group, Severn Trent, SSE, Standard Life, Tesco, Unilever, United Utilities Group, Vodafone Group, Weir Group, Whitbread	Experian, Glencore International, Petrofac Ltd, Polymetal International, Randgold Resources Ltd, Resolution Ltd, Shire, Wolseley, WPP Group

What can we make of this?

Probably not much. It's unlikely that, say, Glencore International is really being run from a room above a chip shop in St Helier.

However, it's possible that companies that share a desire to register their addresses in, say, the Channel Islands may also share other characteristics. And it might be interesting to compare the performance of companies with such shared characteristics with other groups.

The following chart plots the performance of three share portfolios since January 2010. Each is an equally-weighted portfolio of all the companies in their respective group.

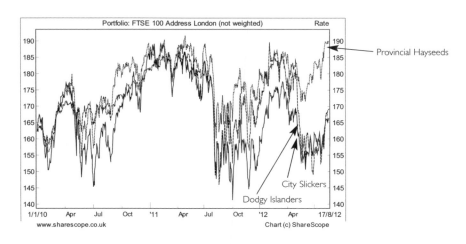

Let's hear it for the Hayseeds. Since January 2010 they've fairly consistently been the better performing group, and recently they have decisively left the City Slickers and the Dodgy Islanders in their wake.

CHANCELLORS AND THE STOCK MARKET

Since 1945 there have been 22 chancellors of the exchequer, 14 of them Conservative and eight Labour.

Which chancellors were the most investor-friendly?

The chart on this page lists the 22 chancellors of the exchequer since 1945 with the years they were in office. For each chancellor, two values are plotted:

1. the percentage change in the value of the FTSE All Share Index during their period in office (white bars), and
2. the above value adjusted by annualising, to allow for comparison of chancellors in office for different lengths of time (black bars).

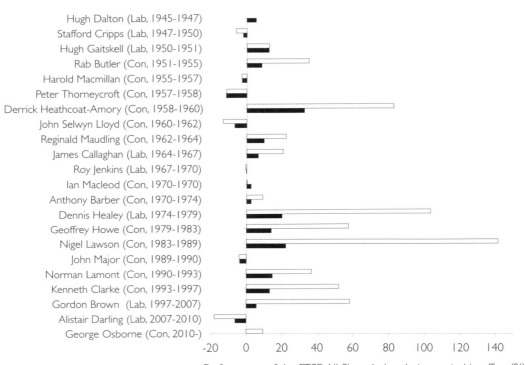

Performance of the FTSE All Share Index during period in office (%)

Observations

1. Six chancellors left office with the market lower than when they started: three of these chancellors were Conservative and three were Labour.

2. The stock market suffered its worst period under the chancellorship of Alistair Darling (although it must be admitted that he did not inherit the soundest of economies).

3. The chancellor seeing the greatest rise in the market was Nigel Lawson; the market rose 141% during his time in office. That performance was followed by Denis Healey and Derrick Heathcoat-Amory.

4. However, looking at the annualised figures we see that the best chancellor for the stock market was Derrick Heathcoat-Amory who become chancellor when Jerry Lewis' 'Great Balls of Fire' was top of the hit parade (7 Jan 1958).

CREDIT CRUNCH FALLOUT

On 14 September 2007 Northern Rock sought liquidity support from the Bank of England and queues formed outside its branches. It was the first run on a British bank for 150 years. In the public eye this was the start of the credit crunch.

The stock market had peaked a couple of months earlier, appropriately on a Friday 13th (13 July). From then the FTSE 100 Index fell 48% to a low on 3 March 2009 and has since then bounced back but (as of the time of writing) failed to recover its pre-crunch level.

Since the 2007 market high many companies have gone bust, been taken over, or (in the case of some banks) nationalised. The table below lists the 11 companies whose share price has fallen more than 99% over this period but are still hanging in there.

Company	TIDM	Price since 13/7/07(%)	Capital (£m)	PE	Sector
AEA Technology Group	AAT	-99.9	1	5.5	Support Services
Hampson Industries	HAMP	-99.9	1	0.0	Aerospace & Defense
Superglass Holdings	SPGH	-99.9	3		Construction & Materials
Styles & Wood Group	STY	-99.8	5	14.2	Support Services
Mouchel Group	MCHL	-99.8	1		Support Services
Helphire Group	HHR	-99.7	4		Financial Services
Hibu	HIBU	-99.7	29		Media
Invesco Property Income Trust	IPI	-99.4	1	0.4	Real Estate Investment & Services
Findel	FDL	-99.3	64	4.2	General Retailers
Independent News & Media	INM	-99.2	81	1.2	Media
UK Coal	UKC	-99.0	17	0.3	Mining

But the credit crunch has not been bad for all companies. The following table lists the 13 companies whose share price has increased at least 200% since July 2007.

Company	TIDM	Price since 13/7/07(%)	Capital (£m)	PE	Sector
Medusa Mining Ltd	MML	458	623	9.0	Mining
Dialight	DIA	453	349	34.2	Electronic & Electrical Equipment
Randgold Resources Ltd	RRS	435	5,707	23.6	Mining
Oxford Instruments	OXIG	354	718	35.5	Electronic & Electrical Equipment
Carclo	CAR	326	326	51.2	Chemicals
Telecom Plus	TEP	320	584	24.7	Fixed Line Telecommunications
Aggreko	AGK	276	6,118	23.8	Support Services
ARM Holdings	ARM	273	7,905	68.9	Technology Hardware & Equipment
Imagination Technologies	IMG	269	1,440	73.7	Technology Hardware & Equipment
Booker Group	BOK	264	1,602	19.6	Food & Drug Retailers
Croda International	CRDA	246	3,308	20.1	Chemicals
Petrofac Ltd	PFC	209	5,112	14.6	Oil Equipment; Services & Distribution
Devro	DVO	204	507	14.9	Food Producers

SUN AND THE STOCK MARKET

When the sun shines do you find yourself hovering over the trading screen enthusiastically adding stocks to your portfolio? Or on cloudy days when the rain beats against the window do you sit morosely at your desk, your finger stabbing at the sell button?

Two academic papers seem to think this is how you behave. The first paper[1], published in 2003, analysed 26 international stock exchanges and found that sunshine was "strongly positively correlated" with market index returns. The authors attributed this to sunny weather fostering an "upbeat mood". They even claimed it was possible (after trading costs) to trade profitably on the weather. A second paper[2], published in 2007, found that the sunshine effect was stronger for stock exchanges further away from the equator (e.g. exchanges in dark, gloomy northern European countries) and that the effect did not exist on the equator itself.

This seemed a fun and easy topic to study, so we dived in.

The chart below plots daily sun hours (at Heathrow) against the FTSE 100 Index return on the same day.

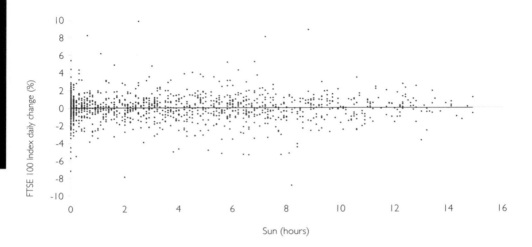

At first glance, you might think that the chart shows no correlation between the two series (i.e. sun hours and index returns). And you'd be right. Even second or third glances will not reveal any positive correlation. In fact, if you look very closely and squint, you may even see a negative correlation – which is not at all what we want.

We should have stopped there. But we were motivated to find some correlation. We'd read the academic papers and also paid a reasonable amount of cash for the weather data (stock tip: if the Met Office is ever privatised…).

So, on we went.

Perhaps the effect does not exist for the FTSE 100 Index which, after all, is heavily influenced by foreign investors, who are trading from their pools in the Caribbean or skyscrapers in Shanghai and who are unlikely to be affected greatly by how sunny it is in Orpington. So, we looked at sun hours and the FTSE 250 Index – an index more closely reflecting UK PLC and possibly attracting more domestic investors. No correlation.

Perhaps the effect really displays itself for smaller stocks? We drafted in the FTSE Small Cap Index. No correlation.

The AIM market – home of optimistic punters with a sunny disposition. Surely the sunshine effect will reveal itself there? Nothing.

OK. Let's start manipulating the data.

We calculated the average daily sun hours for the winter and summer periods and then adjusted the daily sun hours data by calculating the daily divergence of sun hours from their seasonal average. After all, just two hours of sunshine in the winter could be considered a sunny day. That should do it. No.

We limited the analysis to just those days with extremes of sunshine (i.e. daily sun hours one standard deviation away from the average). Nothing.

Perhaps the change in sun hours from one day to the next would work? In other words, the effect would kick in when a sunny day followed a cloudy day, or vice versa. Nada.

In desperation to rescue something from all the research, we looked at sun hours against daily trading volumes. If the curmudgeonly UK investor wasn't inspired by the sun to increase his net equity exposure, perhaps he at least punted around a bit more. Well, finally, on this one... no. No correlation.

At the end of everything the best we could do was the chart below – the FTSE 250 Index plotted against the change in sun hours from the previous day.

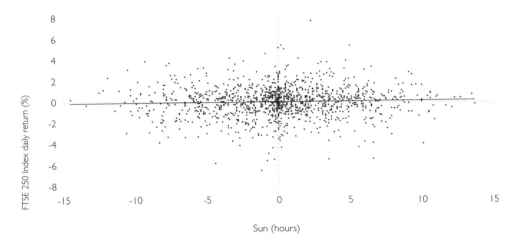

Sun (hours)

Hardly much of an improvement on the first chart – still just a random mass of uncorrelated dots. At least the correlation is (minutely) positive, but we wouldn't recommend trading off of it.

Summary

So, who is wrong, the papers or our research? It's difficult to say. Our data covered the period 2007-12, while the first academic paper looked at data for the period 1982-97. Possibly the effect has changed in the intervening years.

But if the academic papers are right, and the sunshine effect does exist, this would seem to conflict with the strongest seasonality effect in the market – whereby the market in the (dark) winter months outperforms the (sunny) summer months. Tricky thing, the market.

---

[1] Hirshleifer, D. and T. Shumway, 'Good day sunshine: Stock returns and the weather', *The Journal of Finance* 58:3 (2003).
[2] Keel, S. P. and M. L. Roush, 'A meta-analysis of the international evidence of cloud cover on stock returns', *Review of Accounting and Finance* 6:3 (2007).

SINCLAIR NUMBERS

FTSE 100 INDEX DAILY PEFORMANCE

Date	Up(%)	Avg Change (%)	Std Dev	Date	Up(%)	Avg Change (%)	Std Dev
2 Jan	56	0.3	1.1	22 Feb	40	-0.1	0.6
3 Jan	69	0.3	1.2	23 Feb	45	-0.2	1.0
4 Jan	55	0.2	1.4	24 Feb	40	-0.1	0.9
5 Jan	45	-0.1	1.0	25 Feb	70	0.4	1.1
6 Jan	60	0.3	0.9	26 Feb	60	0.3	0.8
7 Jan	30	-0.2	1.0	27 Feb	45	-0.2	0.9
8 Jan	45	-0.1	0.7	28 Feb	45	-0.2	1.1
9 Jan	40	-0.1	1.0	29 Feb	40	-0.1	1.4
10 Jan	35	-0.1	0.9	1 Mar	65	0.3	1.1
11 Jan	35	-0.2	0.7	2 Mar	50	-0.1	1.4
12 Jan	40	-0.3	0.7	3 Mar	55	0.1	1.0
13 Jan	35	-0.2	0.9	4 Mar	60	0.4	1.2
14 Jan	60	-0.1	1.5	5 Mar	50	0.0	1.3
15 Jan	60	0.2	1.3	6 Mar	55	0.2	1.0
16 Jan	60	0.2	0.9	7 Mar	45	-0.2	0.8
17 Jan	55	0.2	0.9	8 Mar	65	0.1	0.8
18 Jan	60	0.2	1.1	9 Mar	45	0.0	0.8
19 Jan	40	-0.2	0.8	10 Mar	70	0.3	1.3
20 Jan	30	-0.5	0.8	11 Mar	45	-0.2	1.0
21 Jan	40	-0.5	1.3	12 Mar	40	-0.3	1.4
22 Jan	50	0.0	1.3	13 Mar	45	0.1	1.6
23 Jan	35	-0.4	0.9	14 Mar	60	0.3	1.3
24 Jan	60	0.5	1.2	15 Mar	50	0.1	1.0
25 Jan	35	-0.2	0.7	16 Mar	45	0.0	1.3
26 Jan	80	0.7	1.1	17 Mar	55	0.0	1.4
27 Jan	50	0.2	1.3	18 Mar	50	0.1	1.2
28 Jan	55	0.1	1.1	19 Mar	65	0.1	0.8
29 Jan	40	-0.2	1.0	20 Mar	50	0.1	1.0
30 Jan	60	0.3	1.1	21 Mar	47	0.1	1.0
31 Jan	65	0.3	0.8	22 Mar	40	-0.4	1.2
1 Feb	65	0.6	1.0	23 Mar	45	0.1	1.0
2 Feb	75	0.3	0.9	24 Mar	50	-0.2	1.4
3 Feb	50	0.3	1.2	25 Mar	47	0.2	1.2
4 Feb	45	-0.2	1.0	26 Mar	55	0.2	1.0
5 Feb	45	-0.2	1.3	27 Mar	53	0.0	1.0
6 Feb	60	0.0	0.9	28 Mar	35	-0.3	0.7
7 Feb	55	0.1	1.2	29 Mar	56	0.2	0.8
8 Feb	55	0.2	1.0	30 Mar	45	-0.4	1.2
9 Feb	55	0.0	0.7	31 Mar	44	0.1	1.4
10 Feb	35	-0.3	0.8	1 Apr	75	0.5	1.2
11 Feb	60	0.4	1.0	2 Apr	67	0.7	1.2
12 Feb	35	-0.1	1.2	3 Apr	43	-0.3	1.1
13 Feb	65	0.2	0.6	4 Apr	53	0.1	0.9
14 Feb	45	0.1	0.7	5 Apr	71	0.3	0.7
15 Feb	60	0.1	0.7	6 Apr	63	0.2	0.7
16 Feb	45	0.2	1.1	7 Apr	45	0.2	1.1
17 Feb	75	0.4	0.9	8 Apr	22	-0.3	0.7
18 Feb	42	0.0	0.7	9 Apr	65	0.3	0.8
19 Feb	45	-0.1	1.1	10 Apr	53	0.3	1.7
20 Feb	40	-0.3	1.1	11 Apr	38	-0.2	0.9
21 Feb	45	0.0	0.8	12 Apr	58	0.1	0.7

Date	Up(%)	Avg Change (%)	Std Dev
13 Apr	59	0.2	0.6
14 Apr	28	-0.3	0.9
15 Apr	65	0.4	0.9
16 Apr	58	0.1	1.2
17 Apr	59	0.0	1.1
18 Apr	50	0.0	1.0
19 Apr	52	0.2	0.7
20 Apr	58	-0.1	1.2
21 Apr	39	-0.1	0.5
22 Apr	47	0.1	0.8
23 Apr	38	-0.2	0.9
24 Apr	50	0.1	1.1
25 Apr	60	0.1	0.6
26 Apr	71	0.3	0.6
27 Apr	50	-0.2	1.1
28 Apr	50	0.1	1.1
29 Apr	47	0.3	0.9
30 Apr	57	0.2	0.7
1 May	50	0.1	0.8
2 May	75	0.6	0.9
3 May	59	-0.2	1.1
4 May	53	-0.1	1.2
5 May	50	0.0	1.0
6 May	63	0.3	1.0
7 May	38	-0.5	0.9
8 May	50	0.0	1.1
9 May	38	-0.1	0.7
10 May	43	0.3	1.5
11 May	52	0.1	1.1
12 May	55	0.0	0.9
13 May	55	0.2	0.9
14 May	33	-0.6	1.4
15 May	52	0.2	0.9
16 May	43	0.1	0.6
17 May	48	-0.2	1.3
18 May	57	0.2	0.9
19 May	55	-0.2	1.4
20 May	50	-0.2	1.0
21 May	57	0.0	0.8
22 May	52	0.0	1.0
23 May	43	-0.3	1.2
24 May	43	-0.1	0.8
25 May	53	-0.2	1.1
26 May	56	0.3	0.8
27 May	41	0.0	1.1
28 May	53	0.1	0.7
29 May	69	0.3	0.7
30 May	18	-0.5	1.3
31 May	59	0.1	0.6
1 June	62	0.4	1.1
2 June	50	0.2	1.0

Date	Up(%)	Avg Change (%)	Std Dev
3 June	63	0.2	0.8
4 June	53	0.0	1.0
5 June	55	0.1	0.8
6 June	57	0.0	1.0
7 June	48	0.0	0.8
8 June	38	-0.1	0.9
9 June	45	0.2	0.8
10 June	50	-0.1	0.7
11 June	52	0.0	1.0
12 June	43	-0.2	0.9
13 June	52	-0.2	0.8
14 June	43	-0.1	1.1
15 June	48	-0.1	1.0
16 June	65	0.2	0.5
17 June	65	0.3	1.0
18 June	38	-0.3	0.7
19 June	48	-0.1	1.0
20 June	38	-0.3	0.8
21 June	57	0.1	0.8
22 June	43	-0.3	0.9
23 June	35	-0.3	0.8
24 June	40	-0.4	0.9
25 June	57	0.1	0.8
26 June	38	-0.5	1.0
27 June	57	0.1	0.8
28 June	67	0.2	0.9
29 June	57	0.1	1.2
30 June	60	0.0	0.9
1 Jul	65	0.3	1.5
2 Jul	57	0.0	1.1
3 Jul	67	0.3	1.2
4 Jul	55	0.3	0.8
5 Jul	40	0.1	1.0
6 Jul	55	0.1	1.0
7 Jul	60	0.4	1.0
8 Jul	25	-0.2	0.9
9 Jul	60	0.1	0.8
10 Jul	35	-0.5	0.9
11 Jul	50	-0.3	1.5
12 Jul	35	-0.1	0.7
13 Jul	70	0.3	0.9
14 Jul	60	0.3	1.0
15 Jul	45	-0.1	1.7
16 Jul	50	0.1	0.8
17 Jul	65	0.3	1.3
18 Jul	35	-0.2	1.1
19 Jul	50	-0.1	1.3
20 Jul	45	-0.1	0.8
21 Jul	45	-0.1	0.9
22 Jul	45	-0.5	1.5
23 Jul	60	0.1	1.0

Date	Up(%)	Avg Change (%)	Std Dev
24 Jul	45	-0.4	1.1
25 Jul	45	0.2	1.2
26 Jul	55	0.0	1.0
27 Jul	55	0.1	1.0
28 Jul	75	0.2	0.6
29 Jul	75	0.5	1.4
30 Jul	55	0.3	0.9
31 Jul	45	0.2	1.0
1 Aug	55	-0.3	1.3
2 Aug	80	0.6	1.0
3 Aug	40	-0.2	1.1
4 Aug	30	-0.4	0.9
5 Aug	50	-0.2	1.3
6 Aug	40	-0.2	1.4
7 Aug	65	0.3	0.9
8 Aug	60	0.1	1.3
9 Aug	55	0.1	1.0
10 Aug	30	-0.6	1.4
11 Aug	45	0.0	1.3
12 Aug	70	0.4	1.1
13 Aug	60	0.2	1.1
14 Aug	70	0.2	1.0
15 Aug	60	0.1	1.2
16 Aug	55	-0.1	1.1
17 Aug	60	0.1	1.2
18 Aug	55	0.0	1.5
19 Aug	45	-0.3	1.3
20 Aug	55	0.1	0.7
21 Aug	65	0.2	1.2
22 Aug	55	0.3	1.0
23 Aug	50	0.0	0.8
24 Aug	75	0.3	0.9
25 Aug	69	0.0	1.0
26 Aug	44	-0.1	0.8
27 Aug	56	0.2	1.1
28 Aug	50	-0.3	1.4
29 Aug	50	0.0	0.8
30 Aug	75	0.4	1.0
31 Aug	63	0.2	1.0
1 Sep	65	0.3	1.2
2 Sep	50	0.0	1.0
3 Sep	55	0.0	1.5
4 Sep	60	0.0	1.0
5 Sep	50	-0.4	1.1
6 Sep	65	0.0	1.1
7 Sep	50	0.1	1.5
8 Sep	40	0.0	1.1
9 Sep	30	-0.3	0.8
10 Sep	40	-0.3	1.2
11 Sep	32	-0.1	0.9
12 Sep	45	-0.3	1.2

Date	Up(%)	Avg Change (%)	Std Dev
13 Sep	50	0.1	0.9
14 Sep	55	-0.1	1.4
15 Sep	50	-0.2	1.4
16 Sep	60	-0.1	1.2
17 Sep	50	0.2	1.6
18 Sep	50	-0.1	1.4
19 Sep	50	0.2	2.3
20 Sep	50	-0.1	1.4
21 Sep	35	-0.4	1.0
22 Sep	50	-0.3	1.4
23 Sep	35	-0.2	1.1
24 Sep	40	-0.1	1.3
25 Sep	45	-0.1	1.1
26 Sep	55	0.3	1.4
27 Sep	75	0.7	1.1
28 Sep	55	0.2	1.2
29 Sep	45	-0.3	1.3
30 Sep	45	-0.2	1.3
1 Oct	75	0.4	1.5
2 Oct	40	-0.1	1.3
3 Oct	55	0.2	1.0
4 Oct	60	0.1	1.1
5 Oct	75	0.3	1.7
6 Oct	55	0.3	2.4
7 Oct	50	0.0	0.7
8 Oct	45	-0.3	1.5
9 Oct	45	-0.2	1.3
10 Oct	45	-0.3	2.2
11 Oct	60	0.3	1.3
12 Oct	50	0.3	1.3
13 Oct	60	0.7	2.0
14 Oct	45	0.1	1.1
15 Oct	45	-0.3	2.2
16 Oct	40	-0.9	2.0
17 Oct	65	0.4	1.6
18 Oct	50	-0.1	0.9
19 Oct	50	-0.2	1.8
20 Oct	50	-0.2	3.3
21 Oct	60	0.4	1.9
22 Oct	35	-0.6	1.8
23 Oct	60	-0.1	1.4
24 Oct	45	-0.2	1.5
25 Oct	35	-0.3	0.8
26 Oct	40	-0.3	1.7
27 Oct	55	0.0	1.3
28 Oct	65	0.1	1.3
29 Oct	55	0.6	2.2
30 Oct	65	0.4	1.4
31 Oct	80	0.5	1.0
1 Nov	55	-0.2	0.9
2 Nov	55	0.2	0.9

Date	Up(%)	Avg Change (%)	Std Dev
3 Nov	55	0.2	1.2
4 Nov	40	0.4	1.6
5 Nov	65	-0.1	1.2
6 Nov	60	-0.2	1.4
7 Nov	50	-0.1	1.0
8 Nov	60	0.2	0.7
9 Nov	45	-0.3	1.1
10 Nov	50	0.0	0.6
11 Nov	55	0.1	1.5
12 Nov	60	0.3	1.3
13 Nov	45	-0.1	1.0
14 Nov	55	0.3	0.7
15 Nov	60	0.2	0.7
16 Nov	65	0.2	0.9
17 Nov	40	-0.2	1.1
18 Nov	60	0.1	0.8
19 Nov	30	-0.6	1.5
20 Nov	50	0.0	1.3
21 Nov	50	-0.1	1.3
22 Nov	45	-0.2	1.0
23 Nov	55	0.3	1.3
24 Nov	55	0.6	2.3
25 Nov	60	0.0	1.0
26 Nov	50	-0.2	1.1
27 Nov	60	0.2	0.8
28 Nov	45	0.1	1.2
29 Nov	70	0.1	0.7
30 Nov	45	-0.2	1.5
1 Dec	55	0.1	1.9
2 Dec	50	0.1	0.9
3 Dec	50	0.1	0.8
4 Dec	35	-0.1	0.7
5 Dec	55	0.3	1.2
6 Dec	50	-0.1	0.8
7 Dec	40	0.0	0.7
8 Dec	60	0.4	1.6
9 Dec	50	0.1	0.9
10 Dec	35	-0.2	0.7
11 Dec	40	-0.2	1.0
12 Dec	45	-0.3	0.9
13 Dec	70	0.1	1.0
14 Dec	55	0.0	0.9
15 Dec	50	0.0	0.7
16 Dec	75	0.6	0.8
17 Dec	45	-0.1	1.0
18 Dec	65	0.2	0.9
19 Dec	55	-0.1	0.9
20 Dec	65	0.1	0.9
21 Dec	60	0.4	1.0
22 Dec	70	0.3	0.6
23 Dec	80	0.4	0.6

Date	Up(%)	Avg Change (%)	Std Dev
24 Dec	80	0.2	0.6
27 Dec	83	0.5	1.2
28 Dec	67	0.2	0.5
29 Dec	75	0.4	1.2
30 Dec	60	0.2	0.9
31 Dec	56	0.1	1.1

FTSE 100 INDEX WEEKLY PERFORMANCE

Week	Up(%)	Avg Change (%)	Std Dev
1	68	1.2	2.6
2	25	-0.5	1.8
3	46	-0.3	2.6
4	54	0.0	1.7
5	64	0.9	2.0
6	61	0.4	2.1
7	61	0.3	1.3
8	50	0.0	2.4
9	54	0.6	2.0
10	54	-0.1	2.4
11	54	0.2	2.3
12	46	0.2	2.7
13	43	0.0	1.9
14	68	0.8	2.0
15	45	0.0	2.2
16	66	0.6	1.4
17	52	-0.1	1.7
18	62	0.3	2.3
19	59	0.2	2.1
20	55	-0.2	2.4
21	45	-0.3	2.1
22	41	0.3	1.9
23	62	0.3	1.8
24	59	-0.3	2.1
25	34	-0.8	1.8
26	45	-0.1	1.9
27	68	0.8	2.1
28	36	-0.6	2.5
29	57	0.2	2.4
30	39	-0.4	2.4
31	79	0.6	2.6
32	50	-0.1	2.4
33	57	0.1	2.2
34	79	0.5	1.9
35	57	0.5	2.3
36	43	-0.6	2.3
37	39	-0.6	2.3
38	43	-0.2	3.0
39	50	0.4	2.7
40	64	0.8	2.5
41	61	-0.4	4.6
42	61	0.1	2.7
43	46	-0.8	4.1
44	54	0.7	3.4
45	68	0.2	2.1
46	61	0.4	1.5
47	46	-0.3	3.2
48	57	1.0	3.3
49	46	-0.3	2.5
50	46	0.0	2.2
51	75	0.8	1.7
52	79	1.0	1.5
53	80	-0.6	2.1

FTSE 100 INDEX MONTHLY PERFORMANCE

Month	Up(%)	Avg Change (%)	Std Dev
January	57	0.3	5.2
February	57	0.9	4.1
March	57	0.6	3.5
April	68	1.8	3.7
May	45	-0.3	4.5
June	41	-0.7	3.5
July	55	0.8	4.3
August	57	0.6	4.8
September	46	-1.0	5.9
October	75	0.7	6.9
November	57	0.7	3.9
December	86	2.6	3.0

ALSO FROM HARRIMAN HOUSE

Free Capital

How 12 private investors made millions in the stock market

By Guy Thomas

Available as paperback and eBook

How to Value Shares and Outperform the Market

A simple, new and effective approach to value investing

By Glenn Martin

Available as paperback and eBook

Cotter On Investing

Taking the bull out of the markets: practical advice and tips from an experienced investor

By John Cotter

Available as paperback and eBook

The Search for Income

An investor's guide to income-paying investments

By Maike Currie

Available as paperback and eBook

ALSO FROM HARRIMAN HOUSE

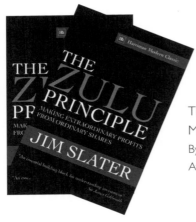

The Zulu Principle
Making extraordinary profits from ordinary shares
By Jim Slater
Available as paperback and eBook

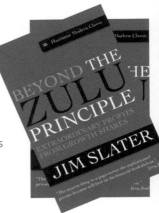

Beyond The Zulu Principle
Extraordinary Profits from Growth Shares
By Jim Slater
Available as paperback and eBook

The Financial Spread Betting Handbook
The definitive guide to making money trading spread bets
By Malcolm Pryor
Available as paperback and eBook

The Investor's Guide to Understanding Accounts
10 crunch questions to ask before investing in a company

Ratios Made Simple
A beginner's guide to the key financial ratios
Both by Robert Leach
Available as paperback and eBook

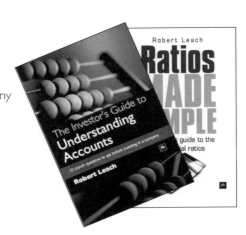